ADVANCED CRIMINAL PROCEDURE

IN A NUTSHELL

SECOND EDITION

By

MARK E. CAMMACK
Professor of Law
Southwestern University School of Law

NORMAN M. GARLAND
Professor of Law
Southwestern University School of Law

THOMSON

WEST

Mat #40333587

Nutshell Series, In a Nutshell, the Nutshell Logo and West Group are trademarks registered in the U.S. Patent and Trademark Office.

© West, a Thomson business, 2001
© 2006 Thomson/West
  610 Opperman Drive
  P.O. Box 64526
  St. Paul, MN 55164–0526
  1–800–328–9352
Printed in the United States of America

ISBN–13: 978–0–314–15893–2
ISBN–10: 0–314–15893–6

TEXT IS PRINTED ON 10% POST
CONSUMER RECYCLED PAPER

To
Anne, Jessie, and Jimmy
MEC

To
Antigone and Melissa
NMG

*

PREFACE

The title of this Nutshell, which is also the usual title of the corresponding law school course, may be misleading. "Advanced Criminal Procedure" would seem to suggest an "Advanced" treatment of issues addressed in "Criminal Procedure." This book is not, however, a further inquiry into the constitutional constraints on police investigation—the subject of Criminal Procedure—but an examination of the procedural aspects of a criminal case once the investigation is complete. The book begins with a discussion of the legal doctrines governing the decision to file formal charges, and ends with the procedures for appeal and collateral attack of the conviction. The Nutshell (and the course) might more accurately be titled "Procedural Aspects of the Prosecution and Adjudication of a Criminal Case," or, less elegantly, "Criminal Procedures from Bail to Jail." Those titles better capture the book's content. However, the label "Advanced Criminal Procedure" is customary, which is why it is used here.

The organization of the book follows the basic chronology of a typical criminal case. The process is set in motion when the police or the prosecutor decide to file criminal charges. The bases for this decision and the decision making process are not ordinarily open to public scrutiny. Nevertheless, the law has developed a limited number of doctrines that can be used to challenge a decision to prosecute, which are the main subject of Chapter 1.

If the charges that are filed against a defendant are at all serious the defendant will be arrested and jailed. Because the accused has not, at this point, been convicted of a crime, the defendant's continued incarceration pending trial must be justified on some basis other than punishment. Chapter 2 discusses both the types of limitations on the defendant's freedom that can be imposed before trial, including bail and pre-trial detention, and the justifications for imposing those restraints.

Chapters 3 and 4 discuss the two most important procedures for screening the prosecution's evidence to determine its sufficiency to require the defendant to stand trial—the preliminary hearing and grand jury review. Although the preliminary hearing and the grand jury review serve similar purposes, they operate very differently. The preliminary hearing is an adversarial public hearing that resembles a bench trial. Both the prosecution and defense are permitted to present evidence, and the decision whether to require the accused to stand trial is made by the judge. The grand jury operates in secret, the defendant is not permitted to present evidence or challenge the prosecution's proof, and the decision regarding the sufficiency of the evidence is made by a group of citizen-jurors.

Chapters 5 through 8 take up a range of procedural issues that arise in the course of preparing for trial. Chapter 5 addresses discovery—the pre-trial exchange of evidence and information between the prosecution and defense. Chapter 6 discusses the legal doctrines that prescribe time limitations within which the defendant must be charged and brought to trial. Chapter 7 treats the rules that govern where a criminal case can be tried, and Chapter 8 addresses rules defining when multiple charges or multiple defendants can be joined together in a single trial.

The subject of Chapter 9 is the constitutional protection against double jeopardy. The double jeopardy rule prevents the government from prosecuting an individual a second time for the same offense following either a conviction or an acquittal, or from punishing an individual twice for the same offense. Despite the seeming simplicity of this rule, the doctrine has developed a complex body of law, which is why Chapter 9 is the longest in the book. Although the double jeopardy principle is applicable to several stages in the processing of a criminal case, its most fundamental importance is as a substantive limit on the criminal process. The doctrine defines basic limits on the government's use of the processes of the criminal law.

Although much of criminal procedure is directed toward an eventual trial, most criminal convictions are the result of the defendant's plea of guilty, rather than a finding of guilt after an adversarial trial. Because a guilty plea results in a conviction with all of the consequences that entails, the law has developed rules and procedures to ensure that judgments entered on the defendant's plea of guilty that are accurate and just. Those rules are the subject of Chapter 10.

Chapters 11 through 13 deal with various aspects of the criminal trial. These chapters all reflect in various ways the distinctively adversarial character of the American criminal trial. The rules discussed in Chapter 11 that require that the accused be provided with assistance of counsel are designed to ensure that the trial functions as a fair contest between rough equals. The requirement that the defendant be afforded assistance of counsel that is "effective" reflects the responsibility of the system as a whole for assuring that the issues are subjected to meaningful adversarial testing.

A fundamental premise of our adversarial procedure is that the partisan presentations of the parties shall be submitted to a neutral third party for decision. Chapter 12 discusses rules and procedures designed to ensure that the decision maker—usually a jury—is impartial. Chapter 13 covers a variety of topics relating to the actual conduct of the trial. Because of its varied content, the themes of this chapter are more diverse. However, one important principle that does emerge in this chapter is that while the criminal trial is structured as an adversarial contest, one of the adversaries—the prosecution— has the burden of proof.

The last two chapters provide relatively brief treatment of topics that are often subject of separate law school courses. The general subject of sentencing, covered in Chapter 14, embraces a wide variety of topics, from probation to the complex body of law governing the death penalty. The treatment of the subject in this Nutshell does not attempt to be comprehensive, but simply to provide an outline of the goals and structure of the sentencing process.

Chapter 15 addresses two subjects: the first, appeal, is a procedure by which a higher court within the judicial hierarchy is requested to review some aspect of the proceedings below; collateral attack, the second topic covered in Chapter 15, is another mechanism for pursuing the same objective. Historically, a collateral attack was a separate civil action filed in a different court from the one that produced the conviction. Although that is no longer generally the case, appeal and collateral attack are still governed by very different rules. Collateral attack in particular is a complex and rapidly changing body of law, and this book provides only an introductory treatment of the subject.

The law that is discussed in the Nutshell does not derive from a single source. The subjects treated in the book are governed partly by constitutional doctrines and partly by non-constitutional local law. (By "local law" we mean simply non-constitutional law that applies only within a single jurisdiction. For example, the Federal Rules of Criminal Procedure are "local law" applicable only within the federal system.) Constitutional doctrines, where they exist, are for the most part applicable in both the federal system and the states. The one exception to that generalization is the Fifth Amendment requirement of indictment by a grand jury, which does not apply to the states.

The primary sources of local law regulating post-investigation criminal procedure are legislation and court rules. Because of the federal nature of the nation's criminal justice system, each jurisdiction—the federal system and all fifty states—has its own local law. It would be neither possible nor helpful to try to describe all of the various rules that govern the subjects covered in this book throughout the United States. This Nutshell thus follows the approach taken in many courses on advanced criminal procedure in focusing primarily on federal law. Focusing on one jurisdiction has the advantage of seeing the doctrines that govern the various stages in the process as part of a system of coherent rules. The federal system is chosen because it is the most visible.

The roles of constitutionally based doctrines and local law in regulating the issues treated in this Nutshell differ depending on the subject matter. The only subject treated in the book that is based entirely on the constitution is the double jeopardy doctrine. For a number of issues, local law provides the primary source of regulation, but constitutional doctrines define limits on how those rules can be applied. For example, the rules governing joinder of charges or defendants discussed in Chapter 8 are contained in the Federal Rules of Criminal Procedure. But in applying the joinder rules consideration must also be given to the Sixth Amendment right of the accused to confront adverse witnesses, since some types of joinder risk violation of that right.

Another pattern of legal regulation found with several of the issues discussed in the book involves overlapping constitutional and non-constitutional rules. For example, the Federal Rules of Criminal Procedure require the prosecution to disclose certain types of evidence to the defendant before trial. The Due Process Clause also imposes disclosure obligations on the prosecution, which can, but do not necessarily overlap with the prosecutor's statutory obligation. The Sixth Amendment right to a speedy trial and the federal Speedy Trial Act provide another example of overlapping or duplicate regulation. Finally, some issues are regulated by a mix of constitutional and non-constitutional rules that fits into no discernable pattern. The critical point for present purposes is that, in reading this book, careful attention should be given to the sources of governing rules and how those rules relate and interact.

We have required a lot of help writing this little book. Professor Cammack would like to thank Southwestern students Stephanie Cohen, Bren Unger, Ed Rathbun, Fiona Woon, and Fanny Tagawa who provided able research assistance and Lisa, Phillip, John, Anne, Hugh, Jenny, Steve, and Westside School of Dance who helped enormously filling in for occupied parents.

Professor Garland would like to thank Southwestern students David Hammond, Craig Hopkins, Craig Kleffman, Laura Krank, Jesica Trotter, and Melinda White, and his wife, Melissa Grossan. Southwestern University School of Law supported the project with a Sabbatical Leave for Professor Cammack and summer research grants for both Professor Cammack and Garland, as well as staff and facilities support.

OUTLINE

OUTLINE

OUTLINE

TABLE OF CASES

References are to Pages

TABLE OF CASES

TABLE OF CASES

TABLE OF CASES

TABLE OF CASES

TABLE OF CASES

*

TABLE OF RULES AND STATUTES

UNITED STATES

UNITED STATES CONSTITUTION

XXXIX

TABLE OF RULES AND STATUTES

UNITED STATES CONSTITUTION

TABLE OF RULES AND STATUTES

UNITED STATES CONSTITUTION

TABLE OF RULES AND STATUTES

FEDERAL RULES OF CRIMINAL PROCEDURE

TABLE OF RULES AND STATUTES

FEDERAL RULES OF CRIMINAL PROCEDURE

FEDERAL RULES OF EVIDENCE

ADVANCED CRIMINAL PROCEDURE

IN A NUTSHELL

SECOND EDITION

*

CHAPTER 1

THE DECISION TO PROSECUTE

A. THE NATURE AND EXTENT OF DISCRETION

In everyday speech we refer to the "enforcement" of the criminal law as if it were a straightforward matter of deploying criminal prosecutions against anyone and everyone who may be liable to criminal penalties. A moments reflection makes clear that this simple model of the criminal justice process is inaccurate. It is not simply that many crimes cannot be prosecuted because they are never reported to law enforcement officials or because the identity of the perpetrator remains unknown. Within the category of reported and solved crimes, many do not result in prosecution because the police or prosecutor elects not to go forward.

A realistic understanding of the criminal justice process recognizes that the decision whether to initiate a criminal prosecution includes a large element of discretion. The discretionary character of the decision to prosecute is both a practical reality and a firmly established legal principle. Prosecutors in the United States are under no legal obligation to prosecute every meritorious case that comes to their attention. The law permits, if not commands, prosecutors to base their decision whether to charge someone with a crime on non-legal considerations. Obviously legal standards—the definition of crimes and the evidence necessary to convict—play an important role in the decision to initiate a criminal case. But other considerations play a role as well. These extra-legal factors influence both the decision *whether* a criminal case will be commenced and, if so, *what* crime or crimes will be charged.

The broad discretionary power granted to prosecutors is arguably in conflict with the bedrock principle that the imposition of criminal penalties shall be based on the rule of law. Any attempt to explain why prosecutors are granted such discretionary powers raises questions that are more sociological than legal. One view holds that substantial discretion is unavoidable in the functioning of a criminal justice system, though this is debatable. It is probable that prosecutorial discretion is both more acceptable and more extensive in the criminal justice system of the United States than in many other countries.

It has also been suggested that non-enforcement of the criminal law is in part a result of over-criminalization. That is, the substantive law reaches more conduct than society is willing or able to punish. One possible reason for this is that the legislature and the political process more generally are using the criminal law to express a conception of public morals that is more demanding than society is actually prepared to live by. This over-abundance of criminal laws is made worse by an insufficiency of enforcement resources. The prosecution and punishment of crime require expenditure for police, prosecutors, courts, and prisons. The public's appetite for criminalization often exceeds its investment in the resources required for full prosecution and punishment.

Finally, non-enforcement of the criminal law responds to a desire to adjust general rules to specific cases in order to achieve results that are felt to be just. In other words, in some instances, it is just not appropriate to prosecute even though the letter of the law might seem to demand it.

It is not possible to specify all the considerations that enter into a decision whether to initiate a criminal case, much less the relative weight that is assigned to the various factors in arriving at a decision. One consideration that is invariably part of the mix, but rarely is solely determinative, is the prosecutor's assessment of the chances of success if the case goes forward. This requires evaluation of the strength of the evidence, its admissibility under the rules of evidence, and the fact-finder's likely response to both the evidence and the case generally. Another set of factors influencing the decision whether to charge someone with a crime has to do with the personal characteristics of the person to be charged. The age, family and community ties, employment or educational status, criminal history, and other personal circumstances may all bear on a prosecutor's decision whether to charge someone with a crime.

Criminal cases are brought in the name of the state, and the victim of crime does not have the right to compel prosecution. Nonetheless, the wishes of the victim sometimes influence a prosecutor's decision whether to charge someone with a crime. The victim's opposition to prosecution frequently persuades police or prosecutors not to bring charges in assault cases involving spouses or other related adults. Pressure from the victim or sometimes from the press or public may also persuade a prosecutor to make an affirmative charging decision in a case that might not otherwise be prosecuted.

Judgments about the relative public costs and benefits of prosecution may persuade a prosecutor not to bring charges. Prosecutors sometimes conclude that criminal prosecution of an obvious offender would not serve the public interest because of social costs—it would impede the person's rehabilitation or interfere with important social relationships. In other cases the high costs of prosecuting a case—because of the difficulty of gathering evidence or securing the testimony of witnesses—does not justify the relatively slight public benefit of prosecution. In weighing costs and benefits of pursuing a criminal case the gravity of the offense is clearly a very important consideration; non-prosecution is much more common for minor offenses than for serious crimes.

In addition to determining whether to initiate criminal charges, prosecutors must often decide what crime or crimes to charge. On this question the prosecutor will often have a range of options.

One reason this choice is available is because the same course of conduct may support several different charges. For instance, an unauthorized entry into a building might be charged as either burglary or the less serious crime of breaking and entering. Prosecutors frequently have the option of charging several offenses arising out of a single course of conduct. Along with the burglary the prosecutor might be able to charge the underlying felony committed inside the building.

Another situation that often entails a choice among potential charges is when the prosecutor has information that a suspect has committed multiple, unconnected crimes—a series of burglaries, for example. The discretion to choose among available charges is the power that enables prosecutors to tailor the punishment to the crime and the offender. In determining what offense is appropriate, prosecutors consider some of the same factors that influence the decision whether to bring any charges at all—most notably the characteristics of the offender and the nature of the criminal conduct.

Charging decisions are also sometimes based in part on strategic considerations. Subject to the constraints imposed by grand jury or other pre-trial review of the sufficiency of the evidence, a prosecutor may file more counts or more serious charges than she deems appropriate in anticipation that the eventual conviction will be for a reduced charge arrived at through a negotiated plea agreement. Sometimes the initial charge is the result of a negotiated bargain.

Another option sometimes available as an alternative to immediate prosecution is a disposition referred to as diversion. Diversion results in a suspension of prosecution with a promise that charges will be dropped upon successful completion of a period of probation. There may be a number of conditions required in exchange for suspending prosecution, such as requiring the offender to submit to supervision, to undergo treatment or counseling, or to maintain employment or education. Failure to abide by the conditions results in reinstatement of criminal prosecution.

As a practical matter, the most important checks on the arbitrary or malicious enforcement of the criminal law are administrative and political constraints, rather than legal rules. Some prosecutors' offices, especially larger ones, have adopted formal internal procedures that set forth guidelines for charging decisions. Offices without formal guidelines usually develop standardized responses to recurring situations as a matter of customary practice. Because prosecutors in the United States are either political appointees or are directly elected, they are, to some extent, politically accountable for their actions.

B. CHALLENGING THE DECISION NOT TO PROSECUTE

Procedures for pre-trial review of the sufficiency of the evidence, principally the grand jury and the preliminary hearing, are reasonably effective in preventing prosecutions that are not based on adequate evidence. The law has not developed comparable mechanisms for ensuring that prosecutions *are* instituted against all persons as to whom there is evidence that would support the bringing of criminal charges.

One vehicle that is sometimes used to attempt to compel the prosecutor to act is a writ of mandamus. Suits seeking a writ ordering a prosecutor to bring a criminal case are rarely successful. See *Inmates of Attica Correctional Facility v. Rockefeller* (2d Cir. 1973). The basic reason given for denying such claims is that the plaintiffs do not possess rights that entitle them to mandamus. The writ of mandamus is available only to compel the performance of a duty that is owed *to the party who is seeking the writ*. The general rule, however, is that "a private citizen lacks a judicially cognizable interest in the prosecution or non-prosecution of another." *Leeke v. Timmerman* (S.Ct.1981). In rejecting suits for a writ of mandamus courts also cite separation of powers principles, arguing that judicial intervention in prosecutorial decision making encroaches on an executive function, and the practical difficulties of judicial oversight of a decision as complex and sensitive as deciding whether to charge someone with a crime. Private prosecution of crime, which was once available, is now rarely permitted. Although grand juries are in theory empowered to bring criminal charges on their own initiative, in practice they almost never act independently of the prosecutor.

Removal of the prosecutor by impeachment or appointment of a special prosecutor are rarely realistic options. In short, prosecutors have what amounts to a monopoly over the prosecution of crime, and there are no effective means for compelling the prosecutor to act.

The prosecutor's power to terminate or "nol pros" (from the Latin *nolle prosequi*) a case once it has been begun is less complete. Many jurisdictions have adopted statutes or rules of court which require judicial approval or, at the very least, a written statement of reasons for a prosecutor's decision to discontinue a prosecution. Federal Rule of Criminal Procedure 48(a), for example, requires leave of court in order for the dismissal of an indictment, information or complaint. The general purpose of such requirements is to prevent harassment of defendants through repeated charges and dismissals. The extent to which such rules impose meaningful checks on the prosecutor's discretion will depend on how rigorously the rules are interpreted and enforced. In some jurisdictions a boilerplate recital that the case is being dismissed "in the interest of justice" is sufficient to satisfy the requirements of the law.

C. CHALLENGING THE DECISION TO PROSECUTE

Although the prosecutor's discretion is broad, it is not entirely unchecked. The two primary constitutional restraints on the prosecutor's discretion are the requirements that it be exercised consistent with the equal protection guarantee of the Fifth and Fourteenth Amendments, and a due process guarantee against prosecutorial vindictiveness. The standards for proving a constitutional violation are demanding, however, and successful constitutional challenges to prosecutorial decisions are rare.

1. SELECTIVE ENFORCEMENT

The Court has recognized that the constitutional guarantee that no person shall be denied equal protection of the laws prohibits both state and federal prosecutors from enforcing criminal statutes in a selective or discriminatory fashion. The requirements for a selective prosecution claim, which draw on ordinary equal protection standards, are typically divided into three elements: An arbitrary classification; purposeful discrimination; and non-prosecution of other similarly situated offenders.

There is some uncertainty over the remedy for a selective prosecution violation. State and lower federal courts have typically ordered dismissal of the charges upon proof that the defendant has been impermissibly targeted for prosecution. The Supreme Court, however, has expressly declined to endorse dismissal as the appropriate remedy.

a. Arbitrary Classification

Neither the Equal Protection Clause nor any other constitutional provision prohibits all selectivity in the enforcement of the criminal law. If it did, there would be an end, or nearly that, to prosecutorial discretion. What the constitution forbids is selection for prosecution that is "deliberately based upon an unjustifiable standard such as race, religion, or other arbitrary classification." *Oyler v. Boles* (S.Ct.1962).

There is no fixed set of selection criteria that have been deemed "arbitrary" for selective prosecution purposes. Under standard equal protection analysis, a different level of scrutiny is applied to different types of classifications. "Strict scrutiny," requiring demonstration that the classification is narrowly tailored to serve a compelling governmental interest, is applied to a limited set of classifications–most notably race, national origin, and the exercise of a fundamental right. Gender-based classifications are subjected to an intermediate scrutiny. The test applied to all other types of classifications is a simple rational relation test. A classification is permissible if it is rationally related to a legitimate governmental purpose.

In the selective prosecution context courts have not emphasized the distinction among suspect, quasi suspect, and non suspect classifications and the different levels of review they entail, though courts occasionally discuss the distinctions. It is reasonable to assume that a claim alleging discriminatory prosecution based on constitutionally suspect criteria more readily triggers review. Most selective prosecution claims, moreover, have alleged discrimination based on classifications that are subject to a heightened level of scrutiny, such as race, religion, gender, political affiliation or views, union membership and the exercise of first amendment rights. In general, however, courts have focused on whether the challenged enforcement practice reflects the application of legitimate law enforcement goals, rather than on the nature of the classification involved. If the pattern of selective enforcement is the result of a legitimate law enforcement objective, the classification created by the enforcement policy will not be deemed to be arbitrary, regardless of the type of classification it creates. On the other hand, if the classification is irrelevant to any law enforcement objective it will be held arbitrary regardless of whether it qualifies as a suspect or quasi suspect classification.

Because a prosecutorial selection criteria is arbitrary whenever it is irrelevant to a legitimate law enforcement purpose, the determination of whether a given classification is arbitrary cannot be answered in the abstract. That is, it cannot be said that an enforcement practice that results in the selective prosecution of one racial group or of women, but not men, is invariably arbitrary. The question in every case is whether the challenged enforcement practice is related to a legitimate governmental purpose.

The approach used in determining whether a prosecutorial classification is arbitrary for discriminatory prosecution purposes is well illustrated by cases alleging gender discrimination in the prosecution of female prostitutes but not their male customers. One challenged practice involves the use of male decoys to catch female prostitutes but not female decoys to catch male customers. Courts have generally rejected arguments that this violates equal protection. They have reasoned that, because a single prostitute might engage several customers on one night, focusing prosecutorial resources on the prostitute is a reasonable method of seeking to maximize the law's deterrent effect. The distinction that is being drawn, on this view, is not based on gender at all. The distinction, rather, is between prostitutes and customers. Since the prostitute-customer classification is rationally related to a legitimate law enforcement objective, it is not arbitrary.

Because the determination of whether a classification is impermissible depends on whether it is rationally related to a legitimate law enforcement purpose, judgments must be made about what qualifies as a legitimate purpose and whether a given prosecution policy is in fact rationally related to the alleged purpose. On the latter question—whether the challenged classification actually furthers the asserted law enforcement objective—the courts generally defer to the judgment of prosecutors on the basis that courts' views about what works in law enforcement are no more reliable than the views of prosecutors. As to what qualifies as a legitimate purpose, there is no fixed list of permissible law enforcement objectives that will justify limiting prosecution to a particular class of offenders. The general justifications that are most often invoked are considerations related to the allocation of prosecutorial resources and the goal of promoting deterrence. Other ends that advance the general purposes of the criminal law also suffice.

One issue that has not been definitively resolved is whether, in order to survive an equal protection challenge, a classification must be related to the purposes of the criminal law under which the person is being prosecuted, or if it is enough that the classification bears a rational relation to *any* permissible governmental purpose. For instance, one case raised the questions whether the enforcement of a bicycle safety law against suspected prostitutes, but not others, must be justified by reference to the purposes underlying the bicycle law, or whether selective prosecution of prostitutes for violating the bicycle law could be justified as a means of eradicating prostitution. In the case the court held that singling out suspected prostitutes for prosecution violated equal protection because the policy of selective enforcement against prostitutes did not further the interest of promoting bicycle safety. But the question whether it is enough for a prosecutorial classification to advance any governmental purpose remains unsettled.

b. Purposeful Discrimination

In order to demonstrate unconstitutional selective prosecution it must be shown that the classification was both arbitrary and deliberate. It is not enough that an arbitrary class of offenders has in fact been singled out for prosecution; it must be shown as well that the practice was carried out with an *intent* to discriminate against the class.

The meaning of the purposeful discrimination requirement was clarified in the U.S. Supreme Court's decision in *Wayte v. U.S.* (S.Ct.1985), a case involving a selective prosecution challenge to the government's policy of "passive enforcement" of the law requiring registration for the draft. Under the policy, the government investigated and prosecuted only those non-registrants who either reported themselves or were reported by others as having failed to register. In challenging his prosecution for failing to register, Wayte argued that the policy impermissibly discriminated against "vocal non-registrants" who were exercising their first amendment right to protest the law. In rejecting the challenge the Court held, among other things, that the defendant had not proven that the government *intended* to discriminate. The Court stated that " 'discriminatory purpose' implies more than intent as awareness. It implies that the decision-maker . . . selected or reaffirmed a particular course of action at least in part 'because of,' not merely 'in spite of,' its adverse effects upon an identifiable group." Although Wayte had presented evidence "demonstrat[ing] that the Government was aware that the passive enforcement policy would result in the prosecution of vocal objectors," he had not shown that "the Government prosecuted him *because of* his protest activities." For that reason his challenge to his prosecution failed.

The discriminatory purpose element of a selective prosecution claim sometimes overlaps with the arbitrary classification requirement discussed in the previous section. In some cases the conclusion that there was no discriminatory intent is simply another way of expressing the conclusion that the enforcement practice did not target an arbitrary class of offenders. That is, if the selective prosecution of one class of offenders was in fact the result of the implementation of a legitimate law enforcement policy, then the targeting of that class for prosecution is clearly not the result of purposeful discrimination. That point is illustrated by an example presented by Professors LaFave, Israel, and King in their discussion of the intent element. LaFave, Israel, & King, Criminal Procedure § 13.4(d) (3d ed. 2000). They point out that a decision to prosecute black gamblers but not white gamblers would clearly be impermissible. But a decision to focus law enforcement efforts on the numbers racket rather than poker in private clubs because of ties between numbers rackets and organized crime would not be improper, even if the effect of the policy was that most of those prosecuted for gambling were black. Professors LaFave, Israel, & King explain that the difference between the two cases is the absence of a discriminatory purpose in the latter case. But the cases could also be distinguished on the basis that no arbitrary classification is involved in the prosecution of numbers rackets, since the pursuit of that form of gambling is rationally related to the legitimate law enforcement objective of combating organized crime.

Although the arbitrary classification requirement and the purposeful discrimination element occasionally overlap, the two should not be treated as identical. A program of selective prosecution which is in fact motivated by a discriminatory purpose is improper even if the same pattern of selective enforcement could result from some legitimate enforcement objective. To return to the gambling example, if the prosecution of numbers rackets was in fact motivated by an intent to discriminate against members of a particular racial group, the fact that it coincidentally relates to a legitimate law enforcement purpose does not make it proper.

c.   Non-prosecution of Others

Standard equal protection doctrine requires proof of both a "discriminatory purpose" and a "discriminatory effect." In the selective prosecution context, the discriminatory effect requirement has been interpreted as requiring proof that other violators of the law who are not members of the arbitrary classification have not been prosecuted. This requirement is described as requiring proof of the non-prosecution of others who are "similarly situated" to the defendant. A person is similarly situated to the defendant for purposes of this rule if the person has committed the same offense as the defendant but does not share the arbitrary feature that is alleged to be the basis of the discriminatory prosecution. For example, if the allegation is that the prosecution has discriminatorily targeted blue-eyed jaywalkers for prosecution, it must be shown that jaywalkers with eyes of a different color have not been prosecuted.

The Supreme Court relied on the defendant's failure to demonstrate the non-prosecution of other similarly situated violators as an alternative basis for its holding that the defendant had not proven an equal protection violation in *Wayte v. U.S.* The defendant in *Wayte* argued that his prosecution for failing to register for the draft was discriminatory because the prosecution's enforcement policy targeted "vocal non-registrants" who were exercising their first amendment right to protest the registration requirement. The Court concluded, however, that the challenged policy did not in fact target vocal non-registrants, since other persons who had not registered but who had not protested had been prosecution. That is, other violators who were similarly situated to the defendant but did not share the arbitrary feature alleged to be the basis for the discriminatory prosecution, i.e., public protest of the registration requirement, had in fact been prosecuted for failure to register. The record indicated that the government had prosecuted all non-registrants who had either reported themselves or were reported by others as having not registered, regardless of whether those persons had expressed opposition to the registration requirement. Additionally, the government had *not* attempted to prosecute those persons who had publicly protested the registration requirement but had not reported themselves or been reported by others as having not registered. Thus, the record showed that the government had treated all *reported* non-registrants similarly, without regard for whether they had protested the registration requirement.

In *U.S. v. Armstrong* (S.Ct.1996) the Court emphasized that the requirement of proof of a discriminatory effect evidenced by the non-prosecution of other similarly situated violators is intended to and does impose a heavy burden on defendants claiming selective prosecution. The defendants in *Armstrong* claimed that they were selected for prosecution for crack cocaine and firearms offenses because of their race. In support of their claim, the defendants had presented an affidavit stating that all of the crack cocaine cases closed by the local Federal Defenders Office in the previous year involved black defendants. The Court held that the defendants' affidavit did not constitute "some evidence" that similarly situated offenders were not prosecuted because it did not identify individuals who were *not black* and who *could* have been prosecuted for the same offenses but were *not prosecuted*. The Court rejected the assumption relied on by the lower courts that "people of all races commit all types of crimes" on the ground that it was contradicted by statistics indicating that a majority of those *sentenced* for federal crack cocaine offenses were black. At best, therefore, the defendants' evidence tended to prove who *was prosecuted* for the same offense as the defendants; it did not prove the existence of other offenders who were not prosecuted. The Court in

Armstrong stated that the similarly situated requirement "does not make a selective-prosecution
claim impossible to prove." But the requirement
clearly poses a formidable obstacle to demonstrating
a constitutional violation, since in most cases it is
very difficult to obtain information about others
who have violated the law and could have been
prosecuted but were not.

The definition of who is "similarly situated" to
the party challenging the prosecution practice is
occasionally disputed. One case raising the issue
involved the prosecution of participants in the
"sanctuary movement" who were charged with violation of the immigration laws for smuggling Central American natives into the United States. The
defendants claimed that they were being targeted
for prosecution because of their political views. In
alleging selective prosecution they claimed that
growers and ranchers who employed undocumented
aliens were similarly situated to them but had not
been prosecuted. The court disagreed with the defendants' characterization of who was similarly situated on the ground that it did not "insure that all
distinctions extraneous to the first amendment expression were removed." According to the court,
those most closely analogous to the defendants were
organized smugglers operating for financial gain.
This group represented the appropriate "control
group" because they posed comparable threats to
the immigration laws in terms of the number of
aliens they smuggle, but they had not engaged in

the political expression that defendants claimed was the motivation for the prosecution.

The requirement that there be proof of non-prosecution of persons outside the class of those claiming selective prosecution has been criticized as overly broad and unduly restrictive. The contention, in effect, is that proof of non-prosecution of other similarly situated individuals may have evidentiary value as proof of discriminatory intent, but should not be required as a separate element of the claim. That is, proof of non-prosecution of similarly situated offenders is relevant evidence that the prosecutions actually undertaken were motivated by a discriminatory intent. But, according to the critics, proof of non-prosecution should not be required in every case, since non-prosecution does not preclude the possibility that the charges against the defendants were based on discriminatory motives. In defense of the requirement, it is argued that proof of non-prosecution of similarly situated offenders provides an objectively verifiable, stabilizing element necessary to prevent intrusive and uncertain inquiries into the subjective motivations of prosecutors.

d.   Problems of Proof

In its cases discussing the requirements for selective prosecution, the Supreme Court has emphasized that courts should be hesitant to interfere with prosecutorial discretion, and has taken great pains to explain that the standard for proving selective prosecution is a "demanding one." The Court has stressed that a "presumption of regularity" supports the decisions of prosecutors, and has stated that "in the absence of clear evidence to the contrary, courts presume that they have properly discharged their official duties."

The defendant bears the burden of proof on all three elements of the claim. Some lower courts and commentators have advocated shifting the burden of proof to the prosecution once the defendant has made some preliminary showing. The justification for such a rule is that the prosecution generally has superior access to facts critical to the defendant's claim. The Supreme Court, however, has never endorsed such a rule, and in its most recent pronouncement on the matter, the Court clearly signaled a reluctance to ease the burden on defendants making selective prosecution claims.

In *U.S. v. Armstrong* (S.Ct.1996) the Court addressed the showing necessary to obtain discovery in a selective prosecution case. The defendants in the case claimed that their federal crack cocaine and firearms prosecution was racially motivated. The Court held that in order to be entitled to discovery from the government, the defendant must present "some evidence tending to show the essential elements of the defense." In explaining the heavy burden required to obtain discovery, the Court stated that the justifications for a rigorous standard for the elements of a selective prosecution claim require a correspondingly rigorous standard for discovery in aid of such a claim. Because, according to the Court, discovery imposes many of the same burdens on the government as responding to a prima facie case, the showing necessary to obtain discovery should itself be a significant barrier to the litigation of insubstantial claims. The Court's reasoning suggests, and lower courts have assumed, that the same rigorous standard applied to discovery must be satisfied before the defendant will be entitled to an evidentiary hearing on a selective prosecution claim.

2. VINDICTIVE PROSECUTION

In *Blackledge v. Perry* (S.Ct.1974) the Court first announced the principle that the Due Process Clauses of the Fifth and Fourteenth Amendments protect criminal defendants from both state and federal prosecutions that are based on vindictive motives. The defendant in that case was initially charged and convicted of misdemeanor assault. After the defendant gave notice of an intent to invoke his right to a trial *de novo*, which under state law nullified the prior conviction and required a new trial, the prosecutor obtained an indictment charging the defendant with felony assault based on the same conduct. The defendant challenged his subsequent conviction on the felony charge as a violation of due process.

The court in *Blackledge* relied on *N.C. v. Pearce* (S.Ct.1969), a case involving a claim of judicial rather than prosecutorial vindictiveness. As explained in *Blackledge,* the due process violation in *Pearce* was "not grounded upon the proposition that actual retaliatory motivation must inevitably exist." Rather, due process requires that a defendant be freed of "apprehension of retaliation" so as not to deter a defendant in the exercise the right to appeal. Although *Pearce* involved the imposition of a harsher sentence by a judge following a successful appeal, the Court in *Blackledge* found the principle stated there equally applicable to prosecutorial charging decisions after the defendant has expressed an intent to seek a trial *de novo*. The Court observed that the prosecutor in such a situation has a considerable stake in discouraging a convicted defendant from seeking a new trial, and held that the *opportunities* for vindictiveness were such as to impel the conclusion that due process required that the more serious charge be barred.

As originally described in *Blackledge*, a due process claim alleging vindictive prosecution is not premised on a conclusion that the charges were in fact vindictive. The rule as initially conceived was intended to protect the defendant from fear of retaliation so as not to deter the defendant in the exercise of his rights. Later cases, however, recharacterized the *Blackledge* (and *Pearce*) cases as establishing a *presumption* of vindictiveness under circumstances where the possibility of retaliation was deemed high. This re-characterization effected a fundamental change in the rule itself. Under the current approach, due process bars prosecutions that are in fact vindictive. The presumption serves as a substitute for proof of vindictiveness, enabling the defendant to prevail on the vindictive prosecution claim without the necessity of presenting evidence of the actual motivation underlying the charges. There is, however, "no presumption of vindictiveness when the first sentence was based upon a guilty plea," and "the second sentence follows a trial." *Alabama v. Smith* (S.Ct.1989).

The reformulation of the due process rule as creating a presumption of vindictiveness is significant because it opens the possibility that the presumption can be rebutted or overcome through the presentation of contrary evidence. In *Blackledge* itself the Court stated that no due process violation occurs when it is shown that the more serious charge could not have been presented at the outset, as when a victim dies after assault charges have been filed giving rise to the possibility of murder charges. In *U.S. v. Goodwin* (S.Ct.1982) the Court stated that the presumption, when it applies, "could be overcome by objective evidence justifying the prosecutor's actions." Although the context of this statement in *Goodwin* raises questions about its meaning, the "any objective evidence" standard has been applied in cases involving claims of judicial vindictiveness, suggesting that the Court will permit prosecutors to rebut the presumption on the same basis.

In addition to re-conceptualizing the rule, post-*Blackledge* decisions have narrowed the scope of its application. The circumstances in which a presumption of prosecutorial vindictiveness will be applied are in fact quite rare. In *Bordenkircher v. Hayes* (S.Ct.1978), the Court held that due process was not violated when the prosecutor carried out a threat made during plea negotiations to indict the defendant on more serious charges if the defendant refused to plead guilty to the existing charge. The Court characterized *Blackledge* as involving "the State's unilateral imposition of a penalty upon the defendant who had chosen to exercise a legal right to attack his conviction." In the plea bargain context presented by *Bordenkircher*, however, there is no equivalent element of punishment or retaliation so long as the accused is free to accept or reject the prosecutor's offer.

Bordenkircher narrowed the situations in which prosecutorial vindictiveness will be presumed to circumstances in which the filing of charges might be used to deter the exercise of a legal right. In *U.S. v. Goodwin*, the Court further limited the importance of the presumption by holding it inapplicable to the entire pre-trial process. In *Goodwin* the defendant was initially charged with misdemeanor assault, but that charge was replaced with a felony indictment after the defendant demanded a jury trial. In rejecting the defendant's due process challenge to the felony charge, the Court drew a sharp distinction between the actions taken by prosecutors during the pre-trial process and their actions after an adjudication of guilt. The pre-trial setting differs from the situation after trial in that charging decisions made prior to trial are shaped by the ongoing investigation and a developing understanding of the case. Furthermore, because pre-trial motions that "burden" the prosecution are common and indeed expected, it is unrealistic to assume that a prosecutor would respond to such motions by seeking to penalize and deter the defendant. For those reasons, the Court concluded, the possibility that charging decisions made before trial will be based on retaliatory or vindictive motives is too unlikely to warrant a presumption of vindictiveness.

The Court's opinion in *Goodwin* strongly suggests that no presumption applies to charging decisions made prior to trial. Although the Court has never repudiated its holding in *Blackledge*, it is unclear whether a presumption applies to post trial contexts other than those presented in *Blackledge*—i.e., when the prosecutor files more serious charges in apparent response to the defendant's exercise of a right to appeal. The Court emphasized in *Goodwin* that the absence of a presumption that the prosecutor acted vindictively does not preclude a defendant from *proving* that the prosecution was vindictive. However, the practical difficulty of demonstrating prosecutorial vindictiveness guarantees that successful vindictive prosecution claims will be rare outside of the narrow situation where a presumption applies.

3.　OTHER CHALLENGES

a.　Waivers of Other Rights

It has never been doubted that a prosecution filed in retaliation against an accused for the assertion of trial rights violates the constitution. Questions sometimes arise over whether prosecutions that are based on a defendant's refusal to waive other rights are improper. For example, in one case the prosecutor offered to dismiss drunk driving charges against the defendant if he would stipulate that there was probable cause for his arrest. The defendant refused, whereupon the prosecutor filed an amended complaint adding a charge of resisting arrest. When the defendant challenged his subsequent conviction for resisting arrest, the prosecutor defended the attempted waiver as a legitimate effort to protect the police against civil suit. The federal court hearing the case on habeas review disagreed, stating that it was improper for the prosecutor to use a criminal prosecution to forestall a civil proceeding.

The law regarding such waivers is not entirely settled, and the outcome in a given case may depend on the facts of that case. In *Town of Newton v. Rumery* (S.Ct. 1987) the Court addressed the enforceability of a "release-dismissal" agreement in which a criminal defendant releases his right to bring a civil action in return for a prosecutor's dismissal of a pending criminal charge. Rumery had been charged with witness tampering for contacts with the alleged victim and likely witness in a sexual assault prosecution. The charges were dropped after Rumery signed an agreement, drafted by his lawyer, not to sue persons connected with his arrest. Despite the agreement, Rumery later filed a civil suit against the municipality alleging a violation of his civil rights. The Town pleaded the agreement as a bar to the suit. In describing the test for enforceability of such release-dismissal agreements, the Supreme Court stated that "a promise is unenforceable if the interest in its enforcement is outweighed in the circumstances by a public policy harmed by enforcement of the agreement." The Court recognized legitimate public policy reasons for such agreements in protecting public officials from having to defend unfounded claims, and concluded that the risk that an accused would be coerced into entering such an agreement was not sufficient to ban them per se. Because Rumery was a sophisticated businessman represented by an experienced lawyer, and because the prosecutor had a legitimate prosecutorial interest in protecting the sexual assault victim from unnecessary embarrassment, the Court held the agreement enforceable.

b. Duplicative Statutory Schemes

The claim is sometimes made that a prosecutor's decision to prosecute a defendant under one rather than another of two potentially applicable "overlapping" or "duplicative" statutes is improper. The leading federal case on the subject is *U.S. v. Batchelder* (S.Ct.1979). The defendant in *Batchelder* was convicted of violating a statute that made it a crime for a felon to "receive any firearm ... which has been shipped or transported in interstate or foreign commerce." He received the maximum possible sentence of five years in prison. Another statute, which applied to any convicted felon who "receives, possesses, or transports in commerce or affecting commerce ... any firearm," carried a maximum two year sentence. The defendant challenged the prosecutor's election to proceed under the statute authorizing the longer sentence on equal protection and due process grounds.

The Supreme Court unanimously rejected all of the defendant's arguments. The Court held that the statutory scheme was not so vague as to violate the due process requirement of fair notice of potential punishment because the two statutes left no more uncertainty over what penalties might be imposed than a single statute authorizing various alternative punishments. The defendant had also argued that the broad discretion exercised by a prosecutor in deciding between identical statutes with different penalties violated due process and equal protection. The Court found, however, that the discretion involved in selecting between identical statutes was not appreciably greater than that involved in deciding between statutes with different elements. Finally, the Court rejected the claim that, because the prosecutor rather than the legislature decides what penalty is appropriate, the statutory scheme constituted an unconstitutional delegation of legislative power to the prosecutor. The Court concluded that, because the statutes at issue plainly demarcate the range of potential penalties, the delegation of power to decide between identical statutes was no broader than the authority routinely exercised by judges and prosecutors.

The Court's opinion in *Batchelder* appears to foreclose any challenge to a prosecution under overlapping statutes based on federal constitutional grounds. Prior to the *Batchelder* decision, however, some states had held that statutes which define the same crime but carry different penalties are unconstitutional. After *Batchelder* states remain free to interpret their own constitutions to prohibit such schemes.

c. Generally Unenforced Statutes

The criminal codes of many jurisdictions include statutes which are rarely if ever enforced. When someone is charged under one of these long unenforced provisions, the question arises whether there exist legal grounds for challenging the prosecution.

The European civil law recognizes a doctrine known as "desuetude," which holds that prolonged non-enforcement of a criminal statute results in its effective repeal. Some commentators have urged adoption of similar principle in the United States, but courts hearing challenges to prosecutions under generally unenforced statutes have rejected any categorical rule that a statute becomes ineffective through long non-use. For example, in District of Columbia v. John R. Thompson Co. (S.Ct.1953) the Court held "[t]he failure of the executive branch to enforce a law does not result in its modification or repeal" because "[t]he repeal of laws is as much a legislative function as their enactment."

A defendant prosecuted under a long dormant statute may, however, be able to challenge the charges on selective prosecution grounds on the basis that the statute has not been enforced against others. As discussed above, however, the requirements for demonstrating selective prosecution are demanding, and successful challenges are rare.

The most fundamental objection to prosecution under generally unenforced statutes is that a general practice of non-enforcement deprives the defendant of the notice required by due process. The argument, in effect, is that an unenforced statute provides no more notice of the conduct it proscribes than does a statute which is vague or uncertain. Indeed, in an extreme case it might be argued that a prolonged practice of non-enforcement carries the message that the conduct which is technically prohibited is actually condoned by the authorities. According to this argument, just as courts prohibit prosecutions under statutes that are unconstitutionally vague, they should also prohibit prosecutions under statutes which no longer provide the necessary notice because of a practice of non-enforcement.

Courts considering challenges to generally unenforced statutes have recognized the potential validity of a due process-no fair notice defense. They have emphasized, however, that a prosecution is not vulnerable to a due process challenge simply because it is based on a previously unenforced statute. In order to prevail the defendant would have to point to circumstances showing why she reasonably believed her conduct was not punishable under the criminal law.

CHAPTER 2

PRETRIAL DETENTION
AND RELEASE

A. THE RIGHT TO A PROBABLE CAUSE DETERMINATION

Criminal prosecutions often, though not always, begin with the arrest of the suspect. If the suspect is not arrested, she will be issued a citation or summons commanding her to appear in court at a specified date. The Supreme Court has held that a suspect who has been arrested may not be held in custody for an extended period unless there has been a determination by a neutral and detached magistrate that there is probable cause to believe the arrestee has committed a crime.

The requirement of a judicial determination of probable cause for detained suspects was first stated in *Gerstein v. Pugh* (S.Ct.1975). The defendants in *Gerstein* were arrested and held in jail under a Florida law that permitted the initiation of criminal proceedings on the basis of a "prosecutor's information," a formal allegation by the prosecutor that a particular person has committed specified crimes. Although the Florida procedure required a pre-trial probable cause determination before the defendant could be *tried*, the law permitted a suspect to be jailed for a month or more pending the preliminary hearing based on the prosecutor's allegations alone.

Relying on the Fourth Amendment protection against unreasonable searches and seizures, the Supreme Court held that the Constitution "requires a judicial determination of probable cause as a prerequisite to extended restraint of liberty." *Gerstein*. A probable cause determination following arrest is also required if pretrial release is "accompanied by burdensome conditions that effect a significant restraint of liberty." *Gerstein*. The requirement does not apply, however, to suspects who have been arrested after having been indicted by a grand jury or on the basis of an arrest warrant. The reason for exempting those who have been indicted or named in an arrest warrant is because a neutral decision maker will have already found probable cause as to those defendants.

The Court in *Gerstein* held that the probable cause determination required by the Fourth Amendment may be based on written submissions and hearsay evidence. The defendant is not entitled to be present at the determination or to be represented by counsel, to confront or cross-examine witnesses, or present evidence. The standard for probable cause is the same as the standard for arrest—"facts and circumstances 'sufficient to warrant a prudent man in believing the suspect had committed or was committing an offense.'" *Gerstein*. Both the non-adversarial procedures and the standard are consistent with the rules governing probable cause determinations for arrest warrants and in grand jury proceedings.

The Supreme Court clarified the time frame within which a judicial determination of probable cause must be made in *County of Riverside v. McLaughlin* (S.Ct.1991). The Court stated that a jurisdiction that provides judicial determinations of probable cause within 48 hours of arrest will, as a general matter, comply with the promptness requirement established in *Gerstein*. The 48 hour rule is not, however, an inflexible standard. A determination may be untimely even if made within 48 hours if it was delayed unreasonably. Examples of unreasonable delay include delays for the purpose of gathering additional evidence to justify the arrest, a delay motivated by ill will against the suspect, or delay for delay's sake. On the other hand, if the determination is made more than 48 hours after arrest, the burden shifts to the government to demonstrate the existence of a bona fide emergency or other extraordinary circumstance.

The Court in *Gerstein* made clear that an unlawful detention does not void a subsequent conviction. The only remedy that has been recognized for a violation of the rule is the exclusion of confessions or the results of consensual searches that occurred during the unlawful detention. Even these sanctions are rarely imposed.

The *Gerstein* decision represents an important statement of principle. In rejecting the argument that the prosecutor's assessment of probable cause provides a sufficient basis for detaining the defendant pending trial, the decision reaffirms the essentially adversary character of the criminal justice system, in which guilt or innocence is adjudicated through a process of partisan presentation before a neutral decision maker. The practical significance of the decision, however, is limited. Although the *Gerstein* requirement has resulted in the development of procedures to assure prompt processing of arrestees in may jurisdictions, the informal procedures required under the decision and the absence of a meaningful remedy for a violation diminish the significance of the rule in individual cases.

The *Gerstein* requirement should be distinguished from the requirement of an *initial appearance*, though the two procedures are often combined into a single proceeding. The *Gerstein* probable cause determination is required by the constitution, and can be accomplished without the defendant being present. The initial appearance, which is also sometimes called the *first* appearance or the *preliminary arraignment*, is required by statute or rule, and necessitates the attendance of the defendant. An initial appearance is required whether or not the defendant was arrested with a warrant, and even if the defendant was not arrested but simply issued a summons.

The purposes and procedures of the initial appearance vary somewhat from jurisdiction to jurisdiction. Rule 5 of the Federal Rules of Criminal Procedure, which governs the initial appearance in the federal system, is typical. Rule 5 requires that an officer making an arrest, with or without a warrant, take the arrested person "without unnecessary delay" before the nearest available federal magistrate judge. The magistrate is required to inform the defendant of the charges, but the defendant is not required to enter a plea. The magistrate also informs the defendant of various constitutional and statutory rights, including the right to counsel, the right to request appointed counsel if indigent, the right to remain silent, and the right to a preliminary examination. If a defendant is not already represented by an attorney, one will typically be appointed at the initial appearance. *See* Fed. R. Crim. Pro. 44(a). From the defendant's perspective, perhaps the most important function of the initial appearance is to determine the conditions of release pending trial.

B.   ASSURING THE DEFENDANT'S APPEARANCE AT TRIAL

1.   THE BAIL SYSTEM

"Bail" refers to a sum of money that the defendant is required to deposit with the court as a condition of release from custody pending trial. If the defendant appears for scheduled court dates, the bail is refunded. Historically, bail was the principal mechanism for assuring that a defendant who had been released pending trial would return to court.

The court has broad discretion in setting what bail shall be required. In principle, the amount of bail is based on an estimate of the minimum sum necessary to induce the defendant to appear. In fixing bail, the court begins with an estimation of the likelihood that the defendant will appear for trial without regard to bail, and then calculates what additional financial incentive will raise the likelihood of the defendant's appearance to an acceptable level.

The calculation of bail requires consideration of a number of factors. The nature of the alleged offense and the strength of the evidence of guilt are both relevant. The seriousness of the alleged crime is relevant, since the greater the potential punishment the stronger the defendant's incentive to flee. The strength of the evidence is also relevant, since the stronger the evidence of guilt the greater the likelihood of conviction at trial. If the defendant believes that her chances for conviction are high, she may be more likely to abscond to avoid conviction.

The other set of factors relates to the individual defendant. The defendant's financial situation is considered relevant, because a person with wealth may be more willing to forfeit some of it to avoid a conviction than would a person without means. The individual's family and community ties are also relevant. A person with strong ties to the locality where the case will be tried will have an incentive to remain in the area apart from the incentive created by the posting of bail. The defendant's character, measured primarily by the number and seriousness of prior convictions and the defendant's record of compliance with pre-trial release conditions in the past, is also considered relevant to the amount of bail.

Decisions regarding bail are typically made at the time of the defendant's first appearance before a judicial officer. In both state and federal courts, the official who presides over such hearings and decides questions about bail is a lower court judge who often does not have the authority to try the case.

The defendant does not have a constitutional right to counsel at a bail hearing. Federal law grants the defendant the right to an attorney by statute. The law and practice relating to the provision of counsel at bail hearings among the states varies. The information relied on by the judge in deciding bail issues need not be admissible under the rules of evidence.

In its actual operation the bail system often deviates in significant ways from the theory. While the theory assumes that the only legitimate purpose of requiring bail is to assure the defendant's appearance at trial, in practice bail is often set at an amount that the defendant cannot pay as a way of keeping the defendant in custody to prevent her from committing crimes while awaiting trial. Rather than tailoring the amount of bail to the individual defendant, bail is often set by reference to schedules which specify standard bail amounts for particular crimes. Most importantly, the basic premises behind the use of bail are undermined by the widespread use of professional bail bondsmen.

A defendant who cannot raise enough cash to make bail may nevertheless be able to win release from custody by engaging the services of a bail bondsman. The defendant pays a fee, typically ten percent of the bail amount, to the bondsman, who then guarantees the full amount of the bail to the court. If the defendant absconds, the *bondsman* forfeits the bail. It is the bondsman, therefore, rather than the defendant, who has the financial stake in the defendant's appearance for trial. Although the court sets the amount of the bail, the bondsman has effective control over who shall be released from custody, since the bondsman will refuse services to defendants who are regarded as posing too great a risk of flight.

Dissatisfaction with the bail system and the influence of bail bondsmen has fueled efforts to reduce reliance on bail as the presumptive method of assuring and the defendant's appearance. Concern that the reliance on the offense charged as the primary factor in fixing bail punishes the poor has encouraged the use of more individualized standards in setting bail.

One alternative to traditional cash bail that has effectively eliminated bail bondsmen in states where it has been introduced permits jailed defendants to obtain release pending trial by depositing ten percent of the bail amount with the court and executing a bond for the remainder. If the defendant absconds, she is liable under the bond for the full amount of the bail. If she complies with the terms of the bond, however, the court refunds the ten percent deposit, less a small administrative fee. "Property bonds" do not require a cash deposit, but do require that the defendant provide security in the form of property for payment of the bond should she fail to appear. The form of release involving the least restrictive financial condition permits the defendant to be released upon the execution of an unsecured bond. The defendant is not required to provide either cash or security initially, but becomes liable on the bond if she fails to appear. Release may be made available subject to nonfinancial conditions, such as remaining in the custody of a relative or other person, reporting to law enforcement, maintaining employment, or undergoing medical or psychological treatment. Finally, the least restrictive form of release is personal recognizance or "release on recognizance" (ROR), which enables the accused to be released based on a bare promise to return for trial.

In addition to reforming the rules regarding bail, many jurisdictions have passed statutes that authorize the pretrial detention of defendants who are deemed dangerous in order to prevent them from committing crimes while awaiting trial. None of the state statutes adopted so far is as broad as the preventive detention provisions of the 1984 Federal Bail Reform Act, discussed below. Typical state statutes make preventive detention available only for defendant's charged with certain categories of serious offenses.

Another approach to the problem of ensuring the defendant's attendance at trial, which is perhaps more accurately regarded as punishment than inducement, and which is used *with* rather than *in place of* the techniques described above, is to impose a criminal penalty for the knowing failure to appear. "Bail jumping" statutes typically link the penalty for non-appearance to the penalty that is authorized for the underlying charge. For instance, if the defendant failed to appear while awaiting trial on a robbery charge, the penalty for non-appearance will depend on the punishment that is authorized for robbery.

2.   CONSTITUTIONAL PARAMETERS

The Eighth Amendment to the United States constitution provides that "excessive bail shall not be required." Although the applicability of this provision to the states has never been squarely addressed, the Supreme Court has "assumed [the Bail Clause] to have application to the States through the Fourteenth Amendment." *Schilb v. Kuebel* (S.Ct.1971). State constitutions typically include bail provisions as well. Although state bail clauses vary, a common pattern creates a right to bail in all but capital offenses. Notably, more than 15 states have amended their constitutions to permit preventative detention in certain situations.

As will be discussed more fully in the next section, the Supreme Court has rejected an interpretation of the Eighth Amendment as guaranteeing a *right* to bail. What the Bail Clause guarantees is that bail, when it is otherwise available, shall not be set at an amount that is "excessive."

The leading United States Supreme Court case on what constitutes excessive bail under the Eighth Amendment is *Stack v. Boyle* (S.Ct.1951). Twelve defendants were accused of conspiring to advocate the violent overthrow of the government. The district court set uniform bail at $50,000 for each defendant. In support of their motion to reduce bail as excessive under the Eighth Amendment, the defendants submitted statements as to their financial resources, family relationships, health, prior criminal records, and other information. The only evidence offered by the government in response to the motion was evidence that four other persons, apparently unrelated to the defendants, who were charged with the same offense had forfeited bail.

In awarding the defendants the right to renew their motion to reduce bail, the Supreme Court stated that "bail set at a figure higher than an amount reasonably calculated to [assure an accused's presence at trial] is 'excessive' under the Eighth Amendment." Although this statement suggests that the only legitimate consideration in establishing the conditions of pre-trial release is assuring the defendant's attendance at trial, that interpretation of the Eighth Amendment has now been rejected. *See* Section C2 below. In *U.S. v. Salerno* (S.Ct.1987) the Court held that the Eighth Amendment does not prohibit the government from pursuing objectives other than assuring the defendant's appearance in setting the conditions of pretrial release. The only limitation imposed by the Bail Clause is that the conditions imposed not be excessive in relation to the objective that is being pursued. "Thus, when the government has admitted that its only interest is in preventing flight, bail must be set by a court at a sum designed to ensure that goal, and no more."

The Court in *Stack* also emphasized that the amount required as bail must take into account the facts of the particular case. The Court stated that the standards relevant to assuring the defendant's attendance at trial must "be applied in each case to each defendant." *Stack*. The "traditional" standards included the nature and circumstances of the offense, the weight of the evidence, the financial ability of the defendant to give bail, and the character of the defendant. In setting uniform bail for all 12 defendants based solely on the nature of the charge, without regard for the circumstances of the individual defendant, the district court in *Stack* had not applied the proper standards.

In *Stack* the Court mentioned the defendant's financial circumstances as a relevant factor in determining the amount of bail. This is based on the common sense assumption that it requires a larger sum of money to induce a rich person to return than to induce a poor person to return. The requirement that the court consider the defendant's financial circumstances does not mean that bail which is otherwise proper is excessive because the defendant is indigent and cannot afford it. The constitution prohibits courts from requiring more bail than is necessary to assure the defendant's attendance at trial. The Eighth Amendment does not require the courts to make release on bail available regardless of the defendant's financial circumstances by setting bail the defendant can afford.

The courts have also rejected the argument that indigent defendants who are unable to win release on bail are denied equal protection because similarly situated defendants with assets are able to make bail.

3.   THE 1966 AND 1984 FEDERAL REFORMS

In 1966 Congress passed the Federal Bail Reform Act. The 1966 Act, which served as a model for reforms passed in many states, made pre-trial release more generally available, and reduced the emphasis on bail or other financial conditions as inducements to return. The statute marked a clear departure from the traditional reliance on bail by establishing personal recognizance as the preferred method of pre-trial release.

In 1984 Congress repealed the 1966 Act and replaced it with the Bail Reform Act of 1984. The 1984 Act preserves many features of the 1966 law, but also introduces two significant changes. First, the law expressly authorizes the judge in establishing the conditions of release to consider whether releasing the defendant would endanger others. Second, the law expressly authorizes the judge to deny pre-trial release in order to assure the defendant's appearance or to prevent the accused from committing crimes while awaiting trial. (The "preventive detention" provisions are discussed in the next section.)

The Bail Reform Act of 1984 authorizes three types of pre-trial release: 1) release on personal recognizance; 2) release upon execution of an unsecured appearance bond in an amount specified by the court; and 3) release on conditions. The Act creates a presumption in favor of release under one of the first two types of release; it instructs the court to release the defendant on recognizance or execution of a bond "unless the judicial officer determines that such release will not reasonably assure the appearance of the person as required or will endanger the safety of any other person or the community."

If the judge decides to release the defendant on conditions, the statute requires that the judge utilize the "least restrictive" set of conditions that will reasonably assure the appearance of the defendant and the safety of others. One condition that is required of every defendant is that she not commit a crime while on release. In addition, the judge may impose one or more of thirteen conditions listed in the statute, as well as any other condition that is necessary to fulfill the purposes of assuring the defendant's appearance and protecting others.

The Act specifies four factors to be taken into account in determining what conditions will suffice to fulfill the purposes of assuring the defendant's appearance and protecting others: 1) the nature and circumstances of the charged offense; 2) the weight of the evidence; 3) the history and characteristics of the accused, including family and community ties, criminal history, record of appearance in previous cases, and whether the alleged crime was committed while the accused was on probation or release pending trial; and 4) the nature and seriousness of the danger to any person or the community that would be posed by the defendant's release.

The statute states that the court may not impose a financial condition that results in the pre-trial detention of the accused. The purpose of this provision, according to the Senate Judiciary Committee Report that accompanied the Act, is to put an end to the practice of setting bail at an amount the defendant cannot afford in order to keep dangerous defendants in custody. If the judge believes that the defendant must be detained to assure her appearance or protect the community, the judge must follow the procedures for preventive detention. The prohibition against imposing a financial condition that results in the defendant's detention does not, however, require the court to make release on bail available regardless of the defendant's financial circumstances by setting bail at an amount that the accused can afford.

The statute authorizes the judicial officer to amend the release order at any time to impose additional or different conditions. Either the defendant or the government may seek review of a magistrate's release order by the district judge, and either may pursue an interlocutory appeal to the court of appeals. The release order must include a clear and specific written statement setting forth all the conditions of the defendant's release, and advise the defendant of the penalties and other consequences of violating a condition of release.

Violation of a condition of release is punishable as contempt. In addition, violation of a release condition may result in the defendant's detention. Detention can be ordered only after a hearing at which the judicial officer makes a finding that no conditions will assure the defendant's appearance or the safety of the community or that the defendant is unlikely to abide by any conditions of release.

C. PREVENTIVE DETENTION

1. PROCEDURAL ISSUES

Notwithstanding the assumption that the only purpose of bail is to ensure the defendant's appearance at trial, courts sometimes set bail at an amount the defendant cannot afford in order to detain persons deemed dangerous. The 1984 Act prohibits this subterfuge by stating that the court may not impose a financial condition that results in the pretrial detention of the person. The Act also makes the sub rosa use of bail to detain the defendant unnecessary by providing for preventive detention directly.

The two general requirements for ordering the defendant's detention pending trial under the 1984 Federal Bail Reform Act are 1) a hearing before a judicial officer and 2) a finding that the defendant poses an unacceptable risk of flight or danger to others or the community. The "judicial officer" referred to by the Act includes either a judge or a magistrate, though detention hearings are usually conducted by magistrates.

The Act specifies a limited set of circumstances that will trigger a detention hearing. First, the court must hold a detention hearing, on motion by the prosecutor, if the defendant is charged with certain types of crimes. The Act specifies four categories of crimes that may trigger a detention hearing: a crime of violence; any crime for which the maximum sentence is life imprisonment or death; a drug crime for which the sentence is ten years or more; and any felony if the defendant has previously been convicted of two or more of the above offenses or equivalent state crimes. In addition, the court shall also hold a hearing on motion of the prosecutor or on its own motion, in cases involving either a serious risk that the person will flee or a serious risk that the person will obstruct justice or intimidate prospective witnesses or jurors.

The Act directs the court to order the defendant's detention if, after the hearing, the judicial officer finds "that no condition or combination of conditions [attaching to release] will reasonably assure the appearance of the person as required and the safety of any other person and the community." It is not clear from the Act precisely what sorts of threats to the safety of others and the community warrant the defendant's detention. The legislative history indicates that Congress was concerned about accused persons committing *crimes* while on release awaiting trial. Whether any crime qualifies is not clear. For instance, it is uncertain whether a defendant who is found to present an unreasonable risk of selling or using drugs represents a threat to the safety of the community that warrants detention.

In determining whether the defendant should be detained, the court is to consider the same four factors used in determining what conditions, if any, should be imposed on the defendant's release, i.e., the charge, the evidence of guilt, characteristics of the accused, and the danger posed by the defendant's release. *See* Section B2 above. In addition to these four factors, the Act establishes two rebuttable presumptions in favor of detention. The "previous violator" presumption applies only in cases where the detention hearing is based on the defendant's having been charged with a particular type of crime; it does not apply when the hearing is ordered because the defendant poses a risk of flight or intimidation of witnesses or jurors. The presumption arises if the defendant, who stands charged with one of the four types of crimes that trigger a detention hearing, has been previously convicted of one of those same crimes while the defendant was on release pending trial. In addition, the prior conviction or release from confinement, whichever is later, must have occurred within the past five years. An accused who qualifies for this presumption is presumed too dangerous to be released.

The "drugs and firearms" presumption may apply regardless of the grounds for convening the detention hearing. It arises if the defendant is charged with a drug felony carrying at least a ten year sentence or with use or possession of a firearm during the commission of a violent felony. When this presumption applies it is presumed that no release conditions will reasonably assure that the defendant will not flee or commit crimes if not detained.

The Act does not clarify the effect of these presumptions beyond stating that they are rebuttable, and the Supreme Court has not interpreted the presumption provisions. The lower federal courts have concluded that the presumptions shift the burden of production to the accused, but do not shift the burden of persuasion. (For an explanation of the different types of presumptions, see Chapter 13, Section D2 below.) Unlike some production shifting presumptions, however, the presumptions established by the Act do not evaporate with the introduction of contrary evidence by the defendant. The presumption retains some force even after it has been rebutted. This means that in weighing the evidence relating to the charge and the accused, the court should bear in mind that persons who fit within the terms of the presumption generally pose a greater risk of flight or danger to others than do persons for whom the presumption does not apply. Courts have suggested that a presumption that shifts the burden of persuasion might violate due process, but have rejected constitutional challenges to the Act's presumptions if construed as shifting only the burden of production.

The detention hearing is to be held at the time of the defendant's first appearance unless the defendant or the government seeks a continuance. Except for good cause, a continuance at the request of the defendant may not exceed five days, and a continuance granted at the request of the government may not exceed three days. The Act authorizes the detention of the defendant pending completion of the hearing.

The Act guarantees the defendant the right to be represented by an attorney at the hearing. If the defendant cannot afford adequate representation, counsel will be appointed by the court. The defendant has the right to testify, to present witnesses, and to cross-examine prosecution witnesses. The Act also gives the defendant the option of presenting information at the hearing by way of "proffer." A proffer in this context typically involves a summary by the accused's attorney of evidence that is available but not actually presented in the form of live witness testimony or documents. Although the Act does not expressly authorize the prosecutor to proceed by way of proffer, some courts have extended this option to the government as well.

The rules regarding admissibility of evidence in criminal trials do not apply to the presentation and consideration of information at the hearing. The Act states that the facts in support of the court's finding that no combination of release conditions will reasonably assure the safety of any other person and the community must be supported by clear and convincing evidence. (The clear and convincing standard apparently does not apply if the detention order is predicated on a conclusion that the defendant presents an unacceptable flight risk.)

If the judge orders the defendant detained she must make written findings of fact and a statement of reasons for the detention. The Act directs that, to the extent practicable, the person be confined separately from persons who have been convicted of a crime. If the detention decision is made by a magistrate, the losing party may seek review by a judge. The Act also authorizes either party to seek appellate review of the decision in the court of appeals.

2.   CONSTITUTIONAL CHALLENGES

Preventive detention is subject to constitutional challenge on several grounds, including substantive due process, procedural due process, the Eighth Amendment prohibition against excessive bail, and equal protection. (The pre-trial confinement of persons who have been charged with a crime but not convicted does not violate the due process presumption of innocence, which the Supreme Court has described as a doctrine that allocates the burden of proof at trial, and is inapplicable to proceedings before trial.)

The United States Supreme Court rejected due process and Eighth Amendment challenges to the preventive detention provisions of the 1984 Federal

Bail Reform Act in *U.S. v. Salerno* (S.Ct.1987). The
defendants in *Salerno*, who were charged with
RICO and other offenses, were detained under the
Act after the district court found that the government had established by clear and convincing evidence that no condition or combination of conditions of release would ensure the safety of the
community or any person. In challenging their detention, the defendants claimed that the preventive
detention provisions of the Act were unconstitutional on their face. The Supreme Court stressed that in
order to prevail on such a challenge, the challenger
must establish that no set of circumstances exists
under which the Act would be valid.

The Court first addressed the contention that the
Bail Reform Act violates substantive due process
because the pretrial detention it authorizes constitutes impermissible punishment before trial. In rejecting this claim, the Court first stated that the
fact that a person is detained does not necessarily
lead to the conclusion that the government has
imposed "punishment." The test for whether a
restriction on liberty constitutes *punishment*, which
may not be imposed prior to a determination of
guilt, or permissible *regulation* looks first to the
intent of the legislature in passing the statute. If
Congress expressly intended that the restrictions be
punitive, the restrictions violate due process. If
Congress did not express an intention to punish,
the court must ask whether the restriction is rationally connected to some alternative, non-punitive
purpose. If an alternative purpose is assignable to

the restriction, the court must determine whether the restriction that is imposed is excessive in relation to that purpose. This final inquiry requires a balancing of the governmental interest served by the restriction against the individual's liberty interest.

In applying this test to the 1984 Bail Reform Act, the Court found that the legislative history to the Act clearly shows that Congress did not intend the preventive detention provisions as punishment for dangerous individuals. Rather, Congress perceived pretrial detention as a potential solution to the legitimate regulatory goal of preventing danger to the community. The Court also found that the incidents of pretrial detention prescribed by the Act are not excessive in relation to the objective sought to be achieved in imposing the restrictions. In support of this conclusion, the Court pointed to several features of the Act: The Act "carefully limits the circumstances under which detention may be sought to the most serious crimes"; the arrestee is entitled to a prompt detention hearing, and the maximum length of detention is limited by the limitations of the Speedy Trial Act; and the detainee is to be confined separately from persons who are incarcerated under a conviction. Finally, in support of its conclusion that the Act's restrictions are not excessive in relation to its purposes, the Court found that the government's interest in preventing crimes by arrestees is "both legitimate and compelling," and outweighs the individual's "strong" interest in liberty.

The Court summarily dismissed the claim that the procedures governing detention hearings violate procedural due process. Quoting from an earlier decision upholding a state statute authorizing pretrial detention of juveniles, the Court stated that "there is nothing inherently unattainable about a prediction of future criminal conduct." (The Court did not address social science studies which have raised questions about the reliability of predictions of future criminality.) The Court then cited the key procedural features of the Act, including: provisions granting the arrestee the rights to counsel, to present evidence and to cross-examine witnesses; the requirements that the judge decide based on specified factors, and provide written findings of fact and reasons for a decision to detain; the requirement that the government prove its case by clear and convincing evidence; and the provisions for immediate appellate review. The Court declared that "these extensive safeguards suffice to repel a facial challenge [on procedural due process grounds]."

Though approving the procedures of the Bail Reform Act, the Court's opinion fails to clarify whether a preventive detention scheme with fewer or less stringent procedural safeguards—e.g., no right to counsel, absence of cross examination, a lower standard of proof—would satisfy constitutional standards of procedural due process. In particular, it is not clear from the opinion whether the non-adversary procedures approved in *Gerstein v. Pugh* for probable cause determinations would satisfy due process if those procedures were used to make preventive detention decisions. At lease one court has held, in a decision that pre-dates *Salerno*, that the Supreme Court's holding in *Gerstein* is controlling in the preventive detention context. In *U.S. v. Edwards* (D.C.App.1981) the court reasoned that procedures which suffice for a probable cause determination are also adequate for a preventive detention decision because the effect of the findings in a detention hearing and a *Gerstein* hearing are the same—each hearing determines whether the accused may be detained pending trial. However, as was pointed out in dissent in that case, there are two important differences between the *Gerstein* probable cause determination and the decision whether to impose preventive detention: 1) the predictive decision about whether the arrestee is likely to commit crimes in the future is much more complex than the determination of whether there is probable cause, and therefore requires a more carefully focused analysis; and 2) the effect of a finding of probable cause is not in fact the same as a decision to detain, since a finding of probable cause only authorizes the detention of the person pending a determination of the person's eligibility for release on bail. The Supreme Court's only comment on the question in *Salerno* was a statement that the procedures required under the Bail Reform Act "far exceed what we found necessary to effect limited post-arrest detention in *Gerstein v. Pugh*." This statement leaves unresolved the question whether *Gerstein*-type procedures would be constitutionally adequate if employed for preventive detention decisions.

Finally, in *Salerno,* the Court held that the preventive detention provisions of the Act do not violate the Eighth Amendment prohibition against excessive bail. The Court adopted a narrow interpretation of the Bail Clause, rejecting the view that the Eighth Amendment grants a right to bail calculated solely on considerations of flight. (The Court also suggested, but did not actually hold, that the Bail Clause is directed exclusively at the *courts,* and does not impose any restriction on the *legislature's* power to grant or deny bail.) The text of the Bail Clause, the Court pointed out, "says nothing about whether bail shall be available at all," and does not specify what objectives the government may pursue in establishing the conditions of pretrial detention or release. *Salerno.* Thus, the Bail Clause does not prohibit the government from pursuing objectives other than ensuring the defendant's appearance at trial, and does not categorically prohibit the government from detaining the defendant to prevent the commission of crimes while awaiting trial. "The only arguable substantive limitation of the Bail Clause is that the government's proposed conditions of release or detention not be 'excessive' in light of the perceived evil." If the government admits that its only interest is in preventing flight, "bail must be set by a court at a sum designed to ensure that goal, and no more." But when the objective is to prevent a dangerous defendant from committing crimes while awaiting trial, the Eighth Amendment does not require release on bail, since pretrial detention is not excessive in relation to that objective.

The Court in *Salerno* emphasized that its holding was limited to the *facial* validity of the preventive detention provisions of the Bail Reform Act. The possibility remains that the Act could be found unconstitutional as applied to the facts of a particular case. For instance, some lower courts have held that a prolonged pretrial detention under the Act could result in a violation of due process.

The Equal Protection Clause provides another possible basis for challenging the Act's preventive detention scheme. The argument underlying such a challenge is that the statute arbitrarily targets one class of dangerous persons—those who have been charged with a crime. Individuals who, though equally dangerous, have not been charged with a crime, are not subject to preventive detention under the Act.

D. POST CONVICTION BAIL

Once the defendant has been convicted of a crime, release on bail pending sentence or appeal is less likely to be available than is pre-trial release. There are several reasons for applying stricter standards to applications for post conviction bail. The temptation to flee is presumably stronger following conviction because the likelihood of punishment is greater. Since the defendant has been found guilty, the presumption of innocence is not implicated. After the trial is over, the defendant can no longer claim that incarceration will prevent her from assisting in the preparation of a defense.

The different approach to post conviction bail is reflected in many state constitutions, which guarantee a right to bail "before conviction." The 1984 Federal Bail Reform Act imposes especially strict standards for obtaining release pending sentence or appeal. The Act directs that a person who has been convicted and is awaiting sentence shall be detained unless the judicial officer finds by clear and convincing evidence that the person is not likely to flee or pose a danger to the safety of any other person or the community. For convicted persons seeking release pending appeal, the judicial officer must find *in addition* that reversal or other disposition favorable to the defendant is "likely."

CHAPTER 3

THE PRELIMINARY HEARING

A. FUNCTIONS AND USES OF THE PRELIMINARY HEARING

The preliminary hearing, also called the preliminary examination, is an adversarial evidentiary proceeding at which the prosecutor must present sufficient evidence of the defendant's guilt of a serious crime (usually limited to a felony) to justify requiring the defendant to either face trial in a superior court or have the case submitted to the grand jury for indictment and subsequent trial. The preliminary hearing is typically conducted before a judge of a court of limited jurisdiction (such as a municipal court), a magistrate, or some other judicial officer who lacks jurisdiction to try the case.

The preliminary hearing is usually held shortly after the arrest and initial appearance of a person charged with a serious crime. At the initial appearance, the magistrate will inform the defendant of the essential elements of the crime charged, the defendant's rights to a preliminary hearing, to counsel, to release on bail or recognizance (which will be fixed at this initial appearance), and also the defendant's privilege against self-incrimination.

Historically, the primary function of the preliminary hearing is to ensure that there exists sufficient evidence to justify detaining the accused and compelling her to submit to review of the charges by a grand jury or a trial. In short, the goal is to screen out weak cases. If the defendant waives preliminary hearing or if the magistrate finds sufficient evidence that the defendant committed the crime or crimes alleged by the prosecutor, the defendant is "held to answer" or "bound over" for the next step in the process.

The effectiveness of the preliminary hearing in screening out baseless charges is debatable. In many jurisdictions the defendant is held to answer on the charge in all but a small percentage of cases. In other jurisdictions as many as thirty percent of cases are dismissed at the preliminary hearing stage. The requirement of a pre-trial or pre-indictment screening procedure may be as important as the screening process itself, since an awareness that a judge will be required to pass on the sufficiency of the evidence may impel prosecutors to engage in a self-screening of charges that accomplishes the basic objectives of the hearing.

In many jurisdictions the screening of charges for trial is the only recognized function of the preliminary hearing. This means that efforts by the defense to achieve other ends, with the hearing will be cut short. Whether permitted or not, the preliminary hearing everywhere serves ancillary purposes that may be more important than the official screening function. The preliminary hearing gives both sides, albeit, principally the defense, an opportunity to assess the respective strengths of their cases. Furthermore, because the preliminary hearing is an adversarial proceeding at which the defendant is present, the hearing provides the defendant an opportunity to obtain discovery of the prosecution's evidence. The effectiveness of the preliminary hearing as a defense discovery device will depend on the type of evidence the prosecutor is required to present, as well as on the defendant's tactical decision whether to risk assisting the prosecution by cross-examining prosecution witnesses. The prosecutor may also use the preliminary hearing as a dry run for later trial testimony or to solidify an eyewitness identification or other testimony.

The preliminary hearing also serves as an important source of impeachment evidence for later use at trial. All jurisdictions permit the credibility of a witness to be attacked through the introduction of evidence of statements made before trial that are inconsistent with the witness's trial testimony. To the extent a witness's preliminary hearing testimony differs from his or her later trial testimony, the discrepancy can be used to argue that the witness is not worthy of belief. The possibility of producing such discrepancies is both the attraction and deterrent of the preliminary hearing. Sometimes defense lawyers use preliminary hearings as a tool to educate their clients. The strength of the prosecution's preliminary hearing can be used as a tool to help a defendant make an informed choice of taking the offered plea bargain. Sometimes defense lawyers use preliminary hearings as a tool to educate their clients. The strength of the prosecution's preliminary hearing can be used as a tool to help a defendant make an informed choice of taking the offered plea bargain.

Finally, the preliminary hearing can be used, primarily by the prosecution, as a means of preserving evidence for trial. An important limitation on the use of the preliminary hearing to preserve evidence is that a witness's preliminary hearing testimony may not be presented at trial unless the witness is unavailable to testify at the trial. This is because the testimony given at the preliminary hearing is "hearsay" when offered at trial, and the former testimony exception to the hearsay rule requires proof of the witness's unavailability. Indeed, under Crawford v. Wash. (S.Ct.2004), the test for whether a prior statement is admissible revolves around whether a defendant had an adequate opportunity to cross-examine. However, in those instances where the prosecutor has any concern that the state's principal witnesses might not be available for trial, calling those witnesses at a preliminary hearing could perpetuate the witnesses' testimony.

B. RIGHT TO A PRELIMINARY HEARING

The Supreme Court held in *Lem Woon v. Oregon* (S.Ct.1913) that the United States constitution does not guarantee a right to a preliminary hearing.

Indeed, the constitution does not require any mechanism for pre-trial screening of charges. Although the Court held in *Gerstein v. Pugh* (S.Ct.1975), that the fourth amendment guarantees a right to a judicial determination of probable cause as a condition to pre-trial detention, the *Gerstein* determination serves a different function and employs different procedures from a preliminary hearing. The *Gerstein* determination protects the defendant's interest against being detained without sufficient cause, whereas the preliminary hearing protects the interest against being tried without sufficient cause; the finding required by *Gerstein v. Pugh* can be based on *ex parte* submissions by the prosecutor, whereas the preliminary hearing is an adversarial procedure where the defendant is entitled to be present and introduce evidence.

Although not required by the constitution, almost all jurisdictions provide for a preliminary hearing by statute or court rule. In many jurisdictions, however, the defendant's entitlement to a preliminary hearing can be preempted by prior presentation of the case to a grand jury.

1. IN THE FEDERAL SYSTEM

The Fifth Amendment requires that the prosecution of felonies in federal court be based on an indictment issued by a grand jury. In addition to the constitutional requirement of grand jury review, Rule 5(a) of the Federal Rules of Criminal Procedure requires a preliminary hearing within ten days after the initial appearance if the defendant is in custody, and within 20 days if the defendant is not in custody. However, no preliminary hearing is required if the defendant is indicted by a grand jury before the deadline for holding the preliminary hearing. The indictment of the defendant by a grand jury, eliminates the necessity for a preliminary hearing. This avoidance of the preliminary hearing can be referred to as the bypass rule.

The original reason for requiring review of the charges both by a grand jury and by a judge at a preliminary hearing was to ensure prompt review by means of a preliminary hearing in those parts of the country where grand juries met infrequently. In many federal districts today, prosecutors are able to avoid a preliminary hearing in most cases by presenting the case to a grand jury before the defendant's entitlement to a preliminary hearing ripens. In short, when the government presents its case to a grand jury, the defendant is not entitled to a preliminary hearing and cannot demand one for the purposes of screening the charges and gaining discovery.

2.   IN THE STATES

The states are about equally divided between states that require grand jury review for all felonies (indictment states) and states that permit the prosecution of felonies based on a sworn allegation by the prosecutor called a "prosecutor's information" (information states). States that require indictment by a grand jury typically have a provision like the federal bypass rule that permits the prosecutor to bypass the preliminary hearing through a prior presentation of the charges to the grand jury. It is a common practice, however, for prosecutors first to present the charges at a preliminary hearing and then a second time before a grand jury.

In information states, the prosecutor typically has the choice of either presenting the charges to a grand jury or conducting a preliminary hearing. In many jurisdictions that offer a choice between grand jury review and a preliminary hearing, the majority of felonies are routinely prosecuted by an information and a preliminary hearing.

A preliminary hearing has advantages for the defendant over grand jury review. Because grand jury hearings are secret, non-adversarial, *ex parte* proceedings, the grand jury does not offer the defendant the same opportunities for discovery or to compel attendance of defense witnesses as the preliminary hearing. Based on these differences, the California Supreme Court at one time held that the equal protection clause of the state constitution guaranteed the right to a preliminary hearing even if the defendant had previously been indicted by a grand jury. That holding, however, was later overturned through an amendment to the state constitution.

C. THE BINDOVER DECISION

The prosecutor has the burden of proving at the preliminary hearing that there is probable cause to believe a crime was committed and that the accused committed it. Though there may be slightly different wording of this burden from jurisdiction to jurisdiction, the essence is the same: proof that a crime has been committed (the *corpus delicti*) and that the perpetrator is the accused. In most jurisdictions, the standard of proof the prosecutor must satisfy is simply probable cause, a lower standard than either proof beyond a reasonable doubt that is required in criminal trials or preponderance of the evidence used in civil cases.

On its face, the probable cause showing required at the preliminary hearing would appear to be redundant and unnecessary, since a prior judicial determination of probable cause will usually have been made either in the issuance of an arrest warrant or as part of a probable cause determination under the principles of *Gerstein v. Pugh*. But the probable cause standard applied at the preliminary hearing is not necessarily identical with the probable cause standard applied at the arrest stage. The differences are related to the different purposes of the preliminary hearing and the procedures for testing the legality of an arrest under the fourth amendment. The preliminary hearing is a "forward looking" proceeding, in the sense that its function is to determine whether the defendant should be required to submit to the burdens and risks of an indictment or trial. In determining the legality of an arrest, the only question is whether the evidence available at the time of arrest establishes a sufficient "fair probability" that the accused committed the crime, whereas the judge at the preliminary hearing must also assess the probability that the prosecution will be able to prove guilt at a grand jury proceeding or trial. Although the prosecution need not demonstrate the existence of admissible evidence sufficient to convict at the time of the preliminary hearing, the defendant should not be bound over if at the time of the hearing there is no reasonable likelihood that the prosecution will be able to indict or convict. Furthermore, because the preliminary hearing is conducted by the prosecutor, a more legalistic evaluation of the evidence is called for at the preliminary hearing stage than is expected of the police at the time of arrest.

A minority of jurisdictions requires the prosecutor to establish a prima facie case of guilt at the preliminary hearing, a higher standard of proof than mere probable cause. Under this standard, the judge decides whether the prosecution's evidence, if believed by the jury, is sufficient to prove the defendant guilty at trial.

In evaluating whether the evidence presented at the preliminary hearing establishes the required probability of guilt, it is necessary to specify how far or in what way the judge should assess the credibility of the evidence. All jurisdictions agree that the judge must consider credibility at least to the extent of deciding whether a reasonable jury could believe the evidence relied on by the prosecution. The courts are divided over whether the defendant should be bound over if the judge concludes that a reasonable juror could find the evidence believable, but the judge does not personally believe it.

D. THE EFFECT OF DISMISSAL

A magistrate's decision not to bind over the accused at a preliminary hearing is almost universally treated as a non final judgment. For that reason the decision cannot be appealed. Moreover, such lack of finality, along with the fact that jeopardy does not attach at the preliminary hearing stage, permits the prosecution to refile the charge or charges.

So, in the vast majority of jurisdictions, the prosecution cannot appeal but can refile against the accused after a dismissal of charges at a preliminary hearing. In most jurisdictions refiling can take place either before a different magistrate or the same magistrate. Some jurisdictions require that the prosecution only refile if presenting additional evidence. Of course, after a decision not to bind over, the prosecution could seek an indictment in those jurisdictions where the grand jury route is available.

Some states by specific statute grant the prosecution the right to appeal a magistrate's decision not to bind over and some states allow appellate review of dismissal at a preliminary hearing by extraordinary writ. However, since the prosecution may still have available the alternatives of refiling or seeking an indictment, the extraordinary writ avenue may be foreclosed.

Many prosecutors do not wish to present too much of their case at the preliminary hearing, holding something back for trial and to avoid complete discovery by the defense. Thus, if the magistrate concludes that the prosecution failed to meet its burden and does not bind the defendant over, the question may arise whether the prosecution should be given another chance and be permitted to refile—even before the same magistrate. The countervailing consideration is that allowing the prosecution to refile after a dismissal undermines the magistrate's authority.

These considerations have led to a variety of rules in various states with respect to refiling. As previously mentioned, the majority rule is that the prosecution can refile at will. A minority of states permit refiling only upon a showing of additional evidence, and most do not require any showing as to why the additional evidence was not presented in the first place.

E. RIGHTS AND PROCEDURES AT THE PRELIMINARY HEARING

1. RIGHT TO COUNSEL

As previously mentioned, the constitution does not mandate a preliminary hearing for an accused in a criminal proceeding. Thus, a state may devise a criminal procedure that does not include a preliminary hearing or a right to one. However, if the state does afford the accused a preliminary hearing, the state cannot restrict the defendant's rights at the hearing in a manner that violates his or her constitutional protections.

In *Coleman v. Alabama* (S.Ct.1970), the United States Supreme Court, after reaffirming that a preliminary hearing is not constitutionally required, declared that a preliminary hearing, if provided by the state, is a "critical stage" in a criminal proceeding. As such, the sixth amendment right to counsel attaches. Thus, the accused, at a preliminary hearing is entitled to the assistance of counsel in order to ensure that he or she gets a fair trial.

In the *Coleman* case, though Alabama did not require a preliminary hearing, one was held for the defendants. They, being indigents, did not hire counsel; nor did the state appoint counsel for them. This, the Supreme Court held, denied the defendants a substantial constitutional right, vacated their convictions, and remanded for a determination of harmless error. In reaching its conclusion, the Court stated that the "guiding hand of counsel" is required at a preliminary hearing to protect an indigent defendant "against an erroneous or improper prosecution," giving the following examples of how counsel helps at a preliminary hearing:

First, the lawyer's skilled examination and cross-examination of witnesses may expose fatal weaknesses in the State's case that may lead the magistrate to refuse to bind the accused over. Second, in any event, the skilled interrogation of witnesses by an experienced lawyer can fashion a vital impeachment tool for use in cross-examination of the State's witnesses at the trial, or preserve testimony favorable to the accused of a witness who does not appear at the trial. Third, trained counsel can more effectively discover the case the State has against his client and make possible the preparation of a proper defense to meet that case at the trial. Fourth, counsel can also be influential at the preliminary hearing in making effective arguments for the accused on such matters as the necessity for an early psychiatric examination or bail.

The mandate of the *Coleman* decision is universally followed in the states.

2.   APPLICABILITY OF THE RULES OF EVIDENCE

There is no uniformity among the states with respect to the applicability of the rules of evidence at a preliminary hearing, except that all states recognize privileges. Essentially, the states take one of three different approaches to the applicability of the rules of evidence.

The majority of states and the federal system do not apply the rules of evidence to preliminary hearings. See, e.g., Federal Rules of Evidence 1101(d) specifically stating that the "rules (other than with respect to privileges) do not apply in ... preliminary examinations in criminal cases...." Under this rule, and state rules following it, no rules of evidence apply. Nonetheless, there are two categories of evidence, admissible at a preliminary hearing but inadmissible at trial, that may be scrutinized by the magistrate at a preliminary hearing: hearsay evidence and evidence obtained illegally.

Federal Rule of Criminal Procedure 5.1 provides, in part: "The finding of probable cause may be based upon hearsay evidence in whole or in part.... Objections to evidence on the ground that it was acquired by unlawful means are not properly made at the preliminary examination." The permissive reference to hearsay evidence suggests that the magistrate judge in the federal system can take into account the hearsay nature of the evidence in assessing probable cause. The reference to illegally obtained evidence suggests that it may be relied upon by the magistrate to evaluate probable cause. However, a magistrate should take into account the likelihood of sustaining a conviction at trial in determining probable cause and a case based on insufficient admissible evidence at trial could appeal to the magistrate to exercise discretion and find probable cause nonexistent.

A small number of states take the approach that the rules of evidence generally apply to preliminary hearings, with exceptions for such categories of evidence as hearsay and illegally obtained evidence, or other categories. In those jurisdictions, the state's statutes specifically permit the probable cause finding to be based on the specified category of evidence. In some instances the magistrate may have discretion to give such evidence limited weight.

An even smaller number of states apply the rules of evidence to their fullest extent at a preliminary hearing. In these states, the erroneous admission of evidence at a preliminary hearing will not necessarily result in an appellate decision overturning a probable cause finding. In the event that the appellate court finds sufficient admissible evidence present in the record, the magistrates decision to bind the defendant over will likely be affirmed. Also, in those states imposing the rules of evidence fully at the preliminary hearing, the defendant can raise a claim that evidence was illegally obtained. The magistrate's ruling on the admissibility of such evidence is not binding on the trial court, though the magistrate's factual findings may be accepted by a subsequent trial court, appellate court, or another magistrate if the prosecutor were to refile.

3. RIGHT OF CROSS EXAMINATION

The right to counsel afforded at a preliminary hearing, in fact mandated by the *Coleman* decision, carries with it the right of defense counsel to cross-examine prosecution witnesses. Whether cross-examination is mandated by the constitution is another question. Since the issues before the magistrate at a preliminary hearing are decided by a standard of probable cause, theoretically there is no need for the full and complete cross-examination of prosecution witnesses that must be permitted at trial. It is not surprising, therefore, that there is no Supreme Court decision that mandates full and complete cross-examination rights be granted by a magistrate to a defendant at a preliminary hearing. Nor does the sixth amendment confrontation clause require such broad cross-examination of prosecution witnesses: the confrontation clause applies at trial, not at a preliminary hearing.

Thus, the magistrate at a preliminary hearing could, within his or her discretion, limit defense counsel's cross-examination to narrowly deal with the basic probable cause questions before the court. The magistrate could limit inquiry into matters such as sources of evidence not presented by the prosecution, names of other witnesses, the manner in which the police investigation was pursued, or other matters that clearly relate to attempted discovery by the defense.

On the other hand, in order for testimony presented at a preliminary hearing to be admissible at a subsequent trial as prior testimony, both under the hearsay rule and the confrontation clause, the defendant must have had an adequate opportunity to fully develop the witness's testimony. This means that a magistrate's limitation of defense cross-examination could later be construed as an interference with full and adequate cross-examination resulting in the exclusion of such preliminary hearing testimony. The prosecution and the presiding judicial officer at a preliminary hearing must keep this in mind. Concerns about perpetuation of witness's testimony at a preliminary hearing thus may lead to more full cross-examination by the defense than otherwise might be required.

4.   DEFENSE EVIDENCE

Universally the defendant has the right to call witnesses and present evidence at a preliminary hearing. Nonetheless there are some limitations, both practical and theoretical, upon this right. One practical limitation is that the case is likely to be bound over in most instances; thus, it serves no viable purpose for the defense to put on a case. Another practical limitation, which may also be behind the first, is that the defense can gain little by putting on a case, but can loose much through revealing defense witnesses and weaknesses to the prosecution.

The major theoretical limitation upon the right of the defense to present evidence at a preliminary hearing is that the questions before the magistrate are narrow and do not permit or require the magistrate to resolve credibility issues in the sense that the ultimate trier of fact does at trial. The language in most jurisdictions is that the defendant "may introduce evidence" on his or her own behalf. A magistrate who personally believes that the prosecution's witnesses could be believed by a jury at trial is going to bind over for trial in most cases in most jurisdictions. There are some jurisdictions where the preliminary hearing is viewed as a mini-trial and the magistrate is charged with the responsibility to evaluate credibility. But even in those jurisdictions, the ultimate credibility decision will be left to the trial jury. In short, these considerations lead to the ability of the magistrate to limit the defense's right to present extensive evidence at the preliminary hearing.

A small number of states specifically grant the magistrate the authority to determine whether the defendant should be permitted to present witnesses. Typically, in these jurisdictions, the defense must convince the magistrate with an offer of proof.

CHAPTER 4

THE GRAND JURY

A. FUNCTIONS OF THE GRAND JURY

The grand jury is a group of citizens that reviews evidence of suspected criminality to decide whether criminal charges are warranted. The formal charging instrument issued by a grand jury is an *indictment*, sometimes also referred to as a *true bill*. If the grand jury decides *not* to indict, it returns what is called a *no true bill*.

The Fifth Amendment to the United States Constitution requires indictment by a grand jury for all federal prosecutions for felonies or capital crimes. The Supreme Court has held that this requirement is not binding on the states. *Hurtado v. California* (S.Ct.1884).

Just under half the states (mostly in the eastern part of the U.S.) make indictment by a grand jury mandatory for all felonies as a matter of state law. Twenty eight seven states give the prosecutor the choice of prosecuting any felony by either a grand jury indictment or a prosecutor's information. In four states, indictments are mandatory only for capital offenses.

The requirement of grand jury review and indictment can be waived by the accused in jurisdictions where it is mandatory. In "information" jurisdictions where the prosecutor has the option of proceeding by way of indictment or information, most cases are prosecuted by information.

There is considerable diversity in the size, voting requirements, and selection methods governing the grand jury. Under federal law, as at common law, a grand jury consists of from 16 to 23 grand jurors, 12 of whom must agree in order to vote an indictment. Some jurisdictions use grand juries as small as 12. A simple majority is sufficient to indict in some jurisdictions, while other jurisdictions require a larger percentage.

Unlike trial or "petit" juries, which are convened for the purpose of hearing a single case, grand juries typically sit for a term, during which they consider several or many cases. Today grand jurors in most jurisdictions are chosen through a process of random selection off voter registration lists or other mass lists, though a small number of jurisdictions continue to select grand jurors through the "key-man system," in which jury commissioners hand pick grand jurors in order to obtain individuals with standing in the community.

Grand juries serve both an investigatory function and a screening function. In their investigatory function grand juries actively gather evidence, by summoning witnesses and compelling production of tangible evidence, in order to determine whether there are grounds for charging someone with a crime. The investigatory powers of the grand jury are very broad. Unlike the courts, which can only act in response to a specific case or controversy, the grand jury defines its own inquiry, and can initiate an investigation on mere suspicion that the law is being violated, or even because the grand jury wants assurance that the law is not being violated. The grand jury need not identify the person it suspects, or even the nature of the offense it is investigating.

In the past grand juries carried out their investigative function on their own, without any guidance or assistance from the public prosecutor. Today investigatory grand juries virtually always act in cooperation with the prosecutor, who convenes the grand jury for that purpose.

Most criminal cases are investigated by the prosecutor or the police without the involvement of a grand jury. In cases where the evidence is developed through the efforts of the prosecutor without the participation of a grand jury, the grand jury may nevertheless be required to screen the evidence to determine whether it merits charging someone with a crime. In the performance of its screening function, the grand jury hears the evidence presented by the prosecutor, and then decides, usually upon a recommendation from the prosecutor, whether to return an indictment charging the commission of a crime. The grand jury also decides, again with the prosecutor's advice, what crimes to charge.

The same group of grand jurors may be involved in both conducting an investigation and screening cases developed by the prosecutor. At the close of its investigation, an investigatory grand jury will have to screen its own evidence to decide whether to bring charges. Likewise, a grand jury involved in screening cases presented by the prosecutor may also conduct an investigation of suspected crimes.

The role of the grand jury, and perhaps its importance, has changed considerably in the two hundred years since the requirement of grand jury review was included in the Fifth Amendment. The primary explanation for the change lies in the emergence of professional prosecutors and police, which did not exist at the time the constitution was ratified. Critics of the grand jury contend that it is now so completely under the control of the prosecutor that it serves as little more than a rubber stamp for the prosecutor's charging decisions. Supporters of the grand jury argue, however, that the requirement that the prosecutor obtain the approval of a group of citizens in order to charge someone with a crime guarantees that prosecutors will themselves engage in a careful screening of their cases before invoking the machinery of the criminal law. According to this view, the fact that grand juries refuse to indict in only a relatively small percentage of cases presented by prosecutors only shows that the system as a whole is effective in ensuring that prosecutors do not bring charges unless there is an adequate evidentiary basis.

The investigatory grand jury survives despite the rise of professional prosecutors largely because a grand jury has investigative tools not normally available to police and prosecutors acting alone. These investigative tools, though most often identified with the investigatory grand jury, may also be used by the grand jury in the performance of its screening function.

The grand jury can exercise the subpoena power of the court that empaneled it to compel the appearance of witnesses (by issuing a subpoena *ad testificandum*) and the production of documents and other tangible evidence (with a subpoena *duces tecum*). The use of a grand jury subpoena to compel testimony or document production is often more effective than simply requesting that the information be turned over voluntarily because, unlike a simple request for information, the subpoena is backed up by the court's contempt power. A person who willfully refuses to comply with a grand jury subpoena can be held for either civil contempt, in which case she is jailed or fined until she complies, or criminal contempt, which can result in criminal penalties. In addition, grand jury testimony must be given under oath subject to penalty of perjury. Unlike a search warrant, which requires probable cause, the use of a grand jury subpoena to obtain tangible evidence or compel the testimony of a witness does not have to be based on probable cause. (Although the Fourth Amendment does not require probable cause for a subpoena, the Fourth Amendment does bar a subpoena *duces tecum* that is "too sweeping to be regarded as reasonable.")

Another advantage of a grand jury investigation is that it enables a prosecutor to grant immunity to obtain the testimony of a witness who asserts a Fifth Amendment right against compelled self incrimination. A grant of immunity, which is extended before the witness testifies, protects the witness from suffering adverse criminal consequences as a result of her testimony. Since immunity removes the only danger that the Fifth Amendment privilege protects, the witness may not refuse to testify by asserting her Fifth Amendment right, and a refusal to answer questions can result in citation for contempt.

Immunity is usually governed by statute. Although the prosecutor must ordinarily obtain a court order to immunize a witness, the court's authority to deny an application for immunity is typically very limited.

There are two basic types of immunity: transactional immunity and use and derivative use immunity. A witness who testifies under a grant of transactional immunity may not thereafter be prosecuted for any transaction about which she has given immunized testimony. One logical and necessary limitation on this sweeping protection is that a witness does not gain immunity from prosecution for transactions adverted to in answers that are totally unresponsive to the question. The witness may also be prosecuted for perjury if she perjures herself during the immunized testimony.

A witness who testifies under a grant of use and derivative use immunity may still be prosecuted for crimes that are the subject of her testimony. The grant of immunity protects against use of both the immunized testimony itself and evidence that is derived from the immunized testimony. The prohibition against derivative use of the witness' testimony prevents the prosecutor from using the witness' testimony as an investigative lead to the discovery of additional evidence. If a witness who has testified under a grant of use immunity is thereafter prosecuted for events that were the subject of her testimony, the prosecution must demonstrate that its evidence was not "tainted" by the protected testimony. To meet this burden, the prosecution must show that it "had an independent, legitimate source for the disputed evidence." *Kastigar v. United States* (S.Ct.1972).

B. RIGHTS AND PROCEDURES IN THE GRAND JURY

In the past grand juries functioned as independent bodies defining and conducting their own inquiries. Today, grand jury proceedings are under the nearly complete control of the prosecutor. The prosecution presents its evidence to the grand jury *ex parte* without opportunity for cross-examination or challenge. The prosecutor also advises the grand jurors on the elements of the offense, and in many jurisdictions is permitted to offer her opinion on the sufficiency of the evidence to support the proposed charges. In some, but not all jurisdictions, the prosecutor's dominance of the grand jury is tempered by an obligation to present exculpatory evidence known to the prosecution. The prosecutor's partisan impulses are also presumably checked by the realization that guilt must eventually be proven beyond a reasonable doubt in an adversary trial, and by her ethical obligation to refrain from seeking convictions that are unjust. Prosecutors obtain indictments in a huge percentage of cases, however; so much so that one judge was moved to make the now famous statement that "a prosecutor who wanted to could indict a ham sandwich."

Although grand jury proceedings are now under the effective control of the prosecutor, remnants of the historical tradition in which the grand jury acted on its own initiative survive, at least in theory if not always in practice. The grand jury can insist on the production of witnesses and additional physical evidence not presented by the prosecutor. Unlike a trial jury, which is supposed to decide based solely on evidence presented in open court, grand jurors can call on their personal knowledge in deciding whether to return an indictment. While the prosecutor conducts most of the questioning of witnesses, grand jurors can and do ask questions of their own.

The judge who empanels the grand jury is not present during the presentation of evidence. Except in rare circumstances, the judge's only communication with the grand jurors is at the very beginning of their service when the judge delivers a general charge about the grand jury's function and duties.

A witness testifying before the grand jury may assert the Fifth Amendment privilege against compelled self incrimination and refuse to answer questions that are either directly incriminatory or would furnish a link in the chain of evidence needed to prosecute the witness for a crime. At trial, the Fifth Amendment privilege prohibits the prosecution from calling the defendant as a witness. The Fifth Amendment does not, however, prevent the prosecution from calling a prospective defendant as a witness before the grand jury, and requiring the individual to assert her Fifth Amendment right to refuse to answer in the presence of the grand jurors. Although a prospective defendant who testifies before the grand jury may have a right to be informed of her Fifth Amendment right not to incriminate herself, she is not entitled to the full set of warnings that are required for custodial interrogations under *Miranda v. Arizona* (S.Ct.1966).

In the federal system and most states neither witnesses nor prospective defendants (should they testify) are allowed to bring an attorney into the grand jury room to advise them during their testimony. A witness may, however, station her attorney outside the grand jury hearing room, and leave the hearing to consult with the attorney in the corridor. Some states now permit defense counsel to be present during grand jury hearings and advise the witness, but do not to permit the attorney to address the grand jury or in any way challenge the prosecution's evidence.

In most jurisdictions the grand jury has the discretion to grant or deny a prospective defendant's request to testify before the grand jury. A minority of jurisdictions grant the target a right to testify and require that she be notified of her right. If the prospective defendant does testify she opens herself up to unprotected cross-examination by the prosecutor, which is why few prospective defendants choose to testify.

The law regarding the applicability of the rules of evidence to grand jury proceedings varies considerably from one jurisdiction to another. All jurisdictions require that testimonial privileges be recognized. In the federal system and the majority of states, the law of evidence, other than the privilege rules, is not applied, and hearsay evidence is freely admissible. Some states apply the law of evidence in full, or with only a few narrow exceptions. A third approach utilizes special rules that prevent the prosecutor from relying on the recorded statements of witnesses, but do not prohibit all hearsay.

The standard of proof required for a grand jury to indict is not as clearly specified or precisely defined as the standard required for a trial jury to convict. The two standards that are recognized, each used in approximately equal numbers of jurisdictions, are probable cause and *prima facie* evidence of guilt. The precise meaning of the probable cause standard, described as probable cause to believe that a crime was committed and the defendant committed it, is usually left unexplained. The prima facie standard is presumably the more stringent of the two; it requires that the evidence, if unexplained and uncontradicted, would warrant conviction.

In a sizable minority of jurisdictions, including the federal system, there is uncertainty as to which standard applies. The reason for the relative ambiguity over this seemingly important point is related to the most fundamental character and function of the grand jury. Part of the justification for using lay grand jurors to decide whether to charge the commission of a crime is to obtain the common sense judgment of ordinary people about whether someone should be prosecuted. The accomplishment of this objective is not thought to require precise legal formulations of evidentiary sufficiency. This conception of the grand jury's function is also reflected in the fact that grand jurors are instructed by the judge at the commencement of their service that they are not *required* to indict even if they find evidence sufficient to support charges.

In most jurisdictions, including the federal system, there is no impediment to a prosecutor's refiling a case after the grand jury has failed to indict on the first submission. In some states re-submission is permissible only with court approval, which typically requires a showing of additional evidence that was not presented to the first grand jury.

C. GRAND JURY SECRECY

Grand jury proceedings are not open to the public. The grand jurors, the prosecutor, and interpreters, court stenographers, clerks or other court personnel who are present during the proceedings are prohibited from disclosing what occurred in the grand jury. The obligation of secrecy does not generally apply to grand jury witnesses. A knowing violation of the secrecy requirement is punishable as contempt.

The reasons for grand jury secrecy include: preventing embarrassment to persons who were investigated but not charged; encouraging uninhibited disclosure by persons who have information about the commission of crime; ensuring the freedom of grand jurors to consider the case without fear of public pressure or influence; and preventing leaks of information to prospective defendants who might be tempted to flee or tamper with witnesses.

All jurisdictions authorize disclosure of grand jury evidence in certain clearly defined circumstances. Rule 6(e)(3) of the Federal Rules of Criminal Procedure states the exceptions to the secrecy requirement for federal grand juries. Among the exceptions listed in the Rule is an exception for disclosure to other members of the prosecutorial team, including attorneys and other personnel, for the purpose of discharging the duty to enforce the criminal law. Disclosure under this provision does not require court approval. The Rule also authorizes disclosure, at the request of the defendant, upon a showing that grounds may exist for a motion to dismiss the indictment because of matters occurring before the grand jury. Disclosure under this provision requires judicial approval, which typically requires some demonstration that there is a valid basis for the challenge. It is understandably difficult to make such a preliminary showing given the requirement of grand jury secrecy. Jurisdictions that permit challenges to the sufficiency of the evidence before the grand jury grant the defendant access to complete grand jury transcripts as a matter of right.

The discovery rules also authorize some disclosure of grand jury evidence for use at trial as possible impeachment evidence. Federal Rule of Criminal Procedure 26.2 requires disclosure to the defendant of the grand jury testimony of witnesses who testify at trial. Many state discovery rules provide broader access to grand jury testimony.

D. THE INDICTMENT

1. THE PURPOSES AND CONTENT OF THE ACCUSATORY PLEADING

The rules governing indictments—the formal accusatory pleadings issued by grand juries—and informations—accusatory pleadings filed by prosecutors, which are a sufficient basis for trying all or most felonies in many jurisdictions—are for the most part the same. The chief differences are in the rules regarding the scope of permissible amendment of the pleading.

In evaluating the adequacy of an accusatory pleading courts apply a "functional test" that looks to whether the information or indictment is drafted so as to serve the essential function of a criminal pleading. The two basic functions of the pleadings in a criminal case are: 1) to provide adequate notice to enable the accused to defend against the charge; and 2) to identify the offense and the act that is the basis for the charge with enough specificity to permit the defendant to invoke the protection of the prohibition against being twice placed in jeopardy for the same offense. The availability of complete verbatim transcripts of trial proceedings has reduced the importance of the pleading in providing double jeopardy protections. Nevertheless, an accusatory pleading must fulfill both of these essential functions to be adequate.

Rule 7(c) of the Federal Rules of Criminal Procedure states that "the indictment or information shall be a plain, concise and definite statement of the essential facts constituting the offense charged." Many states use rules that are similar or identical to the federal standard.

In order to comply with the Rule 7(c) standard the indictment or information must satisfy two requirements: 1) the essential elements requirement, and 2) the factual specificity requirement. In evaluating whether a particular pleading meets these requirements, courts ask whether the indictment or information fulfils the basic functions of notice and double jeopardy protection.

The *essential elements* rule requires that the pleading allege the existence of each of the essential elements required for the commission of the crime. The elements of the offense are determined by the substantive criminal law, and typically include a mental state element and a conduct element, and possibly also an attendant circumstances element or a result element.

A pleading that tracks the language of the statutory definition of the crime will often, but not always, sufficiently allege the essential elements of the crime. If judicial interpretation has supplied an element not directly stated in the statute, as sometimes occurs with respect to *mens rea* requirements, that element must be alleged in the pleading. Likewise, if judicial interpretation has modified or clarified the meaning of a statutory term to the point that the language of the statute does not provide notice of the nature of the crime, that term must be alleged as interpreted by the courts, rather than as stated in the statute.

The *factual specificity* rule requires that the pleading contain a sufficiently specific factual description of the acts alleged to constitute the crime to enable the defendant to defend against the charge. It does not, however, require the prosecution to disclose its evidence in the pleading. In determining whether a given pleading is sufficiently detailed, the defendant is presumed to be innocent, and therefore ignorant of all facts relating to the alleged crime.

The degree of factual specificity necessary depends on what is required to provide the defendant with notice necessary to prepare a defense under the circumstances of the particular case. This will vary based on, among other things, the nature of the offense. In *Russell v. U.S.* (S.Ct.1962), the Court addressed the adequacy of an indictment that charged the defendants with the federal crime of refusing to answer questions while testifying as a witness before Congress. Conviction for the offense required proof that the witness refused to answer questions that were "pertinent to the question under inquiry" by the Congressional committee. Although the indictment specified the precise questions the defendants refused to answer, the Court held that it was defective because it did not disclose the subject that the Congressional committee was investigating at the time the witnesses testified, and therefore did not adequately allege that the refusal was to questions that were "pertinent to the question under inquiry" by the committee.

The degree of specificity mandated in *Russell* is clearly not required in all situations. In some cases an allegation framed in the language of the statute will provide the defendant with adequate notice of the facts. For instance, an indictment or information charging that the defendant "assaulted" a named person at a specified time and place provides the defendant with the notice necessary to prepare a defense. Customarily, the precise time and place have not been required, so that allegations in the language of "on or about" a time and place will suffice.

Under Rule 12(b) of the Federal Rules of Criminal Procedure, an objection to an indictment or information based on a lack of factual specificity must be raised before trial or it is waived. A claim that the pleading fails to allege the essential elements of the offense, however, may be raised at any time during the pendency of the proceedings, even after conviction. The no-waiver rule for the essential elements requirement reflects the "jurisdictional" underpinnings of that requirement. In addition to serving a notice function, the inclusion of the essential elements of the offense in the pleading is said to serve the function of establishing the formal jurisdiction of the court to try the case. There are two appellate standards available to defendants who raise essential elements objections. The first, when a defendant fails to object at trial and raises the issue solely on appeal. In this instance, the court looks to the prosecution's case with "liberal construction" of the facts and elements used in the government's indictment of information. When a defendant, in fact, objects at trial, the defendant is afforded a de novo review by the appellate court. If this defendant prevails upon the essential elements claim, courts typically grant an automatic reversal.

In *U.S. v. Cotton* (S.Ct.2002) the Court explicitly found that indictment omissions do not "deprivate a court of jurisdiction." Therefore, the standard for their appellate review is plain error that requires the lower court's decision be overturned when, among other things, the error "seriously affect[s] the fairness, integrity, or public reputation of judicial proceedings."

The rule permitting an objection for failure to allege essential elements to be raised at any time gives defendants an incentive to sit on their objections until after trial so as to have two chances at an acquittal. In order to deter defendants from withholding their objections until after trial, many courts have adopted a rule of construction providing that when an objection based on failure to allege a crime is raised for the first time after trial, the pleading shall be "liberally construed" in favor of the validity of the pleading.

a. Bill of Particulars

An accused who needs more information or "particulars" about the crime than is contained in the information or indictment may file a motion with the court to require the prosecution to provide a bill of particulars. See Fed. R. Crim. Pro. 7(f). The motion typically includes a list of questions about the events that are the subject of the charge. The bill of particulars or "bill" is the prosecutor's response to those questions.

The defendant is not entitled to a bill of particulars as a matter of right. The decision whether to grant a defense request for a bill is discretionary with the court. The standard for deciding whether to order the prosecution to file a bill is whether the information sought by the motion is necessary to prepare the defense and avoid prejudicial surprise.

The purpose of the bill of particulars is to provide the defendant with enough information about the *allegations* against her to enable her to prepare a defense. It is not intended to be a vehicle for discovery of the *evidence* by which the prosecution will seek to prove those allegations. Thus, as Professors

LaFave, Israel, and King point out, "a court may be willing to grant a motion asking that the government identify those persons who participated in the conduct it seeks to establish, but not a motion asking for a list of the government's witnesses." LaFave, Israel, and King, Criminal Procedure § 19.4 (3d ed. 2000).

The bill of particulars limits the prosecution's proof at trial to the same extent as the indictment or information. Thus, the rules regarding "variance" between pleading and proof, to be discussed below, apply equally to the bill of particulars and the formal charge. A bill of particulars cannot be used to salvage an information or indictment that is defective because it fails to allege the essential elements of the crime. Whether a bill of particulars is commonly used to cure a claim lacking factual specificity, it can be used to supply necessary factual specificity lacking in the formal charge is uncertain.

b. Amendments

Rule 7(e) of the Federal Rules of Criminal Procedure provides that the court may permit amendment of an *information*, before verdict, if two conditions are satisfied: 1) the amendment may not charge the defendant with an additional or different offense from that contained in the original pleading; and 2) amendment is not permitted if it will prejudice substantial rights of the accused. Rule 7 says nothing about the amendment of an *indictment*. (The Rule does authorize the court to strike "surplusage" from the indictment, but this presumably refers to material that is both unnecessary and in some way prejudicial to the accused, since the party authorized to request that the surplus language be removed is the defendant, rather than the prosecution.) Although federal law does not prohibit all amendments to indictments, the ability to amend an indictment in federal court is more limited than the 7(e) standard for amending informations. Most states, however, apply the same two-part test that is stated in Rule 7(e) to the amendment of both the information and indictment.

The first prong of the Rule 7(e) test, which disallows amendments that charge different or additional offenses, clearly prohibits adding a charge that is based on a different statutory provision from the existing charge. The rule also prohibits an amendment that results in a charge based on an altogether different occurrence from the original pleading. Courts disagree, however, on the permissibility of an amendment that changes neither the statutory nor the factual basis for the charge, but alleges a different method of committing the crime under a statute that includes more than one alternative. For instance, some courts would regard an amendment that shifts the prosecution's theory from intentional murder to felony murder as charging a different offense, while other courts would consider such an amendment permissible.

In applying the prejudice prong of the test, courts focus primarily on whether permitting the amendment will cause prejudicial surprise to the accused.

Because surprise can usually be alleviated if the defendant is granted additional time to prepare, defense claims that an amendment of the pleading is prejudicial are usually rejected where a continuance was either granted or not requested.

The federal courts and a minority of states apply more restrictive rules to the amendment of indictments than to the amendment of informations. The reason for limiting the prosecutor's power to amend the indictment is to protect the grand jury's charging function. To the extent the prosecutor can alter the charge through amendment of the indictment, the grand jury has been deprived of its authority to determine how the accused shall be charged.

All jurisdictions permit amendments to correct technical or formal errors in the indictment, such as misnomers or misspellings. In some states amendments that go beyond matters of form are not permitted. The federal system permits a somewhat broader scope for the amendment of grand jury indictments under what is still referred to as the "*Bain* rule," though the case from which the rule takes its name, *Ex Parte Bain* (S.Ct.1887), is now no longer strictly followed.

The Supreme Court clarified the current standard for amending an indictment in federal court in *U.S. v. Miller* (S.Ct.1985). The defendant in that case was charged with defrauding his insurance company. The indictment alleged that he perpetrated the fraud in two distinct ways: by arranging for a burglary of his place of business, and by misrepresenting the value of the resulting loss. At trial, the prosecution offered no evidence that the defendant had prior knowledge of the burglary to support its first theory. The prosecution did, however, prove that the defendant misrepresented the loss, which was by itself sufficient to support conviction under the statute. Before the case was given to the jury, the prosecution moved to amend the indictment to strike the allegation of a staged burglary. Relying on Supreme Court precedents prohibiting all substantive amendments to an indictment, the trial court denied the motion to amend. The defendant then successfully challenged the ensuing conviction under the unamended indictment on the ground that it violated his Fifth Amendment right to indictment by a grand jury. In overturning the conviction the Court of Appeals reasoned that, since the case was presented to the grand jury on the basis that the defendant engaged in both forms of deception, there is no assurance that the grand jury would have indicted based on the misrepresentation of the loss alone. The resulting conviction, therefore, was for a crime for which the defendant had not been indicted.

The Supreme Court reversed the Court of Appeals and redefined the standards for amending an indictment. The Court reaffirmed that an indictment may not be amended to add different or additional charges. Nor may an indictment be amended to allege a different method of commission of the crime. Thus, citing its holding in a prior "variance" case (See Part 4 below), the Court reiterated that an indictment that charged interference with interstate commerce by means of burdening the importation of sand into Pennsylvania could not be amended to charge interference with commerce by burdening the movement of steel out of Pennsylvania. Amendment will be allowed, however, provided it does not result in prejudicial surprise, *if the amendment narrows the indictment by removing allegations which are unnecessary to an offense that is clearly and fully set out in the original indictment.* Since the allegation that the defendant in *Miller* misrepresented the value of the loss was sufficient to allege the crime for which he was charged, the allegation that he also committed the same crime by arranging the burglary was unnecessary. The prosecution's proposed amendment dropping that allegation should therefore have been permitted.

Traditionally the remedy for a violation of the Bain rule was a reversal of the defendant's conviction notwithstanding whether the error had a prejudicial impact on the trial. LaFave, Israel and King, Criminal Procedure § 11.4(c) (3d ed. 2000). However, U.S. v. Cotton (S.Ct.2002) has called this standard into question because in Cotton the court applied a harmless error standard and found the error in the indictment to be a harmless error. Id.

c. Variance

A variance between the pleading and the proof occurs when the prosecution's evidence at trial differs from the allegations contained in the indictment or information. For instance, a variance exists if the indictment alleges that the defendant committed robbery by threatening the victim with a gun, but the trial evidence establishes that the defendant threatened the victim with a knife. A variance can occur either because the trial evidence proves matters that are not contained in the pleading (e.g., the pleading alleges A but the proof establishes B or A and B), or because the pleadings include matters that are not proven at trial (e.g., the pleading alleges A and B but the trial evidence establishes A only).

The courts have distinguished two different types of variance. A variance that amounts to a "constructive" or "unconstitutional" amendment of the indictment requires automatic reversal. A "mere variance" that does not rise to the level of a constructive amendment requires reversal only if the defendant was prejudiced by the variance.

A variance constitutes a constructive amendment of the pleading and requires automatic reversal if, under the rules governing the amendment of pleadings, the indictment could not have been amended to conform to the proof at trial. The rationale for this rule is that the principles that underlie the rules limiting the scope of permissible amendments require that the prosecution not be permitted to accomplish indirectly by means of a variance that which it is not allowed to do directly with a motion to amend the pleading.

To determine whether a variance results in a constructive amendment the court compares the trial evidence with the allegations of the pleading, and asks whether an amendment incorporating the differences between the two would be possible under the standard stated in *U.S. v. Miller*, discussed above. Applying that standard, a variance that adds new material not included in the indictment constitutes a constructive amendment, but a variance that simply omits proof of allegations that are unnecessary to prove a charge that is clearly set forth in the indictment is not.

Thus, in *Stirone v. U.S.* (S.Ct.1960), a case decided before *Miller* but cited with approval in *Miller*, the Court found that the variance between the indictment and the trial evidence resulted in the conviction of the defendant for a crime for which he had not been indicted. The defendant was charged with a federal crime that included, as one of its elements, an interference with interstate commerce. The indictment alleged that the defendant interfered with interstate commerce by impeding the importation of sand into Pennsylvania for use in making concrete. At trial, however, the government was permitted to seek to prove the element of interference with commerce with evidence that the defendant impeded the movement of steel out of Pennsylvania. Applying its precedents regarding the scope of permissible amendments to grand jury indictments, the Supreme Court held that submission of the case to the trial jury on a factual theory not approved by the grand jury destroyed the defendant's substantial right to be tried only on charges for which he had been indicted. This was so even though the variance did not produce a new offense, but only a new factual element that had not been passed on by the grand jury.

The test for whether a variance that does not constitute a constructive amendment requires reversal was established in *Berger v. U.S.* (S.Ct.1935). Under the *Berger* standard, a "mere variance" not amounting to a constructive amendment requires reversal of the conviction only when the inconsistency between the pleadings and the proof affects the substantial rights of the accused. In evaluating whether the defendant's substantial rights have been affected the court must determine whether the failure of the trial evidence to conform to the allegations contained in the indictment undermined the basic functions of criminal pleadings. This entails a two part inquiry: 1) did the variance deprive the defendant of the notice necessary to prepare a defense and not be taken by surprise by the evidence at trial; and 2) was the difference between the pleadings and the proof such as to jeopardize the defendant's rights under the Fifth Amendment Double Jeopardy Clause.

In assessing whether the defendant was deprived of notice, the courts look to the record to determine if the defendant was misled or otherwise prejudiced as a result of the prosecution's presentation of evidence that differed from the allegations of the indictment. If the defendant did not object to the variance, was made aware of the prosecution's evidence through pre-trial discovery, or presented a defense at trial that was not affected by the existence of the variance, the courts are likely to find that the defendant did not suffer prejudice as a result of the variance.

A variance requires reversal without regard to actual prejudice at trial if the trial evidence alters the focus from what is set forth in the pleadings in a way that places the defendant at risk of losing the protection of the Double Jeopardy Clause. The Double Jeopardy Clause of the Fifth Amendment protects the defendant against being prosecuted twice for the same offense. In determining whether a second prosecution is for the "same offense" as an earlier prosecution, courts look to the pleadings that were the basis for the first prosecution to determine what events and charges constituted the "offense." (At least that is the assumption underlying the variance rule. In reality, courts can now look to the trial record to determine what the defendant was in fact tried for.) If, however, the trial evidence differed from the allegations of the pleadings, the pleadings may not accurately reflect the "offense" that the defendant was actually tried for. Under those circumstances there is a risk that the defendant, having already been prosecuted for a crime at variance with the formal pleading, could be formally charged in a second pleading with the offense that was the subject of the first trial, lose her double jeopardy argument because the previous indictment charged a different offense, and end up being tried twice for the same offense.

In order to determine whether a variance requires reversal because it exposes the defendant to the risk of double jeopardy, it is necessary to apply the rules regarding what constitutes the "same offense" for double jeopardy purposes. Those rules are the subject of Chapter 9.

E. CHALLENGES TO GRAND JURY COMPOSITION

The equal protection guarantee of the Fifth and Fourteenth Amendments of the Constitution prohibits purposeful discrimination in the selection of grand jurors. Although the states are not constitutionally required to provide any grand jury screening of criminal charges, *Hurtado v. California* (S.Ct. 1884), insofar as states make use of grand juries, state selection procedures are subject to the same equal protection limitations as are imposed on federal grand juries.

The requirements for proving an equal protection violation in the selection of grand jurors are the same as the requirements for proving an equal protection violation in the selection of trial jurors. (Since peremptory challenges are not a part of the process of selecting a grand jury, the equal protection limitations on their use have no application to the grand jury.) As with the trial jury, it is not enough to show that members of a particular racial group or other suspect class were under-represented on the grand jury; it must be proven that the under-representation was the result of purposeful or deliberate discrimination.

To prove a *prima facie* case of purposeful discrimination the defendant must show that a racial group or other suspect class had been excluded or substantially under-represented on grand juries over a significant period of time. This is typically done by comparing the proportion of the group in the general population to the proportion of the group called to serve as grand jurors. Thus, in *Castaneda v. Partida* (S.Ct.1977), the Court held that the defendant had proven a *prima facie* case of discrimination with evidence that the county from which the grand jurors were summoned was 79 percent Mexican–American, but over an 11 year period only 39 percent of those summoned for grand jury service were Mexican–American. Once a *prima facie* showing of discrimination has been made by the defendant, the burden then shifts to the prosecution to prove that the exclusion or under-representation was not the result of purposeful discrimination. If the prosecution is unable to carry this burden, the defendant is entitled to a dismissal of the indictment without regard to the sufficiency of the evidence to support the charge.

In a number of cases involving equal protection challenges to grand jury selection procedures the Supreme Court stated that the defendant challenging the jury selection practice must herself be a member of the excluded group. In a recent decision, however, the Court disavowed that requirement, holding that a White defendant can assert an equal protection challenge to the purposeful exclusion of Blacks from the grand jury. *Campbell v. Louisiana* (S.Ct.1998). The rationale for this rule, which had earlier been applied to the use of peremptory challenges in the selection of the trial jury, is that the equal protection rights at issue are the rights of the excluded jurors, and not the rights of the defendant. And while the defendant has not herself suffered an equal protection violation, she has third-party standing to assert the equal protection rights of the excluded jurors.

In *Vasquez v. Hillery* (S.Ct.1986) the Court held that racial discrimination in the selection of the grand jury requires reversal of a subsequent conviction by a trial jury, even though the trial jury was properly selected. The Court majority rejected the dissent argument that the risk of prejudice to the defendant caused by the exclusion of racial groups from the grand jury is eliminated when a trial jury that is not tainted by discriminatory selection procedures finds the defendant guilty beyond a reasonable doubt. The Court reasoned that a subsequent jury conviction does not dispel the possibility of prejudice from an illegally constituted grand jury because the grand jury's role is not limited to determining the existence of probable cause to believe that the defendant committed a crime. The grand jury has the power to decide which crimes to charge among those that are supported by the evidence, and is not required to indict in every case where a conviction can be obtained. "Thus, even if a grand jury's determination of probable cause is confirmed in hindsight by a conviction on the indicted offense, that confirmation in no way suggests that the discrimination did not impermissibly infect the framing of the indictment and, consequently, the nature or very existence of the proceedings to come." Although the Court's reasoning would appear to apply to any challenge to the composition of the grand jury, subsequent decisions have raised doubts about whether the *Vasquez v. Hillery* rule applies outside of the context of race discrimination.

In addition to prohibiting discrimination in the selection of grand jurors, the constitution also prohibits race and gender discrimination in the selection of who among the grand jurors shall serve as foreperson. *Hobby v. United States* (S.Ct.1984). The reason the selection of the grand jury foreperson raises constitutional issues, and the selection of the foreperson of the trial jury does not, is because the grand jury foreperson is usually selected by the court, whereas the foreperson of the trial jury is chosen by the jurors themselves.

Although the constitution guarantees a right against discrimination in the selection of the grand jury foreperson, a violation of that right does not invariably require a dismissal of the indictment. Whether dismissal is the appropriate remedy appears to depend on two factors: the functions assigned to the foreperson in the jurisdiction; and the constitutional provision under which the discriminatory selection was challenged. The Supreme Court has held that dismissal is *not* required where, as in the federal system, the foreperson performs only "ministerial" or "clerical" functions such as administering oaths and signing indictments, *and* the challenge to the discriminatory selection is based on the Due Process Clause. The Court has expressly left open the question whether dismissal is required where the discrimination involves the selection of a foreperson who exercises powers not possessed by the other grand jurors, such as the power to subpoena witnesses, or when the challenge is based on an equal protection violation.

In contrast to the situation where the judge picks a foreperson from among those who have already been chosen as grand jurors, in some jurisdictions the judge selects the grand jury foreperson from outside the grand jury, and then places that individual on the jury as foreperson. When the foreperson is appointed from outside the grand jury, discriminatory selection affects not only the determination of who shall perform the duties of foreperson, but also affects the composition of the grand jury. Although the Court found it unnecessary to decide the issue, it has "assume[d] ... that discrimination with regard to the selection of only the foreman requires that a subsequent conviction be set aside, just as if the discrimination proved had tainted the selection of the entire grand jury venire." *Rose v. Mitchell* (S.Ct.1979).

The composition of the grand jury can also be challenged on grounds other than equal protection. The Supreme Court has recognized in several cases that the exclusion of "large and identifiable groups" from serving on grand juries implicates "representational" interests protected by the Due Process Clause. The Due Process Clause offers a potentially broader basis for challenging the composition of the grand jury than the Equal Protection Clause because it reaches a broader category of groups (an equal protection challenge is presumably limited to discrimination against groups subject to heightened scrutiny), and may not require proof of discriminatory intent. At one time a due process challenge also offered an advantage over an equal protection challenge because the defendant did not have to be a member of the excluded group in order to establish standing. Since the Supreme Court has now held that a defendant who does not share the group identity of the allegedly excluded jurors nonetheless has standing to raise an equal protection challenge, that advantage no longer exists.

There is considerable uncertainty whether other jury selection doctrines that govern the trial jury apply to the selection of grand jurors. It is now well established that a trial jury must be drawn from a group that represents a fair cross section of the community. *Taylor v. Louisiana* (S.Ct.1975). That requirement is now understood to be based on the Sixth Amendment right to trial by jury, and therefore presumably does not apply to the grand jury. It is also unclear whether a defendant has a right to an impartial grand jury, or whether exposure to pretrial publicity regarding the defendant or the crime is a basis for challenging the grand jury's indictment.

F. CHALLENGES TO GRAND JURY EVIDENCE

The principles governing a challenge to an indictment based on the evidence presented to the grand jury that is applied in the federal courts was established in *Costello v. United States* (S.Ct.1956). The defendant in *Costello* was indicted for tax evasion. The only evidence presented to the grand jury that returned the indictment was hearsay not admissible under the rules of evidence. The defendant's pretrial motion to dismiss the indictment was denied, and the defendant was convicted of the charges at trial. In the Supreme Court the defendant claimed that an indictment based entirely on inadmissible evidence violated either 1) his Fifth Amendment right to indictment by a grand jury or 2) the standards governing the grand jury that are promulgated under the Supreme Court's supervisory power over the federal judiciary.

The Supreme Court rejected the claim that the indictment violated the Fifth Amendment, and refused to use its supervisory powers to require that a grand jury indictment be supported by admissible evidence. In support of its decision the Court emphasized the historical character of the grand jury as "a body of laymen, free from technical rules." This justification for not requiring that the grand jury's charge be supported by admissible evidence has been criticized on the ground that, unlike the situation in the 18th century when the Fifth Amendment was adopted, professional prosecutors trained in the law of evidence now exercise considerable control over the presentation of evidence to the grand jury. The Court also suggested that granting the defendant a right to challenge the indictment based on the competency of the evidence before the grand jury would have only minimal benefits in improving the grand jury's screening function, but would impose substantial administrative costs on the courts in litigating challenges to grand jury indictments.

Several justifications not mentioned by the Court have been suggested as underlying the *Costello* rule. One argument for allowing an indictment to stand although it rests in whole or in part on inadmissible evidence rests on an understanding of the grand jury's function as protecting only the factually innocent from having to stand trial, and not protecting those who, though guilty, cannot be convicted because of an absence of admissible evidence. It has also been suggested that the grand jury needs to hear the same evidence that is available to the prosecutor, including information on matters such as the defendant's criminal record and general character that cannot be admitted at trial, in order to effectively evaluate the prosecutor's decision to charge the defendant with a crime. Finally, the point has been made that prosecutors, aware that conviction at trial requires proof of guilt based on admissible evidence, are unlikely to expend scarce prosecutorial resources indicting persons who cannot be convicted because of a lack of admissible evidence.

The defendant's challenge to the indictment in *Costello* related solely to the *admissibility* or "*competency*" of the evidence supporting the indictment. The defendant did not contest the *sufficiency* of the evidence presented to the grand jury which, though hearsay, concededly established probable cause to believe that he committed tax evasion. The Supreme Court framed its opinion, however, so as to foreclose challenges based on either the competency or the sufficiency of the evidence. The Court stated that "[a]n indictment returned by a legally constituted and unbiased grand jury, like an information drawn by the prosecutor, if valid on its face, is enough to call for trial of the charge on the merits." A concurring opinion in the case expressed the view that an indictment could not stand if the grand jury had before it "no substantial or rationally persuasive evidence" to support the charges. Lower courts, however, have generally read the *Costello* majority opinion's stress on the facial validity of the indictment as the sole requirement for a valid charge as precluding any evidentiary challenge to an indictment.

Despite the sweeping terms of the *Costello* holding, some lower courts continued to entertain challenges to indictments that at least indirectly addressed evidentiary issues under the guise of protecting "the integrity of the judicial process." By characterizing the challenge as one involving the misconduct of the prosecutor, rather than the content of the evidence, these courts were able to bring the claim under the language of *Costello* that recognizes the possibility of challenges on the basis that the grand jury that returned the indictment was biased. Under the broadest understanding of the courts' power to protect the integrity of the grand jury process, the types of misconduct that warranted dismissal of the indictment went beyond such familiar forms of prosecutor misconduct as the prosecutor's knowing presentation of false testimony to the grand jury or inflammatory comment by the prosecutor that prejudiced the grand jurors against the defendant. Some courts also found misconduct warranting dismissal if the prosecutor presented the evidence in an unfair or deceptive manner, as when a grand jury witness recites hearsay testimony in such a way as to give the impression that she has first hand knowledge of the facts. However, in the case of *U.S. v. Williams* (S.Ct.1992), discussed in the next section, the Court imposed new limits on misconduct challenges in federal court, precluding any such challenge not based on a violation of either 1) the constitution or 2) other federal law.

Costello v. U.S. concerned a challenge to the indictment based on the inadmissibility of the grand jury evidence under the law of evidence. In subsequent cases the Supreme Court has also rejected efforts to quash the indictment on the basis that the evidence presented to the grand jury included unconstitutionally obtained evidence that is inadmissible at trial under the constitutional exclusionary rule. *U.S. v. Calandra* (S.Ct.1974). In refusing to extend the exclusionary rule to grand jury proceedings the Court expressed concern over the administrative burden involved in litigating suppression issues during the grand jury's consideration of the case, and questioned whether excluding unconstitutionally obtained evidence would have a meaningful deterrent effect on police misconduct. Critics have argued that unconstitutionally obtained evidence should be treated differently from other types of inadmissible evidence because 1) refusing to exclude unconstitutionally obtained evidence in grand jury proceedings does not entail real administrative savings, since the suppression issue will have to be litigated for purposes of the trial; and 2) a prosecutor can frequently improve upon the hearsay presented to the grand jury by calling live witnesses at trial, but no such remedy is available to cure the defects in unconstitutionally obtained evidence.

The majority of states impose the same strict limits on judicial review of grand jury evidence as are applied in the federal system under *Costello*. A minority of states, however, permit much broader review that extends to both the competency of the evidence under the admissibility rules and the sufficiency of the evidence to support the charges. Jurisdictions that permit challenges based on the competency of the evidence do not necessarily apply the law of evidence in grand jury proceedings to the same extent as they are applied at trial. Moreover, the presentation of inadmissible evidence to the grand jury does not usually require dismissal, provided that the charges are supported by some admissible evidence. In reviewing the sufficiency of the grand jury evidence, courts seek to defer to the grand jury's evaluation of the evidence, and rarely dismiss unless there is a complete lack of evidence supporting some essential element of the crime.

G. MISCONDUCT CHALLENGES

Courts in most if not all jurisdictions have recognized that some types of misconduct by the prosecutor are grounds for dismissal of the indictment. Misconduct challenges have been mounted based on a wide variety of prosecutorial actions, including knowing or negligent presentation of false evidence, presentation of evidence in a way that conceals defects in the evidence, inflammatory or inappropriate comment by the prosecutor before the grand jury, failure to present exculpatory evidence to the grand jury, and violation of grand jury procedures, such as rules governing secrecy.

In *U.S. v. Williams* (S.Ct.1992) the Court clarified and narrowed the definition of what qualifies as "misconduct" for purposes of challenging a grand jury indictment in the federal system. The district court in the case had dismissed the indictment on the grounds that the prosecutor had failed to comply with a judicially fashioned rule applied in the Tenth Circuit requiring the prosecution to disclose to the grand jury "substantial exculpatory evidence" in its possession. The rule that was the basis for the misconduct claim was created by the Tenth Circuit Court of Appeals under the court's supervisory power over the judiciary. In its decision reinstating the conviction, the Supreme Court held that the prosecutor's failure to disclose the exculpatory evidence was not "misconduct" because the courts do not possess the authority to prescribe rules governing procedures applicable to the grand jury. The Court of Appeals's attempt to impose a disclosure obligation on the prosecutor was therefore invalid. The reason the supervisory power of the courts to formulate rules of procedure does not extend to the grand jury is "because the grand jury is an institution separate from the courts." The grand jury "belongs to no branch of the institutional government, serving as a kind of buffer or referee between the Government and the people." Thus, while the courts can exercise their supervisory powers to enforce or vindicate rules applicable to the grand jury, they lack the power to prescribe what the rules shall be.

The holding in *U.S. v. Williams* restricts but does not entirely eliminate challenges to grand jury indictments based on the misconduct of the prosecutor. First, the *Williams* decision does not affect a defendant's right to raise a misconduct challenge based on an alleged violation of the constitution. The Due Process Clause requires that the conduct of the prosecutor before the grand jury comports with "fundamental fairness." Courts applying the fundamental fairness standard have found due process violations where the prosecutor used grossly improper argument before the grand jury or purposefully presented critical perjured testimony. It has also been suggested that a pattern of misconduct that infringes the independence of the grand jury could violate due process.

The conduct of the prosecutor before the grand jury may violate constitutional protections other than due process. For example, courts have found violations of the Fifth Amendment privilege against compelled self incrimination when the prosecutor commented on the prospective defendant's failure to testify before the grand jury. In *U.S. v. Williams*, however, the Court held that the constitution does not require the prosecutor to present exculpatory evidence to the grand jury, and a refusal to inform the grand jurors of evidence favorable to the prospective defendant cannot be the basis for challenging the indictment.

In addition to a constitutional violation, the *Williams* Court also recognized that a misconduct challenge can be based on a violation of one of the " 'few, clear rules which were carefully drafted and approved by [the Supreme] Court and by Congress to ensure the integrity of the grand jury's functions.' " In a footnote to its opinion, the Court cited portions of Rule 6 of the Federal Rules of Criminal Procedure, which governs procedures in the grand jury, and several provisions of the United States Code as examples of non-constitutional federal laws prescribing standards of conduct for federal prosecutors. The Rule 6 provisions cited by the Court prohibit any person, other than the jurors, from being present while the grand jury is deliberating and voting, and place controls on disclosure of matters occurring before the grand jury. The cited U.S.

Code provisions include federal statutes setting forth standards for granting a witness immunity from prosecution, criminalizing false declarations before the grand jury, prohibiting grand jury use of unlawfully intercepted wire or oral communications, and criminalizing subornation of perjury.

The Supreme Court's holding in *U.S. v. Williams* limiting misconduct challenges in federal court to violations of either the constitution or other federal law does not prevent the states from granting defendants broader rights to challenge grand jury indictments based on prosecutor misconduct.

A finding of misconduct by the prosecutor before the grand jury does not necessarily entitle the defendant to a dismissal of the indictment. In *Bank of Nova Scotia v. U.S.* (S.Ct.1988) the Court held that prosecutorial misconduct before the grand jury, not involving a violation of the constitution, does not require dismissal of the indictment unless the defendant was prejudiced by the prosecutor's actions. Prejudice requiring dismissal exists " 'if it is established that the violation substantially influenced the grand jury's decision to indict' or if there is 'grave doubt' that the decision to indict was free from the substantial influence of such violations." Under this standard a finding of prejudice is warranted, notwithstanding the fact that the evidence presented to the grand jury clearly supported the finding of probable cause, if there is a sufficient likelihood that the misconduct influenced the grand jurors' decision. The question for the court reviewing the misconduct challenge is not "Was the grand jury's decision to indict correct given the evidence before it," but rather, is there a "grave doubt" that the decision to indict was "substantially influenced" by the prosecutor's misconduct, regardless of the strength of the evidence.

In announcing its holding in *Bank of Nova Scotia* the Court made clear that it was not addressing what if any prejudice showing is required when the challenge to the indictment is based on a violation of the constitution. The Court reiterated its holdings in previous cases that the defendant need not demonstrate prejudice to be entitled to a dismissal if it is shown that racial groups or women were illegally excluded from serving on the grand jury. However, the Court distinguished the jury composition cases from the prosecutorial misconduct challenge in the case before it on the basis 1) that defects in the composition of the grand jury compromised the "structural protections of the grand jury" and 2) assessing the possible impact of the composition of the grand jury on the decision to indict is too speculative to be practical. These considerations suggest that demonstrating prejudice will not be required to secure a dismissal, regardless of whether or not the violation was of constitutional dimension, whenever the error undermined the structure of the grand jury or when measuring the effect of the error requires "unguided speculation." On the other hand, the *Bank of Nova Scotia* approach suggests that even constitutional errors would not require dismissal in the absence of prejudice if those factors are not present.

In *U.S. v. Mechanik* (S.Ct.1986) the Court held that in some situations a conviction renders the prosecutor's misconduct in presenting the case to the grand jury harmless without regard for the effect of the misconduct on the grand jury's decision to indict. The defendant in *Mechanik* discovered during the trial that two of the witnesses before the grand jury had appeared and testified at the same time. The defendant promptly moved for a dismissal of the indictment on the ground that the simultaneous presence and testimony of two grand jury witnesses violated Rule 6(d) of the Federal Rules of Criminal Procedure. The District Court denied the motion, and the defendant was convicted by the jury. In its decision reinstating the conviction, the Supreme Court held that in light of the conviction at trial there was no need to consider the possible impact of the joint appearance of the two witnesses on the grand jury's decision to indict. The Court observed that the purpose of the rule against the simultaneous appearance of two witnesses is to protect against the danger that a defendant will be indicted for a crime for which there is no probable cause to believe him guilty. But the trial jury's subsequent guilty verdict means not only that there was probable cause to indict, but also that the defendant was guilty as charged beyond a reasonable doubt. The Court acknowledged that the defendant in the case could not reasonably be expected to discover the Rule 6 violation any sooner than he had, because the defendant became entitled to a transcript of the witness's grand jury testimony only when the witness was called to testify at trial. The jury's guilty verdict, however, conclusively established that the defendant was not harmed by the prosecutor's misconduct in the grand jury, and no useful purpose would be served by requiring that the defendant be reindicted and retried.

As discussed above, the Supreme Court has held that a subsequent conviction does not cure a violation of the constitutional requirement that the selection of the grand jury be free from purposeful racial discrimination. It is not certain what if any other challenges to the indictment remain viable notwithstanding a conviction on the charge.

CHAPTER 5

DISCOVERY AND DISCLOSURE

Discovery is the pre-trial process by which the parties to a criminal proceeding exchange information and examine, inspect, and copy evidence in the possession of their adversary. Through discovery of the other side's evidence, the parties are better able to evaluate the merits of their case and prepare for trial.

The law relating to discovery specifies what information a party must disclose, and under what conditions. The rules governing discovery have their source in the constitution, legislation, court rules, and judicial decisions. The discovery obligations of the defense and the prosecution are not always equal or reciprocal. This is because the obligation of a defendant to disclose information may be limited by her Fifth Amendment right against compelled self-incrimination as well as rights under the Sixth Amendment and the attorney work product doctrine. The constitution also imposes limits on what information the defendant can be required to disclose to the prosecution.

A. THE EXPANSION OF CRIMINAL DISCOVERY

Until the mid-twentieth century, there were no formal rules regulating discovery in criminal cases. The only ways the prosecutor and defense counsel could obtain information about the other side's case were through their own factual investigations, pre-trial proceedings such as preliminary hearings, and informal exchange of information, if any.

Beginning with the enactment of Rule 16 of the Federal Rules of Criminal Procedure in 1946 and the occurrence of parallel developments in the states, discovery in criminal cases has expanded gradually over the course of the last half century. Discovery in criminal cases is still, however, much more limited than in civil cases. Several reasons are given for this difference, though not everyone finds these reasons persuasive. First, the development of broad discovery in criminal cases has been resisted because of the view that fairness requires discovery to be reciprocal, which is not possible in criminal proceedings. In addition, it is sometimes argued that defense discovery of the prosecution's case will lead to perjury and witness tampering. Finally, other avenues of discovery in criminal cases, like the preliminary hearing, are thought to justify the absence of formal discovery procedures.

The advocates of broader discovery in criminal cases claim several benefits from pre-trial disclosure of the other side's evidence. A fuller understanding of the merits of one's case enables the parties to engage in more informed plea bargaining. Regulating the exchange of information through discovery rules helps level the playing field by reducing the importance of personal relationships between the prosecutor and defense counsel, and promotes efficient use of attorney resources by reducing the need to find alternative methods of discovery. By reducing the element of surprise at trial, pre-trial discovery makes the trial process more rational, and avoids delays and waste of time associated with continuances at trial.

B. THE PROSECUTION'S CONSTITUTIONAL DUTY TO DISCLOSE

1. THE DEVELOPMENT OF THE RULE

The Supreme Court has held that the Due Process clauses of the Fifth and Fourteenth Amendments require the prosecution to disclose certain types of evidence to the defense. This constitutional disclosure requirement, known as the *Brady* rule, operates independently of the prosecution's statutory discovery obligations. The constitution does not impose a comparable discovery obligation on the defense.

The roots of the *Brady* doctrine can be traced to the early case of *Mooney v. Holohan* (S.Ct.1935). In that case the Court held that due process requires the prosecutor to alert the court and the defendant if the prosecutor knows or should know that government witnesses are presenting false testimony.

If the prosecutor fails to reveal that a witness has testified falsely, and a conviction results, the conviction must be set aside if there is a reasonable likelihood that the false testimony affected the jury's verdict. As the Court stated in *Mooney*, the requirement of due process "cannot be deemed to be satisfied by mere notice and hearing if a state has contrived a conviction through the pretense of a trial which in truth is but used as a means of depriving a defendant of liberty through a deliberate deception of court and jury by the presentation of testimony known to be perjured."

Three decades later, in *Brady v. Maryland* (S.Ct. 1963), the Court built on the principle established in *Mooney* to create a general duty of the prosecutor to disclose to the defense exculpatory evidence in the prosecution's possession. In *Brady,* defense counsel had requested the prosecutor to provide statements made by the defendant's co-defendant. The prosecutor turned over some of the co-defendant's statements, but failed to disclose a statement in which the co-defendant admitted that he, rather than Brady, was the actual killer. Although this fact had no bearing on Brady's guilt or innocence, its disclosure might have affected the decision on sentencing.

The Supreme Court held that the prosecutor's failure to disclose the statement in response to the defendant's request violated Brady's constitutional rights. The Court stated that "suppression by the prosecution of evidence favorable to an accused upon request violates due process where the evidence is material either to guilt or the punishment, irrespective of the good faith or bad faith of the prosecution."

In addition to the requirement that the evidence be "favorable to the accused," the disclosure obligation established in *Brady* is subject to two qualifications. First, under *Brady*, the prosecutor is required to disclose exculpatory evidence only when the defense makes a request for the evidence, and second, disclosure is required only of evidence that is "material" to guilt or punishment.

In *U.S. v. Agurs* (S.Ct.1976) the Court expanded the prosecution's disclosure obligations by eliminating the requirement of a defense request as an absolute prerequisite to discovery. The Court also attempted to clarify the requirement that the evidence be "material," and linked the prosecution's disclosure obligation to the materiality of the evidence at issue, establishing three different standards of materiality applicable to three different discovery situations. As the Court uses the term, materiality is a measure of the potential impact of evidence on the outcome of the case. The greater the probability that an item of evidence could or did influence the jury's decision, the more material the evidence. Evidence that is less likely to affect the decision is less material. As the Court has pointed out, materiality determines both whether the evidence must be disclosed, and therefore defines the prosecution's disclosure obligations, and whether non-disclosure of an item of evidence requires a reversal of the defendant's conviction, and therefore defines a harmless error standard.

Under the three-tiered structure established in *Agurs*, the prosecution's disclosure obligation is highest, and the degree of required materiality is least, in the situation addressed in *Mooney v. Holohan*, where the prosecution knows or should know that its evidence is false. In that situation the prosecution is required to disclose the falsity of the evidence if there is "any reasonable likelihood" that the evidence could affect the decision, and the prosecution's knowing presentation of false or perjured testimony requires reversal on appeal unless it is shown that the presentation of the evidence was harmless beyond a reasonable doubt.

At the other end of the spectrum, the highest standard of materiality is required in situations where the defendant has either made no request for exculpatory evidence, as occurred in *Agurs*, or only a "general" request for "all exculpatory evidence" or "all *Brady* evidence." The materiality standard stated in *Agurs* for this situation requires that evidence must be disclosed, or non-disclosure requires reversal, if the evidence "creates a reasonable doubt that did not otherwise exist."

Finally, the *Agurs* Court prescribed an intermediate standard of materiality for situations in which the defense has made a specific request that puts the prosecution on notice of the evidence it is seeking. The Court reasoned that a lower standard of materiality is appropriate in this circumstance, since the defendant's request affirmatively identifies certain evidence as important to the defense. Because the facts of *Agurs* did not raise this issue, the Court did not define the materiality standard for this situation.

2.   THE BAGLEY STANDARD

The standards that currently govern the prosecution's constitutional duty to disclose exculpatory evidence were established in *U.S. v. Bagley* (S.Ct. 1985). While reaffirming much of the previous doctrine, the Court in *Bagley* eliminated the distinction created in *Agurs* between general request and specific request situations, and prescribed a single standard of materiality applicable to both.

The defendant in *Bagley* was indicted on charges of violating federal narcotics and firearms statutes. In a pre-trial discovery motion, Bagley requested disclosure of "any deals, promises or inducements made to [government] witnesses in exchange for their testimony." In its response, the government did not disclose that any "deals, promises or inducements" had been made to two informants who became the government's principal witnesses at trial. The government also produced signed affidavits by these witnesses recounting their undercover dealing with the accused, and concluding with the statement that the affidavits were made without any threats, rewards or promises of reward.

After his conviction, Bagley used the Freedom of Information Act to obtain copies of contracts the

government had entered into with these informants, in which the government promised them
money in exchange for gathering evidence and providing testimony. Bagley then moved to vacate his
sentence, alleging that the government's failure to
disclose these contracts, which he could have used
to impeach the witnesses' credibility, violated his
right to due process under *Brady*.

The discovery motion in *Bagley* requested specific
evidence, which would have triggered a heightened
obligation of disclosure under the approach developed in *Agurs*. (The Court had previously held that
impeachment evidence qualifies as *Brady* material if
it meets the necessary standard of materiality.)
Rather than apply the *Agurs* analysis, however, the
Court abolished the distinction between "specific"
and "general" request situations, and applied a
single standard of materiality to both.

The Court concluded that the test developed in
Strickland v. Washington (S.Ct.1984) for demonstrating prejudice in ineffective assistance of counsel claims was "sufficiently flexible to cover the 'no
request,' 'general request,' and 'specific request'
cases of prosecutorial failure to disclose evidence
favorable to the accused." Under that test, evidence
is material "only if there is a reasonable probability
that, had the evidence been disclosed to the defense,
the result of the proceeding would have been different." The Court defined a "reasonable probability"
as "a probability sufficient to undermine confidence
in the outcome."

In a subsequent case, *Kyles v. Whitley* (S.Ct. 1995), the Court stressed that a demonstration of materiality "does not require demonstration by a preponderance that disclosure would have resulted ultimately in the defendant's acquittal." The Court also made clear that, in determining whether the non-disclosed evidence is material, the evidence must be considered cumulatively, not item-by-item. Finally, once a court has found that the prosecution's failure to disclose evidence at trial violated the *Bagley* standard, there is no need for further harmless error review, since a finding of error necessarily includes as well a determination of prejudice.

Although the *Bagley* Court prescribed a single standard of materiality regardless of whether the defendant made a request for evidence, the Court agreed that a request for specific evidence by the defense may nonetheless be relevant in determining whether the prosecution's non-disclosure adversely affected the defense. This is because "the more specifically the defense requests certain evidence . . ., the more reasonable it is for the defense to assume from the non-disclosure that the evidence does not exist, and to make pretrial and trial decisions on the basis of that assumption."

In several cases the Court has addressed the prosecutor's obligation to disclose evidence not in the actual possession of the attorney assigned to the case. In *Giglio v. U.S.* (S.Ct.1972) the Court held that in determining what evidence is subject to disclosure, the prosecutor's office should be treated as an entity. As applied to the facts of that case, this means that evidence known to one prosecutor within the office is deemed within the possession of the prosecutor trying the case, even if that individual was not personally aware of the evidence.

In *Kyles v. Whitley* (S.Ct.1995) the Court extended the prosecutor's disclosure obligation to include evidence in the possession of the police and not known to any prosecutor. Quoting from *Giglio*, the Court stated that "procedures and regulations can be established to carry [the prosecutor's] burden and to insure communication of all relevant information on each case to every lawyer who deals with it." Federal Rules of Criminal Procedure, Rule 16, provides for disclosure of all items "within the government's possession, custody, or control" and includes evidence known to the prosecutor and that which could be learned about through due diligence.

C. CONSTITUTIONAL LIMITATIONS ON DEFENSE DISCLOSURE

In the *Brady* line of the cases, the Court recognized that the constitution imposes discovery obligations on the prosecution that do not apply to the defense. The Court has also recognized that the defendant may be protected from the obligation to disclose certain types of information to the prosecutor. The limitations on defense disclosure are governed primarily by the Fifth Amendment privilege against compelled self-incrimination, and the attorney client and work product privileges.

Williams v. Florida (S.Ct.1970) involved a Fifth Amendment challenge to a notice of alibi statute. The statute at issue required a defendant who planned to offer an alibi defense to provide pre-trial notice of that intent, together with information regarding where he or she claims to have been at the time of the crime and the names and addresses of any alibi witnesses. In holding that this requirement did not amount to compelled self-incrimination in violation of the Fifth Amendment, the Court reasoned that the notice rule, at most, "compelled the defendant to accelerate the timing of his disclosure, forcing him to divulge at an earlier date information that [he] from the beginning planned to divulge at trial."

In another case, *Wardius v. Oregon* (S.Ct.1973), however, the Court invalidated a notice of alibi provision that required the defense to disclose its alibi witnesses, but did not require the prosecution to disclose the witnesses it intended to call to rebut the defendant's alibi. Relying on the Due Process Clause, the Court stated that "[i]t is fundamentally unfair to require a defendant to divulge the details of his own case while at the same time subjecting him to the hazard of surprise concerning the refutation of the very pieces of evidence which he disclosed to the State."

Although the holding in *Williams* related to a notice of alibi provision, the Court's reasoning in the case would seem to apply to other types of defense discovery as well. That is, *Williams* suggests that a defense discovery requirement does not violate the Fifth Amendment if it does no more than require pre-trial disclosure of information that will eventually be revealed at trial.

One piece of information that may be protected from disclosure under the Fifth Amendment is information about the defendant's intent to testify at trial. Support for that view can be found in *Brooks v. Tennessee* (S.Ct.1972). At issue in *Brooks* was a state statute that required that a defendant who wished to testify must do so before any other defense evidence was presented. The Court held that this requirement violated both the Fifth Amendment and the Due Process right to "the guiding hand of counsel." This is because requiring the defendant to decide whether to testify deprived the defendant of the benefit of being able to make that decision in light of the impact of the defense case on the decision maker. It could be argued that, if a defendant cannot be forced to decide whether to testify at the end of the state's case, she certainly cannot be forced to decide before the trial even begins.

In *U.S. v. Nobles* (S.Ct.1975) the Court addressed both Fifth and Sixth Amendment challenges to a trial court order requiring the defendant to disclose the pre-trial statements of one of its witnesses. The defendant, charged with bank robbery, called a defense investigator for the purpose of eliciting statements the investigator had obtained from bank employees who had testified for the prosecution. The trial court ordered defense counsel to provide the prosecution with a copy of a report the investigator had prepared. The report contained the results of the investigator's interviews with the bank employees. The trial court ordered disclosure of the report for use by the prosecutor in cross examining the investigator. Defense counsel refused, however, asserting several grounds for protection from disclosure of a report prepared on behalf of the defendant. The trial judge then prohibited the defense from calling the investigator as a witness.

The Supreme Court rejected all of the defendant's arguments for withholding the report, and upheld the trial court order precluding the investigator's testimony. First, the Court held that the report was not protected from disclosure under the Fifth Amendment, since the privilege against compelled self incrimination is personal to the accused, and does not protect statements by third parties. Moreover, the fact that the statements of third parties were elicited by a defense investigator on the defendant's behalf does not convert them into the defendant's personal communications protected by the Fifth Amendment.

The Court also rejected various arguments grounded in the Sixth Amendment. The Court held that the disclosure requirement did not interfere with the defendant's right to assistance of counsel by inhibiting effective preparation for trial, since the disclosure order resulted from the defendant's voluntary decision to make testimonial use of the investigator's report. Finally, the Court held that the disclosure order did not violate the defendant's rights under the work product doctrine, since the defendant waived the privilege against disclosure of attorney work product by calling the investigator as a witness.

D. PRESERVATION OF EVIDENCE

The *Brady* rule requires the prosecution to disclose exculpatory evidence within its possession. A related question is whether the Due Process Clause requires the government to preserve evidence that might prove useful to the defense. The Court has held that, while the prosecution's destruction of potentially exculpatory evidence will in some situations violate the defendant's due process rights, the government's duty to preserve evidence is much narrower than its duty to disclose.

In *California v. Trombetta* (S.Ct.1984) defendant claimed that his due process rights were violated because the prosecution failed to preserve a breath sample to enable him to re-test the sample for evidence of intoxication. In rejecting the defendant's claim, the Court first observed that there was no evidence that the prosecution had acted in bad faith in failing to preserve the sample. The Court then stated that the prosecution's constitutional duty to preserve evidence is "limited to evidence that might be expected to play a significant role in the suspect's defense." To meet this requirement, "the evidence must both possess an exculpatory value that was apparent before the evidence was destroyed, and also be of such a nature that the defendant would be unable to obtain comparable evidence by other reasonably available means."

In the later case of *Arizona v. Youngblood* (S.Ct. 1988) the Court appeared to hold that a due process violation for failure to preserve evidence could never be established absent a showing that the government acted in bad faith in destroying evidence. The defendant in *Youngblood* claimed a violation of due process in the prosecution's failure to refrigerate semen samples found on the sexual assault victim's underwear. The failure to refrigerate the samples resulted in degradation of the evidence that prevented the defendant from performing tests that might have exonerated him.

The Court acknowledged that the evidence in *Youngblood* had a greater potential for exoneration than that in *Trombetta*, since the semen sample in *Youngblood* had never been analyzed. Nonetheless, the Court held that, "unless a criminal defendant can show bad faith on the part of the police, failure to preserve potentially useful evidence does not constitute a denial of due process."

The semen samples at issue in *Youngblood* were eventually tested in 2000. At that point Youngblood had been released after serving 10 years in prison for the 1985 conviction, but was being prosecuted for failing to comply with a state law requiring registration of sex offenders. Using DNA testing techniques not available at the time of the trial, the tests on the sample conducted in 2000 showed that

Youngbood was not the donor of the semen on the victim's underwear.

More recently, in *Illinois v. Fisher* (S.Ct. 2004), the Court found no due process violation where the police destroyed drug evidence seized during a traffic stop eleven years before trial. The Court found that since the defendant was a fugitive during this period, which caused the delay in the case coming to trial, and the police followed their regular guidelines for the destruction of evidence, the police acted in good faith

E. SPECIFIC TYPES OF DISCOVERY

Most jurisdictions now have rules that authorize discovery of specific categories of evidence from both the prosecution and the defense. This section summarizes the major discovery requirements under the Federal Rules of Criminal Procedure, referred to here as the Rules.

Discovery rights and obligations established by statute or court rule can and sometimes do overlap with requirements under the *Brady* doctrine. Thus, in deciding whether an item of evidence is discoverable, consideration should be given to both applicable local law and the constitution.

1. NOTICE

a. Alibi Defense

Rule 12.1(a) creates a notice requirement and a procedure for exchange of information when the defendant intends to present an alibi defense at trial. In order to set the procedure in motion, the prosecutor must file a written demand for notice on the defense. This demand must set forth the time, date, and place at which the alleged offense was committed. Upon receipt of the government's demand, the defendant must serve a written notice of the defendant's intention to offer a defense of alibi. This notice must be served within 10 days of the government's demand, and must state the specific place or places at which the defendant claims to have been at the time of the alleged offense, and the names and addresses of the witnesses upon whom the defendant intends to rely to establish the alibi.

Rule 12.1(b) requires the prosecution to respond to the defendant's notice of alibi by providing the names and addresses of the witnesses it intends to use to establish the defendant's presence at the scene of the alleged offense or otherwise rebut the defendant's alibi. If either side fails to comply with the notice requirements, the court may exclude the testimony of the undisclosed witness. The rule does not, however, permit the court to exclude the testimony of the defendant.

b. Insanity Defense

Rule 12.2 requires that a defendant who intends to present an insanity defense, or to introduce expert testimony relating to a mental condition of the defendant bearing on the defendant's guilt, must give the prosecution written notice of that intent. Failure by the defendant to give the required notice can result in exclusion of the insanity defense or the testimony of the expert.

The purpose of the requirement that the defendant give notice of an intent to raise an insanity defense or present other evidence on her mental condition is to give the prosecution the opportunity to have the defendant examined by a neutral expert. Thus, the Rule authorizes the prosecution to move for a court order to require the defendant to submit to a mental examination.

2.   THE DEFENDANT'S STATEMENTS AND CRIMINAL RECORD

Rule 16(a)(1)(A) requires the government, upon the defendant's request, to disclose four different types of prior statements of the defendant. The Rule requires the prosecution to permit the defendant to inspect or copy:

1) any relevant written or recorded statements made by the defendant that are within the possession of the government and the existence of which is know, or by the exercise of due diligence may become known, to the attorney for the government;

2) the recorded testimony of the defendant before a grand jury relating to the offense charged;

3) that portion of any written record containing the substance of any relevant oral statement made by the defendant in response to interrogation by a person the defendant knew to be a government agent; and

4) the substance of any relevant oral statement made by the defendant in response to interrogation by a person the defendant knew to be a government agent, provided the prosecution intends to offer the statement in evidence.

Note the differences between the last two types of statements: number "3" requires disclosure of oral statements made in response to official interrogation that have been reduced to writing, while number "4" requires disclosure of unrecorded statements, but only those that the prosecution intends to offer in evidence.

The Rule does not require disclosure of all defendant statements possessed by the prosecution. For example, the Rule does not require disclosure of an oral statement, which was not made in response to interrogation by a government agent, or which was made in response to interrogation by a government agent who was acting undercover, and therefore not known to be a government agent by the defendant.

Rule 16(a)(1)(B) requires the prosecution, on request by the defendant, to furnish the defendant with a copy of the defendant's prior criminal record, if that record is in the possession, custody or control of the government, and its existence is known or discoverable through due diligence.

3. DOCUMENTS, TANGIBLE EVIDENCE, TEST RESULTS AND SUMMARIES OF EXPERT TESTIMONY

a. Documents and Tangible Evidence

Rules 16(a)(1)(C) and 16(b)(1)(A) provide for reciprocal discovery of documents and tangible evidence by both the prosecution and defense. The discovery obligations of the prosecution and defense are not, however, exactly equal.

Rule 16(a)(1)(C) governs the disclosure obligations of the prosecution. It requires the government to permit the defendant to inspect or copy and photograph documents or tangible objects that are within the possession, custody or control of the government, provided that one of three conditions is present: 1) if the evidence is material to the preparation of the defendant's defense; 2)if the evidence is intended for use by the government as evidence in chief; or 3) if the evidence belongs to or was obtained from the defendant. In order to obtain discovery under this Rule, the defendant must make a request for the evidence.

The defendant's obligation to disclose documents or tangible evidence arises only if the defendant has requested such evidence from the government, and the government has complied with that request. If that happens, and the government makes a request on the defendant, the defendant must grant the prosecution access to documents and tangible evidence, but only that evidence which the defendant intends to introduce as evidence in chief at trial.

b. Test Results

Rules 16(a)(1)(D), (F) and 16(b)(1)(B) provide for reciprocal discovery of results of certain types of tests. Both Rules permit the other side to inspect, copy or photograph results or reports of physical or mental examinations and of scientific tests or experiments that are within the possession, custody, or control of the party, and are known or through the exercise of due diligence can become known. Both Rules also require a request from the other side before disclosure is required.

The Rule governing disclosure by the government requires disclosure of tests which are either material to the preparation of the defense, or are intended for use by the government as evidence in chief at trial. The Rule governing disclosure by the defendant requires disclosure only if the defendant has availed herself of the right to request discovery from the government, and requires disclosure only of those test results that the defendant either intends to introduce as evidence in chief, or were prepared by a witness the defendant intends to call at trial and relate to that witness's testimony.

c. Expert Witnesses

Rules 16(a)(1)(E), (G) and 16(b)(1)(C) provide for reciprocal disclosure of written summaries of expert testimony that either side intends to use at trial. As with other Rule 16 provisions, the prosecution is required to disclose the summaries only if the defendant makes a request, and the defense is required to disclose its summaries only if the defense has made a request and the prosecution has complied. The Rule requires disclosure of three types of information—the opinions of the experts, the information relied on in reaching those opinions, and the experts' qualifications.

4.　WITNESS STATEMENTS

In *Jencks v. U.S.* (S.Ct.1957) the Supreme Court exercised its supervisory power over the federal courts to require disclosure by the prosecutor of prior statements of government witnesses. Later that same year, Congress enacted the *"Jencks* Act" codifying the Court's decision. In the 1970s the rule was expanded to require disclosure to the government of statements by defense witnesses other than the defendant. The expanded rule was then incorporated in the Federal Rules of Criminal Procedure as Rule 26.2. Despite its placement in the Rules, the witness statement Rule is commonly referred to as the *"Jencks* Act," and material subject to disclosure under the Rule is referred to as *"Jencks"* material.

The purpose of requiring disclosure of a trial witness's prior statements is to facilitate cross-examination and impeachment. But while the purpose of the rule is to aid in impeachment, the obligation to disclose witness statements does not depend on showing that the prior statement is inconsistent with the witness's trial testimony or otherwise relevant to impeachment.

Rule 26.2 differs from the disclosure requirements under Rules 12 and 16 discussed above in that disclosure of a witness's prior statements under Rule 26.2 is required *during* rather than before trial. Under the Rule, disclosure is not required until after the witness has testified on direct examination. Because the party receiving the witness's prior statements will often need time to study them before beginning cross-examination, the Rule authorizes the court to grant a recess "to examine the statement and prepare to use it in the proceedings."

The requirement of disclosure arises only upon a request by any party who did not call the witness. Upon request, the party who called the witness must turn over any statement that is in their possession and that relates to the subject matter concerning which the witness has testified.

The most difficult issues in applying Rule 26.2 involve determining what qualifies as a "statement" within the meaning of the Rule. The Rule defines three types of statements:

1) a written statement made by the witness that is signed or otherwise adopted or approved by the witness;

2) a substantially verbatim recital of an oral statement made by the witness that is recorded contemporaneously with the making of the oral statement that is contained in a stenographic, mechanical, or other recording or a transcription thereof; or

3) a statement, however taken or recorded, or a transcription thereof, made by a witness to a grand jury.

The definition of a statement requires either a written statement that was made, adopted or approved by the witness, or a substantially verbatim record of what the witness said. This would not include an interviewer's summary of what the witness said. The reason for requiring that the statement capture the witness's own words or a version of the what the witness said that the witness expressly approved relates to the use that will be made of the prior statement at trial. The purpose of the disclosure requirement is to permit the impeaching party to explore the consistency between the witness's prior statements and trial testimony. Permitting impeachment with a prior statement that is not an accurate recital of what the witness said does not advance the search for truth.

If either party fails to disclose a witness's prior statements, the Rule requires the court to strike the testimony given by the witness on direct examination. If the prosecutor fails to comply with the Rule, the court is instructed to declare a mistrial if required by the interest of justice.

F.   DISCOVERY SANCTIONS AND REMEDIES

The specific discovery rules contained in the Federal Rules of Criminal Procedure typically prescribe

the sanctions for failure to comply with that particular Rule. In addition to these specific remedy provisions, Rule 16(d)(2) contains a general sanctions
provision. This Rule is typical of provisions governing remedies for discovery violations in granting
broad discretion to the trial judge to fashion an
appropriate response to the violation. The Rule
authorizes the judge to order the defaulting party to
permit the discovery or inspection, grant a continuance, prohibit the party from introducing the evidence not disclosed, or enter such other order as it
deems just under the circumstances.

In addition to statutes or court rules regarding
sanctions for discovery violations, consideration
should also be given to the constitutional constraints on the types of sanctions that can be imposed on the defendant. The Supreme Court has
held that a criminal defendant has a constitutional
right to testify and give evidence in her defense. *See
Rock v. Arkansas* (S.Ct.1987). This right stems from
three sources—the Due Process Clause, the Sixth
Amendment right to compulsory process, and the
Fifth Amendment privilege against compelled self-
incrimination. Although the right is not absolute
and can be restricted to accommodate "legitimate
interests in the criminal process," restrictions on
the right to present evidence "may not be arbitrary
or disproportionate to the purposes they are designed to serve."

In *Taylor v. Illinois* (S.Ct.1988), the Court recognized that in some circumstances a discovery sanc-

tion that entirely excludes evidence offered by the
defense may violate the defendant's constitutional
right to present evidence. The Court in *Taylor* also
held, however, that the preclusion order issued in
that case did not abridge the defendant's constitutional rights. The discovery law in Illinois where the
case was tried required the defendant to disclose to
the prosecution the names and addresses of prospective defense witnesses. When defense counsel
attempted to call a witness not included on the
witness list, counsel sought to excuse the failure to
disclose the witness by first claiming to be unaware
of the witness, and then representing that he did
not know the witness's address. When both of those
claims were shown to be false, the trial judge concluded that defense counsel's violation of the discovery rules was both blatant and willful, and disallowed the witness's testimony.

In the Supreme Court, the defendant argued that
a preclusion order is never an appropriate sanction
for violation of pre-trial disclosure rules, since less
drastic sanctions are always available. Specifically,
the trial judge can minimize prejudice to the prosecution by granting a continuance, and deter future
violations of the rules through disciplinary sanctions against the defendant or defense counsel.
While acknowledging that in most cases alternative
sanctions would be adequate and appropriate, the
Court stated that the alternatives to preclusion are
also less effective, and in some instances failure to
order preclusion "would perpetuate rather than
limit the prejudice to the State and the harm to the
adversary process." Because the trial judge had

found that Taylor's discovery violation was "blatant and willful," the Court found that the severest sanction was appropriate.

In *Michigan v. Lucas* (S.Ct.1991) the Court addressed a claim that an order prohibiting the defendant from offering evidence of a rape victim's past sexual conduct because of failure to comply with a pre-trial notice requirement violated his rights under the Sixth Amendment. The trial judge barred the defendant from testifying to his sexual relationship with the victim because of the discovery violation. The state appeals court reversed, holding that the notice requirement violates the Sixth Amendment in all cases where it is used to preclude evidence of past sexual conduct between the rape victim and a defendant. The state court based this conclusion on its determination that the notice provision serves no useful purpose when the evidence the defendant wishes to offer relates to his own past conduct with the victim.

The Supreme Court rejected a *per se* ban on preclusion as a remedy for failure to comply with the notice requirement. Noting that notice serves the legitimate state interests of protecting against surprise, harassment, and undue delay, the Court held that failure to comply with the requirement may in some cases justify preclusion. Because the state appeals court had decided the case on an erroneous *per se* rule, the Supreme Court remanded for a determination of whether on the facts of this case the defendant's Sixth Amendment rights were violated.

CHAPTER 6

TIME LIMITATIONS

Both the constitution and various statutes protect the accused against undue delay in the prosecution of criminal cases. In applying these protections it is necessary to distinguish between two kinds of delay. First is pre-accusation delay—the delay between the commission of the crime and arrest or the filing of charges. Second is post-accusation delay—the delay between arrest or the filing of charges and the commencement of the trial. Because post-accusation delay is relatively more significant, it is discussed first.

A. SPEEDY TRIAL

1. CONSTITUTIONAL GUARANTEE

A mainstay of the Anglo–American criminal justice system, stemming from the Magna Carta, the right of a criminal accused to a speedy trial, is guaranteed by the Sixth Amendment to the constitution of the United States. The Sixth Amendment provides that "[i]n all criminal prosecutions the accused shall enjoy the right to a speedy ... trial." The Supreme Court has acknowledged that the Sixth Amendment right applies to federal prosecutions, *Beavers v. Haubert* (S.Ct.1905), and applies to the states through the Due Process Clause of the Fourteenth Amendment, *Klopfer v. N.C.* (S.Ct. 1967). In *Klopfer*, the Court noted that the right to a speedy trial "is as fundamental as any of the rights secured by the Sixth Amendment."

The defendant has a variety of interests in securing a speedy trial. First, delay in trial can lead to extensive incarceration under conditions that are more onerous than post conviction incarceration. Though less burdensome than incarceration, release on bail or other conditions may also interfere with the defendant's freedom, and any person against whom charges are pending is likely to suffer public disgrace as a result.

In addition, the effect of delay on evidence can be substantial: physical evidence may be lost or destroyed and witnesses may disappear or suffer memory loss. Finally, speedy trial minimizes the anxiety for the accused caused by an unresolved criminal accusation. This interest is implicated even if the defendant has been released pending trial. These interests in a speedy trial were summarized by the Court in *Smith v. Hooey* (S.Ct.1969):

Suffice it to remember that this constitutional guarantee has universally been thought essential to protect at least three basic demands of criminal justice in the Anglo–American legal system: "(1) to prevent undue and oppressive incarceration prior to trial, (2) to minimize anxiety and concern accompanying public accusation and (3) to limit the possibilities that long delay will impair the ability of an accused to defend himself."

Society also has an interest in promoting speedy trials of criminal defendants. Prompt prosecution prevents judicial backlogs and improves the chances of obtaining just convictions, reduces the risk that the accused will escape or commit crimes while awaiting trial, speeds up the initiation of rehabilitative measures for the defendant, and helps minimize the costs of prosecution. The Supreme Court has also noted that a deprivation of the right to a speedy trial may in fact work to the defendant's advantage, since delay often results in lost witnesses or faded memories, and the prosecution bears the burden of proof at trial.

2. WHEN THE RIGHT ATTACHES

By its terms, the Sixth Amendment right to a speedy trial cannot attach unless a person has been accused of a crime. So, when a prosecution has begun, either by an arrest or the bringing of formal charges, then the accused's right to a speedy trial attaches. It does not apply to the period between the commission of the crime and the arrest of the defendant or the filing of charges (the pre-accusation period).

A delay in launching a prosecution cannot be the basis for a speedy trial claim. For example, in *U.S. v. Marion* (S.Ct.1971), the Court held that a 38 month pre-charge delay did not trigger the speedy trial right. In *Marion,* the trial court dismissed the indictment for lack of speedy prosecution since the government had the information to indict for three years prior to seeking an indictment. In reversing the trial court, the Court stated: "In our view, the Sixth Amendment speedy trial provision has no application until the putative defendant in some way becomes an 'accused,' an event that occurred only when the appellees were indicted."

The Court further noted that until a person is accused they suffer no restraint on liberty, and are not the subject of public accusation. Even though the passage of time, whether before or after arrest, may impair memories, cause evidence to be lost, deprive the defendant of witnesses, and otherwise interfere with his ability to defend herself, the Sixth Amendment provides a remedy only when a prosecution has begun.

Remedies other than the speedy trial right under the Sixth Amendment protect against delays in instituting prosecutions: Statutes of limitation and the Due Process Clause of the Fifth Amendment. (See Section B below.)

Generally determination of when the right of speedy trial attaches is fairly straight forward: The right attaches at the time of arrest or formal charge, whichever occurs first. For example, if the defendant commits a burglary on January 1 but is not arrested or charged with the crime until June 1, the speedy trial clock begins to run on June 1.

There may, however, be complications even with this straight forward rule. For example, if the charge is initiated by sealed indictment, the date of the unsealing is the date of attachment of the speedy trial right, since no incarceration or public accusation occurs until then. When there is a dismissal of charges followed by reindictment, the measure of the speedy trial right will still be from the date of the initial arrest or charge, unless the dismissal was at the behest of the defendant.

Problems may also arise if the defendant is arrested for one offense and is later charged with another. The question is the relationship of the offense charged to the offense for which the defendant was originally arrested. Even though the ultimate offense charged may differ, if it relates to the offense for which the defendant was arrested, then the speedy trial time should begin to run from the time of arrest, not formal charge. Similar problems can arise where the jurisdiction of arrest and the jurisdiction of formal charge differs. Dual sovereignty principles suggest that there is a separation time of attachment of the speedy trial right by jurisdiction as well. However, where there is close cooperation between sovereigns, be they state or federal, there is a strong argument that speedy trial rights should attach upon the earliest act by either sovereign.

3. DISMISSAL REMEDY

The Supreme Court has held that the only remedy for a violation of the Sixth Amendment speedy trial right is a dismissal of the charges. Other possible remedies, such as a reduction of the defendant's sentence, have been held to be inadequate. Thus, a pre-trial determination that the defendant's speedy trial rights have been violated prevents the prosecution from trying the defendant, and a defendant whose conviction has been reversed on speedy trial grounds cannot be retried.

The absolute and inflexible nature of the remedy for a speedy trial violation has affected courts' interpretation of the underlying right. Because a finding that the defendant's speedy trial rights have been violated prevents the state from prosecuting her, courts have been hesitant to find a denial of the right to a speedy trial except in the most egregious cases.

4. THE SPEEDY TRIAL BALANCING TEST: *BARKER v. WINGO*

In *Barker v. Wingo* (S.Ct.1972), the Court established a four factor balancing test to be used in evaluating whether a defendant's Sixth Amendment right to a speedy trial has been violated. The defendant in the case, Barker, was accused of a double murder committed with another person named Manning. The prosecution's case against Manning was stronger than its case against Barker. In order to improve its chances of convicting both defendants, the prosecution decided to try Manning first in hopes that it could then compel Manning to testify against Barker. As a result of two hung

juries and two re-trials following appellate reversals, it took six trials and more than four years
before the prosecution finally succeeded in convicting Manning for the two murders.

Barker was free on bail for all but ten months of
the four-year period during which the prosecution
was seeking to obtain convictions against Manning.
Barker raised no objection to eleven prosecution
requests to postpone or "continue" his trial during
this period. But when the state moved for a twelfth
continuance one month before Manning's conviction for the first of the two murders, Barker objected to the postponement, and moved for dismissal of
the charges. The trial court granted the continuance and denied the dismissal motion, and then
granted two additional prosecution continuance requests, to which Barker did not object. After Manning's conviction for the second murder, the case
against Barker was finally scheduled for trial nearly
four and one-half years after he had been indicted.
But on the day the trial was to begin, the prosecution again moved for a continuance, this time based
on the illness of a key prosecution witness. This
fifteenth continuance was granted over Barker's
objection. The prosecution requested yet another
continuance when the witness was still unable to
testify three months later, which continuance was
also granted despite the defendant's objection.
When the case finally came to trial just over five
years after Barker was indicted, he moved to dismiss the charges on the ground that his right to a
speedy trial had been violated. The trial court de-

nied the dismissal motion, and Barker was convicted.

In its opinion addressing Barker's claim that his speedy trial rights were violated, the Supreme Court refused to interpret the Sixth Amendment as requiring that the state try the defendant within some specified time period, such as six months. The Court also rejected what it termed the "demand-waiver doctrine," according to which the speedy trial clock does not begin to run until the accused demands a trial. In preference to either of these "rigid" approaches, the Court established a case-by-case balancing test, and identified four factors to be weighed in determining whether a delay violates the Sixth Amendment.

The four factors are: 1) the length of the delay; 2) the reason for the delay; 3) whether and when the defendant asserted her right to a speedy trial; and 4) whether the defendant was prejudiced by the delay. No one of these factors is either invariably necessary or sufficient to establish a speedy trial violation. Rather, all four must be considered together with other relevant circumstances.

The first factor—the length of the delay—serves initially as a "triggering mechanism." The Court explained that until there is some delay which is "presumptively prejudicial" there is no necessity for consideration of the other factors. In a subsequent case the Court stated that lower courts have found post-accusation delay presumptively prejudicial at least as it approaches one year. *Doggett v. U.S.*

(S.Ct.1992). A delay of five months or less is generally not enough to trigger further inquiry.

In addition to its function as a threshold for further inquiry, the length of the delay is also relevant in assessing the other three factors. Whether a delay is based on adequate reasons—factor number two—will often depend on the length of the delay, and the necessity for the defendant to demand trial in order to succeed on a speedy trial claim will depend on how long the accused has waited before making the demand. The length of the delay is also relevant to the question of the prejudice suffered by the defendant, the fourth factor in the Court's balancing test, since the longer the delay the stronger the presumption of prejudice.

The second factor is the reason for the delay. The Court explained that different weights should be assigned to different reasons, and distinguished three broad categories according to the magnitude of the infringement on the defendant's Sixth Amendment right. First, a deliberate attempt by the prosecution to delay the trial in order to gain unfair advantage at trial is weighed most heavily against the prosecution. As the Court later explained in *Doggett*, when the prosecution acts in bad faith, relief is "virtually automatic." Second, the Court stated that a "more neutral" reason, such as negligence or overcrowded courts, should be weighted less heavily against the prosecution. The weight that is assigned to negligent delays, such as a failure to locate a defendant whose whereabouts is easily determined, compounds over time, since the longer the delay the greater the presumption of prejudice. Finally, a valid reason, such as a good faith interlocutory appeal, would ordinarily serve to justify appropriate delay. Even if the prosecution's reason for the delay is a valid one, a finding that the defendant's speedy trial rights have been violated is still possible if the other factors warrant such a finding.

The third factor is whether and at what point the defendant asserted the right to a speedy trial. Although the Court rejected a rule that the accused waives the speedy trial right for any period before the right is asserted, the defendant's assertion of the right is to be given "strong evidentiary weight," and a failure to assert the right to a speedy trial will make it difficult to prove that the right was violated. To the extent a demand for trial is a purely tactical move in order to claim the right to a speedy trial that the defendant does not genuinely want, it should count for little in the determination of whether the defendant's right has been violated.

The fourth factor is the prejudice to the defendant caused by the delay. The Court explained that prejudice is to be assessed in light of the interests the right to a speedy trial is designed to protect. Those interests are i) preventing oppressive pretrial incarceration; ii) minimizing anxiety to the accused arising from the existence of an unresolved criminal charge; and iii) limiting the possibility that the defendant's ability to defend at trial will be impaired. Because impairment of the defense undermines the fairness of the system of determining guilt or innocence, it is the most serious form of prejudice.

In applying these factors to the facts of Barker's case, the Court observed with respect to the first factor that the "extraordinary" five year delay of Barker's trial was plainly long enough to trigger an inquiry into Barker's speedy trial claim. As for the second factor—the reason for the delay—the Court noted that only seven months of the five years was attributable to a strong justification, the illness of the police witness who was in charge of the investigation. The Court conceded that some delay may have been permissible to allow the state to seek to convict Manning and thereby secure his testimony against Barker. But the four-year postponement the prosecution actually obtained was excessive, especially since the length of the delay was a result of the prosecution's failure or inability to try Manning under circumstances that comported with due process.

Although the length of the delay weighed in favor of the defendant, the Court found that the remaining two factors weighed in favor of the government. First, the prejudice to the defendant was minimal. Although he was free on $5,000 bond during most of the period before trial, the defendant did suffer some prejudice from having spent 10 months in jail. The Court also stated that the defendant was "prejudiced to some extent by living for over four years under a cloud of suspicion and anxiety." But with respect to the third form of prejudice, the defendant made no claim that any defense witnesses had become unavailable, and the trial transcript revealed only two minor memory lapses, neither of which were significant to the outcome of the trial.

The most important factor in the Court's analysis was the fourth. The Court gave decisive significance to the fact that the defendant apparently did not want a speedy trial. Although he was represented by competent counsel throughout the five-year delay, it was not until after Manning had been convicted that the defendant made a serious demand to be tried. The reason he did not object to the prosecution requests for continuance was because he was gambling on Manning's acquittal, which would have prevented him from being tried. The Court concluded that, barring extraordinary circumstances such as severe prejudice or absence of competent counsel, a speedy trial violation will not be found where the defendant's failure to request a speedy trial indicates that she did not want one.

5. STATUTORY RULES

Constitutional speedy trial guarantees are not always effective in insuring that the accused is expeditiously brought to trial. Because the ill-defined constitutional balancing test is often inadequate, Congress and most state legislatures have passed speedy trial statutes which, unlike the Sixth Amendment, require that the accused be brought to trial within a fixed time frame. As a practical matter, these statutes, rather than the constitutional provisions, provide the primary protection against excessive delay in prosecution of criminal cases.

Typically, speedy trial statutes define some starting point—such as arrest or the filing of formal charges—that starts the speedy trial clock running, and a time limit within which the accused must be brought to trial. The statutory time limit may be stated in days, months, or court terms. The statutes also typically provide for flexibility in applying these rigid time limitations through provisions that exclude certain types of delay from the calculation of the time between the starting of the speedy trial clock and the trial. Because the speedy trial clock, once started, does not necessarily run continuously, it is common for trials to be delayed beyond the time limit stated in the statute. Proper application of speedy trial statutes must begin with an analysis of the reasons for any trial postponements to determine whether they count against the prosecution's allowable time. It must then be determined whether the remaining "includable" time exceeds the statutory limit.

There are significant differences among speedy trial statutes, and application requires close attention to the wording of the particular statute. The federal Speedy Trial Act of 1974, 18 U.S.C. §§ 3161–3164, provides an example of how such statutes work. The Act requires that an indictment or information be filed within 30 days from the date an individual is arrested or served with a summons. If the defendant pleads not guilty, the trial must commence within 70 days from the filing date (and making public) of the information or indictment, or the date the defendant appears before a judicial officer, whichever occurs last. Thus, the presumptive time limit from arrest to trial is 100 days.

The primary focus of the Speedy Trial Act is protection of the defendant against delay in bringing the case to trial. But the Act also includes a provision protecting the defendant against being forced to go to trial too quickly, which might impair the defendant's ability to defend against the charge. Unless the defendant consents in writing, the trial may not commence less than 30 days from the date the defendant first appears either through counsel or *pro se* if she elects to represent herself.

In calculating whether the commencement of the trial is within the allowable time limits, postponements granted for certain statutorily defined reasons are defined as "excludable," and therefore do not count against the time allotted to the prosecution to bring the defendant to trial. The Act contains a list of specific exclusions and a catchall provision to address situations not covered by the more specific rules. The specific exclusions are defined in detail in the statute. In general they exclude: delays caused by other proceedings concerning the defendant; deferral for the purpose of permitting the defendant to demonstrate good conduct; delay resulting from the absence or unavailability of the defendant or an essential witness; delay resulting from the fact that the defendant is mentally incompetent or physically unable to stand trial; treatment of the defendant pursuant to statutes governing civil commitment and narcotics addicts; the period during which charges are dismissed, on the motion of the government, and then refiled; a "reasonable period of delay" resulting from joinder of the defendant with a co-defendant as to whom the time for trial has not run; and a delay of not more than one year to obtain evidence located in a foreign country. The catchall provision excludes any period of delay resulting from a continuance granted by a judge upon the judge's own motion or at the request of either the defendant or the government, if the judge finds that the ends of justice served by taking such action outweigh the best interest of the public and the defendant in a speedy trial. The Act specifies factors to be considered by the judge in deciding whether to grant a continuance, and requires that the reasons for the decision be set forth orally or in writing. The Act expressly prohibits consideration of general congestion of the court's calendar or the government's lack of diligent preparation or failure to obtain available witnesses as grounds for a continuance.

The remedy available under the Speedy Trial Act is more flexible than under the Sixth Amendment. The defendant whose statutory speedy trial rights have been violated is entitled to a dismissal, but the Act authorizes the judge to choose between a dismissal with prejudice, which prevents the prosecution from seeking a new indictment for the same charge, and dismissal without prejudice, which does not bar a re-prosecution.

In deciding whether to dismiss with or without prejudice, the Act instructs the judge to consider three factors. First, the judge must consider the seriousness of the offense. The more serious the offense the less willing the judge should be to dismiss with prejudice. Less serious offenses will more often be dismissed with prejudice. Second, the judge must consider the facts and circumstances of the case which led to dismissal. This includes a determination of who is responsible for the delays that caused the violation, the prosecution or the defendant, and an assessment of the level of the prosecution's culpability in failing to bring the defendant to trial in a timely manner, whether it was intentional, negligent, or inadvertent. As a part of this inquiry the judge should also consider how long beyond the statutory time period the defendant's trial was delayed. Third, the judge should consider the impact of a reprosecution on the administration of the Speedy Trial Act and the administration of justice.

In *U.S. v. Taylor* (S.Ct.1988), a case construing the Act's remedy provision, the Court emphasized that in deciding upon the appropriate sanction judges must carefully consider the statutory factors as applied to the facts of the case and set forth their findings on the record. A trial court's decision on sanctions will not be reversed on appeal provided the court's factual findings are supported by the record and support the court's decision. In *Taylor*, however, the trial court failed to explain its consideration of the statutory factors, and the Supreme Court held that the trial court's dismissal of the charges with prejudice was an abuse of discretion. In determining that dismissal with prejudice was not appropriate in that case, the Court stressed that "[d]ismissal without prejudice is not a toothless sanction," and rejected the lower court's view that dismissal without prejudice would tacitly condone the government's failure to afford the defendant a speedy trial.

B. PRE–CHARGE DELAYS

The Sixth Amendment speedy trial guarantee and the Speedy Trial Act protect the accused against delay between the initiation of the prosecution and the commencement of the trial. Although pre-accusation delay poses some of the same risks of prejudice to the accused as post-accusation delay, neither the Sixth Amendment nor the Speedy Trial Act applies to the period between the occurrence of the offense and the filing of charges.

One mechanism for protecting the defendant against prejudice from pre-charge delays is the statute of limitations. Statutes of limitations require that most crimes be charged within some fixed time period after they are committed or they cannot be prosecuted at all. The time period allowed for the bringing of charges typically varies with the seriousness of the offense: Less serious crimes have shorter statutes of limitations; more serious crimes have longer limitations periods. Some especially serious crimes, such as murder, are not subject to a statute of limitations.

In addition to statutes of limitations, the Due Process Clause of the constitution also protects the accused against prejudice from pre-accusation delay. However, the requirements for establishing a due process violation are strict, and successful due process challenges are rare.

The basis for a due process claim is that delay impairs the defendant's ability to defend herself. With the passage of time, memories fade, witnesses become unavailable, and tangible evidence is lost or undiscoverable. Because the effects of delay begin with the occurrence of the offence, the length of the delay for due process purposes is calculated from the time the offense is complete to the commencement of the trial. Thus, a due process claim embraces both pre-accusation delay and post-accusation delay.

To establish a due process violation the defendant must demonstrate both 1) that she was prejudiced by the delay and 2) that the delay was based on inadequate or improper reasons. Prejudice for due process purposes means an actual impairment of the defendant's ability to present an effective defense. In effect, the delay must work to the prosecution's advantage by improving its chances of winning a conviction. It is not enough, for example, for the defendant to show that a witness became unavailable as a result of the delay; the defendant must also demonstrate that the witness would have testified and that the testimony would have aided the defense. Whether a due process claim can be predicated on presumed prejudice is not clear. The

Supreme Court has held that prejudice for purposes of the Sixth Amendment's Speedy Trial Clause can be presumed from a long delay, but many lower courts have held that actual prejudice must be shown to establish a due process violation.

With respect to the second prong of a due process claim, the Supreme Court has not clearly specified what reasons will or will not justify a delay in the filing of charges. The Court has held, however, that delay for the purpose of conducting further investigation does not violate due process, even if the defense was "somewhat prejudiced by the lapse of time." *U.S. v. Lovasco* (S.Ct.1977). This means that the prosecution is not required to file charges as soon as it has sufficient evidence to prove the defendant's guilt at trial. The prosecution may delay charging and continue to investigate even after it has enough evidence to convict, because thorough investigation protects both defendants and the courts against unnecessary prosecutions, and requiring the prosecution to file charges at the earliest possible date would preclude the prosecution from giving full consideration to the desirability of not prosecuting at all. Moreover, the Court has made it clear that it will not second guess the prosecutor's decision that further investigation is necessary.

Thus, *Lovasco* holds that the prosecutor's good faith determination that further investigation is necessary justifies delaying charges as long as the investigation continues. Although the Court has not ruled on what qualifies as insufficient reasons for delay, its pronouncements suggest that the second prong of a due process claim can be established by showing that the prosecution either 1) intentionally delayed charging to gain some tactical advantage or to harass the defendant, or 2) acted in reckless disregard of circumstances, known to the prosecution, suggesting the existence of an appreciable risk that delay would impair the ability to mount an effective defense. Whether a due process violation can be established with proof of prosecutorial negligence, that is, proof that the prosecution should have known that delay would impair the defense, is not clear.

C. POST CONVICTION DELAYS

The right to a speedy trial has also been applied to post-conviction proceedings. In *Pollard v. United States* (S.Ct.1957), the Court held the Sixth Amendment right to speedy trial is applicable to delays in sentencing. The rationale of this case is consistent with *Barker*, where the Court stressed that delay in punishment "may have a detrimental effect on rehabilitation" and thus be harmful to the particular defendant and to society at large. Although the specific right to a speedy parole violation hearing has not been addressed by the Supreme Court, in *Morrissey v. Brewer* (S.Ct. 1972), the Court found that parole revocations are subject to due process limits.

CHAPTER 7

THE LOCATION OF THE PROSECUTION

A. VENUE

Venue refers to the physical location or judicial district in which the prosecution will take place. Venue rules are set forth in statutes, court rules, and the constitutions of the United States and many states. The basic policy considerations underlying the specification of venue are ensuring fairness to the accused by not requiring that she submit to trial in a remote location, and promoting accurate fact-finding by conducting the trial at a place where witnesses and circumstances relevant to the determination of the issues are available.

The concept of venue must be distinguished from two other principles that may also affect the determination of where the case will be prosecuted. *Jurisdiction* refers to the power or authority of the court to decide the case. As it relates to the location of the prosecution, the most important limitation on the jurisdiction of courts is geographical. Courts can only enforce enactments of the legislature, and as a general rule legislatures may not criminalize conduct that occurs outside the geographic boundaries of the political entity. (Congress, however, has a limited extra-territorial jurisdiction to protect and punish United States citizens.) Therefore, courts generally lack jurisdiction to try cases occurring outside the geographic region in which the court is located.

The concept of venue must also be distinguished from the concept of *vicinage*. Vicinage refers to the geographical area from which jurors will be drawn for trial of the case. The concept of vicinage has historically required that the jurors be selected from the vicinity in which the crime was committed in order to insure that the jurors who decide the case are familiar with local values and circumstances. It is possible, albeit rare, for the jury to be drawn from a different district or geographic location from the place where the case is being tried.

1. FIXING VENUE—THE CRIME COMMITTED FORMULA

The most common approach to venue is to divide the jurisdiction into geographical regions and place venue in the region where the crime was committed. Article III, section 2 of the United States Constitution mandates this "crime committed" approach to setting venue for federal prosecutions by requiring jury trials for criminal cases to be held "in the State where said Crimes shall have been committed." This provision was added in direct response to the British colonial practice of forcing the accused to stand trial in England or some other location far from the place where the crime was committed.

During the debates over the ratification of the constitution, the Article III jury trial provision was criticized on the ground that it did not adequately assure trial by jury *of the vicinage.* The critics considered the state as a whole too large an area to serve as the district for the selection of jurors. This criticism was answered through the addition of the in the Sixth Amendment requirement of trial "by an impartial jury of the state *and district* wherein the crime shall have been committed." The delineation of judicial districts, which were obviously intended to be smaller than the whole state, was left to Congress. Although the Sixth Amendment guarantee of a jury drawn from the district where the crime was committed was intended as a jury selection provision rather than a rule specifying the place of trial, the Sixth Amendment implicitly serves as a venue provision as well, since standard practice is to conduct the trial in the same location from which the jury is selected.

Rule 18 of the Federal Rules of Criminal Procedure states that "the prosecution shall be had in a district in which the offense was committed." Because federal judicial districts often cover a large geographic area, and because a single judicial district may have courthouses in more than one location, it is often necessary to decide where within the district the trial shall be held. Rule 18 directs that the court shall determine the place of trial within the district based on 1) "the convenience of the defendant and the witnesses" and 2) "the prompt administration of justice."

State venue rules typically place venue in the county or parish in which the crime was committed. In addition to these general venue provisions, most or all jurisdictions have statutes that specify venue for some set of specific crimes. Typically these special venue provisions explicitly provide that certain crimes—conspiracy or bigamy, for example—can be tried in more than one judicial venue.

2. MULTI–VENUE AND CONTINUING CRIMES

The "crime-committed" formula for the determination of venue does not necessarily specify a single location for the trial of every crime. Some kinds of crimes can be "committed" in more than one place, and therefore tried in more than one district. When the law permits venue to be laid in more than one district, the prosecutor must choose where the case will be brought. If the accused is dissatisfied with the prosecutor's choice of venue, she must seek a change under the rules governing change of venue.

One category of crimes that can cross borders and occur within more than one judicial venue are is"continuing crimes." Kidnaping, for example, is regarded as beginning when the victim is seized and continuing until the victim is no longer under the kidnappers' control. For venue purposes, therefore, the crime of kidnaping is committed in any district where the victim is taken or held.

Crimes can also touch more than one place, and therefore offer a choice of trial venue, if the crime consists of two or more parts that can occur in different places. Crimes like murder that include both an action by the accused and a consequence of that action can typically be tried either in the location of the act or the location where the consequence occurs. Thus, a defendant who mailed a letter bomb from one judicial district that exploded and killed the victim in another district could ordinarily be tried for murder in either place. In some jurisdictions, significant preliminary acts of planning or preparation to commit the crime are considered acts of commission of the crime for purposes of setting venue. Thus, in the mail bomb example, venue may also be proper in the district where the bomb was constructed, even if different from the place where it was mailed or exploded.

The courts have developed two general approaches to the problem of determining where a crime was committed for purposes of applying the venue rules. One approach focuses on a formal, literal interpretation of the statutory language of the crime to determine precisely what conduct constitutes the crime. Under this approach courts analyze the statutory language to identify the "key verb" that specifies the basic conduct prohibited by the statute. The crime is deemed to have been committed in the place where this prohibited conduct occurred.

A leading example of the literalist approach is *Travis v. U.S.* (S.Ct.1961). The statute at issue in *Travis* penalized any person who knowingly makes any false statement "in a matter within the jurisdiction of any department or agency of the United States." The defendant, a union official, was accused of violating the act by filing a false non-Communist affidavit, which was executed and mailed in Colorado and received and filed in the offices of the National Labor Relations Board in Washington. The prosecution argued that the offense was begun in Colorado with the execution and mailing of the affidavit, and therefore venue in Colorado was proper. In holding that the offense could only be committed in Washington where the affidavit was filed, the Court found it significant that the Act under which the affidavit was filed did not impose a legal obligation to file such an affidavit.

If the charge had been based on a statute requiring the filing of a non-Communist affidavit, the Court said, the whole process of filing, including the use of the mails, might be construed to constitute the offense. The statute, however, did not impose such an obligation, but made the voluntary filing of the affidavit a prerequisite to invoking the procedures of the National Labor Relations Board. Under those circumstances, the Court reasoned, "the filing must be completed before there is a 'matter within the jurisdiction' of a [government agency]," and therefore the crime could only be committed at the place of filing, and not at the location from which the affidavit was mailed.

The other major approach to determining venue where the nature of the crime and the acts by which it was committed implicate more than one location is the "substantial contacts" test. This test assumes that there may be more than one appropriate venue for the trial of a criminal case, and requires consideration of several factors to determine what venue or venues are proper. The first factor is the site of the defendant's acts. The presence of the criminal acts by itself provides substantial contacts with the district to ensure that it is as suitable for fact finding as any other.

Consideration of the other factors may lead to the conclusion that there are other permissible venues as well. The second factor looks to the elements and nature of the crime. If, for example, the charge is based on a failure to take some required action, such as appearing for a scheduled court date, the crime is "committed" at the location where the defendant's presence was required. The third factor looks to the location of the effect of the criminal conduct. Under this factor, a federal crime requiring an effect on interstate commerce as an element of the crime could be tried where that effect occurred, even if the defendant's criminal acts were committed elsewhere. The fourth factor is the suitability for accurate fact finding of the district identified through the other three factors. This fourth factor is not an independent basis for establishing venue, but is to be considered in connection with the other factors

In two recent decisions applying the federal venue rules, the Supreme Court has implicitly rejected the rigid formalism of the key verb test, but has not endorsed the substantial contacts test used by some lower federal courts. In both cases the Court stressed that the determination of the location of the offense for purposes of fixing venue requires consideration of two factors: 1) the nature of the crime alleged; and 2) the act or acts that constitute the offense. The defendant in *U.S. v. Cabrales* (S.Ct.1998) was charged with money laundering. Although the currency that was alleged to have been laundered derived came from drug sales in Missouri, the bank transactions that were the basis of the money laundering charges occurred entirely in Florida. In holding that venue was not properly laid in Missouri, the Court relied on the fact that the money laundering statute interdicts only the financial transactions, not the anterior criminal conduct that yielded the funds allegedly laundered. The Court acknowledged that money laundering might arguably qualify as a "continuing offense" triable in more than one place if the launderer acquired the funds in one district and transported them into another, but observed that the facts of the case before it did not fit that pattern.

The second decision, *U.S. v. Rodriguez–Moreno* (S.Ct.1999), involved a prosecution under the federal statute that punishes one who, "during and in relation to any crime of violence . . ., uses or carries a firearm. . . ." The "crime of violence" that was the basis for the charge was a kidnaping that began in Texas and then continued in New York, New Jersey, and finally Maryland. The firearms charge was based on the defendant's having threatened the kidnaping victim with a gun in Maryland. The issue before the Court was whether on these facts venue could properly be laid in New Jersey on the basis that the underlying kidnaping was "committed" there, even though the firearm was used only in Maryland. Applying the verb test, which focuses on the verb used in the statute as specifying the acts that constitute the crime, the lower court had held that the statute penalizes the "use" of a firearm, which occurred only in Maryland, and therefore venue was not proper in New Jersey.

The Supreme Court rejected this approach, and construed the statute to include two distinct conduct elements—the use and carrying of a gun and the commission of a kidnaping. The Court then applied the rule that a crime consisting of distinct parts can be tried in any locality where any part of it took place, and held that venue for the charge was appropriate in any place where the kidnaping was committed.

The prosecution must prove facts establishing venue at trial. This means that the jury must find based on evidence presented at the trial that the facts establishing venue occurred within the geographical area in which the venue is set. A failure by the defendant to timely object to the absence of proof of venue results in a waiver or forfeiture of the objection.

B. CHANGE OF VENUE

All jurisdictions grant the defendant a right to seek, and the trial judge to grant, a change of venue from the venue initially chosen by the prosecution. The two basic grounds on which the accused can obtain a change of venue are 1) for the convenience of the parties and witnesses or in the interests of justice, and 2) to escape the influence of local prejudice, typically resulting from pre-trial publicity regarding the case.

1.   TRANSFER FOR CONVENIENCE OR IN THE INTERESTS OF JUSTICE

Rule 21(b) of the Federal Rules of Criminal Procedure provides that, upon motion by the defendant, the court may transfer the proceedings to another district "for the convenience of the parties and witnesses, and in the interest of justice." In ruling on transfer motions made under this Rule, the federal courts have generally relied on nine factors: 1) the defendant's residence or the location of a corporate defendant; 2) location of possible witnesses; 3) location of events likely to be in issue; 4) location of documents and records likely to be involved; 5) disruption of defendant's business unless the case is transferred; 6) expense to the parties; 7) location of counsel; 8) relative accessibility of the place of trial; and 9) docket condition of the district or division involved. *Platt v. Minnesota Mining & Mfg. Co.* (S.Ct.1964).

The courts have held that it is *not* appropriate in ruling on transfer requests to consider the possibility that a jury in a different location will be more favorably inclined toward either the defense or the prosecution. Thus, the court may not weigh sympathy for the defendant as a factor in favor of transfer or deny a defense request for transfer because the prosecution believes that a jury in a different location will be unsympathetic to its position.

2. TRANSFER BECAUSE OF PRE-TRIAL PUBLICITY

In a small percentage of sensational or high profile cases, media coverage of the crime or the prosecution may jeopardize the defendant's ability to obtain a fair trial by disposing potential jurors to believe the defendant guilty even before the trial begins. When members of the public are then called for jury service, these prospective jurors may not be able to put aside their feelings or convictions and judge the defendant's guilt or innocence solely on the basis of the trial evidence.

One method of seeking to protect against the adverse effects of pre-trial publicity is to change the trial venue to a different location where publicity and public passion are less intense. Other commonly used remedies for hostile pre-trial publicity are a postponement or continuance of the trial to permit public feeling to abate, and jury selection procedures that enable the defendant to identify and exclude jurors who have been prejudiced against the defendant through exposure to pre-trial publicity.

A change of venue is an effective solution to the problem of pre-trial publicity in some cases, but for obvious reasons accomplishes little when press coverage of the case is not confined to the locality where venue was placed initially. Moving the trial out of the locality where the crime was committed is also perceived as entailing disadvantages, since the community where the crime occurred has the greatest interest in a just resolution of the case, and may be better able fairly to judge the issues.

The standards governing change of venue are primarily a matter of local law. Federal Rule of Criminal Procedure 21(a) governs change of venue because of prejudice against the defendant in the federal system. The Rule provides that the court shall transfer the proceeding to another district if the court is satisfied that "there exists in the district where the prosecution is pending so great a prejudice against the defendant that the defendant cannot obtain a fair and impartial trial."

Although change of venue is regulated primarily by non-constitutional rules, under some circumstances the denial of the defendant's request for a change of venue will violate the defendant's constitutional rights. The leading Supreme Court precedent is *Rideau v. Louisiana* (S.Ct.1963). Two months before Rideau's capital murder trial, a local television station broadcast Rideau's 20 minute taped confession to police. In the confession Rideau personally admitted in detail the commission of the crimes for which he was later tried and convicted. The tape was broadcast three times over the space of three days. It was estimated that one of the broadcasts was seen by 53,000 people. The Louisiana parish in which the case was tried had a population of approximately 150,000. The defendant moved for a change of venue, but the request was denied.

The Supreme Court held that the trial court's denial of the defendant's change of venue motion deprived him of due process of law, stating that the repeated broadcast of the taped confession rendered the defendant's trial a "hollow formality." Although three of the trial jurors admitted they had seen the broadcast (but also claimed it would not prevent them from acting impartially), the Court indicated that its holding did not rely on that fact, and suggested that the denial of Rideau's change of venue motion would have violated due process even if none of the jurors had seen the tape. The Court did not explain this position, however, and it is at least questionable whether the Court would find a constitutional violation in a case where none of the jurors was actually exposed to the prejudicial publicity, no matter how inflammatory.

Rideau presents an unusual and extremely compelling case for change of venue. The Supreme Court characterized the defendant's taped confession as tantamount to a guilty plea that was broadcast to tens of thousands of people. Lower courts have generally applied the doctrine sparingly, finding a due process right to a change of venue only in cases in which the community has been saturated with pretrial publicity that is particularly inflammatory in nature.

CHAPTER 8

JOINDER AND SEVERANCE

A. JOINDER OF CHARGES

It is often more efficient to try two or more charges in a single proceeding than to conduct separate trials for each charge. The savings in time and resources from conducting a joint trial of several charges will be greater if the charges are similar or related to each other in some way, since multiple trials of similar or related charges would typically require a duplication of witnesses and evidence that could be avoided at a single trial.

In order to take advantage of these efficiencies, all jurisdictions authorize the consolidation or "joinder" of charges for trial under some circumstances. Thus, a defendant who is suspected of having committed an assault in the course of a robbery could ordinarily be charged with both crimes in a single indictment or information, and tried on both charges in a single proceeding.

Joinder of charges saves time and resources, but the adjudication of multiple charges at a single trial sometimes poses a risk of prejudice or unfairness to the accused. In recognition of this risk, all jurisdictions have procedures for separating or "severing"

183

offenses after they have been joined but before trial in order to protect the defendant's right to a fair trial.

1. GROUNDS FOR JOINDER OF CHARGES

Federal Rule of Criminal Procedure 8(a) governs joinder of offenses in the federal system. (Under Rule 13, offenses or defendants that can be *charged* together in a single charging instrument can also be *tried* together.) The Rule authorizes joinder in two circumstances. First, offenses may be joined under the Rule if they are "of the same or similar character." Thus, two or more burglary charges alleged to have been committed by the same defendant could be joined under this provision, even though the burglaries were not related to each other, and were committed at distinct times and places.

Second, the Rule authorizes joinder of two or more offenses in a single indictment or information if they are "based on the same act or transaction, or are or two or more acts or transactions connected together or connected with or constitute parts of a common scheme or plan." This language permits the joinder of offenses that are related in several different ways. Crimes can be joined if they occur either simultaneously or as part of a sequence of events occurring at the same time and place. In order to qualify for joinder under this part of the rule, it is not necessary that the joined charges be for the same or similar crimes, or that the crimes be connected as part of a common plan.

However, crimes can also be joined if they are parts of a common scheme or plan. The critical requirement for joinder under this provision is a logical or motivational connection between the joined offenses. For instance, a theft charge based on stealing a gun could be joined with a homicide charge in which the gun was used, even though the two crimes occurred at different times and places.

Ordinarily the decision regarding whether to charge more than one offense in a single charging instrument and, if so, what charges to join is made by the prosecutor. Rule 13, however, authorizes the trial judge to consolidate two or more indictments or informations for trial "if the offenses, and the defendants if there is more than one, could have been joined in a single indictment or information." In addition, a small minority of states *require* joinder of multiple charges against a single individual if the offenses are based on the same transaction or event.

2. CIRCUMSTANCES REQUIRING SEVERANCE OF JOINED OFFENSES

One circumstance in which offenses must be severed is when the initial joinder was not proper under the joinder rules. The improper joinder of offenses (or defendants) is referred to as "misjoinder." Even where the initial joinder was proper, however, a severance may be ordered on the ground that the joinder is prejudicial.

Federal Rule of Criminal Procedure 14 authorizes the trial court to order a severance of offenses that have been joined under Rule 8(a) "if it appears that a defendant or the government is prejudiced" by the joinder. The rule does not define prejudice, and trial judges have considerable discretion in determining whether prejudice has been demonstrated. The courts, however, have recognized three general types of prejudice to the defendant requiring a severance of charges. First, the defendant may be entitled to a severance if she interposes different defenses to the separate charges, and a joint trial would impair her ability to defend against one of the charges.

In *Cross v. U.S.* (D.C.Cir.1964), for example, the defendant sought a severance of two robbery charges on the ground that he wished to testify with respect to one of the charges but not the other. The motion was denied. At the trial the defendant testified convincingly that he was a victim rather than a perpetrator of one of the robberies, and the jury acquitted on that count. However, the defendant's answers on cross-examination with respect to the other charge were plainly unconvincing and evasive, and the jury returned a verdict of guilty. The appeals court held on these facts that the trial court's denial of the defendant's severance motion was an abuse of discretion, since the joinder had "embarrassed and confounded" him in making his defense.

It is clear from subsequent cases, however, that a defendant is not automatically entitled to a severance whenever she wishes to testify on some charges but not others. The defendant must demonstrate that she has important testimony to offer with respect to some charges and good reasons not to testify regarding others.

The second type of prejudice the courts have recognized under Rule 14 recognizes that a defendant is entitled to a severance if a trial on multiple charges would result in the admission of prejudicial character evidence that would not be admissible if the charges were tried separately. This is simply an application of the general principle from the law of evidence prohibiting the use of evidence of the defendant's bad character or criminal disposition to prove the defendant's conduct on a particular occasion. See Federal Rule of Evidence 404.

In the case of separately charged offenses, the character evidence rule prohibits the prosecutor from introducing evidence of the accused's uncharged crimes or bad acts if the only relevance of the evidence is as proof of the defendant's character. Evidence of uncharged crimes is admissible, however, if it is offered to prove something other than character, including motive, opportunity, intent, preparation, plan, knowledge, identity, or absence of mistake or accident. The courts have generally held that a defendant is entitled to a severance if the joined offenses would not have been admissible under the rules for uncharged misconduct evidence if the charges had been tried separately.

When offenses are joined on the ground that they are "based on the same act or transaction" or on the ground that they are "parts of a common scheme or plan," the evidence of one offense would ordinarily be admissible at a separate trial for the other. This is because the circumstances giving rise to the joinder coincide with recognized grounds for admission of uncharged misconduct evidence.

Problems arise, however, when offenses are joined because they "are of the same or similar character." The "similarity" of crimes is not itself a basis for admission under the rules governing evidence of uncharged misconduct, though several of the theories of admissibility do look to the similarity between the charged and uncharged offenses as an indication of the necessary logical relationship. But in all cases in which the defendant seeks a severance based on a claim that she is prejudiced by the admission of character evidence, the propriety of the joinder must be determined by reference to evidence doctrines relating to the admissibility of uncharged misconduct evidence.

The third general category of prejudice claims relies on an argument that joinder of offenses prejudices the defendant by causing the jury to "cumulate" evidence. What is meant by cumulation of the evidence is a failure by the jury to limit its consideration of the evidence to the charge on which it was admitted. These types of claims are rarely successful.

B. DOUBLE JEOPARDY AND JOINDER OF CHARGES

Under some circumstances a failure to join related offenses before trial can result in a double jeopardy bar to a subsequent prosecution of the offenses that were not included in the original charge. For that reason, a prosecutor should decide not to join related offenses only after considering two double jeopardy doctrines—the "same offense" doctrine and the "collateral estoppel" doctrine.

The Fifth Amendment Double Jeopardy Clause protects against multiple prosecutions for the "same offense." The Supreme Court has held that in some cases two crimes can be the "same offense" for double jeopardy purposes even if they do not share all of the same elements. As a result, when two crimes constitute the same offense for double jeopardy purposes, the prosecutor must either join the charges in a single prosecution, or forego prosecution of the crime that has was not joined. An exception may exist, however, where the "State is unable to proceed on the more serious charge at the outset because the additional facts necessary to sustain that charge have not occurred or have not been discovered despite the exercise of due diligence." *Brown v. Ohio* (S.Ct.1977). An example of this is *Diaz v. United States* (S.Ct.1912), where the defendant was convicted of assault and battery. This earlier conviction did not bar the charge and conviction for murder brought after the victim died.

The Supreme Court has interpreted the double jeopardy prohibition as including a collateral estoppel principle. Under this principle, an acquittal bars a subsequent prosecution if the verdict at the first trial resolved in the defendant's favor an ultimate issue of fact that is a necessary element of the prosecution's case in the second prosecution.

In the leading case on the subject, *Ashe v. Swenson* (S.Ct.1970), the Court held that the prosecution of the defendant for the robbery of victim X was precluded by the defendant's earlier acquittal on charges of having robbed victim Y, where it was conceded at trial that a robbery had been committed against both X and Y, and the only issue for the jury was whether the defendant was among those who carried it out. Since the jury's verdict acquitting the defendant of robbing Y necessarily meant that he did not participate in the robbery of X, the prosecution was estopped from charging him with that crime. Because the grounds for the jury's decision are rarely apparent from the jury's general verdict of acquittal, the scope of the collateral estoppel doctrine is quite narrow. A more detailed treatment of both the same offense rule and the collateral estoppel doctrine is contained in Chapter 9.

C. JOINDER OF DEFENDANTS

Just as it is often more efficient to combine charges it is often more efficient to join two or more defendants for trial in a single proceeding. Under some circumstances, it is permissible to join both charges and defendants. As with joinder of charges, joinder of defendants presents risks of unfair prejudice that can require a severance of defendants, even though the initial joinder was proper.

1. GROUNDS FOR JOINDER OF DEFENDANTS

Federal Rule of Criminal Procedure 8(b) provides that two or more defendants can be charged together "if they are alleged to have participated in the same act or transaction or in the same series of acts or transactions constituting an offense or offenses." It is not necessary under this Rule that all of the joined defendants be charged with all of the offenses. Thus, the fact that two defendants are alleged to have been part of the same conspiracy is a sufficient basis for charging them together for both the conspiracy and any substantive crimes committed by either of the defendants in furtherance of the conspiracy. This means that defendant A can be charged with crime X in the same proceeding in which defendant B is charged with crime Y, provided that crimes X and Y were both in furtherance of a conspiracy in which both A and B participated.

Although it is not required that all of the joined defendants be charged with the same crimes, it is necessary that all of the crimes charged in a multi-defendant proceeding be related as parts of the same act or transaction or series of acts or transactions. This means that the Rule 8(a) provision authorizing joinder of *similar* offenses cannot be combined with the Rule 8(b) provision governing joinder of defendants so as to try together two defendants charged with having acted together to commit two similar but unconnected crimes, e.g. two bank robberies committed against different banks at different times.

It is also permissible to join defendants who, though acting independently of each other, commit crimes that are so closely related in time and place that proof of one of the crimes will inevitably require reference to the other. LaFave, Israel, and King, Criminal Procedure § 17.2(a) (4th ed. 2004) offer as an illustration of this kind of joinder vehicular homicide charges against two drivers who both collided with the same victim.

2. CIRCUMSTANCES REQUIRING SEVERANCE OF DEFENDANTS

If the initial joinder of the defendants was improper a severance is of course required. Apart from the misjoinder situation, however, Rule 14 authorizes a severance of defendants whose initial joinder was permissible upon a showing that the defendant or the government would be prejudiced if the defendants were to be tried together. One situation that may engender prejudice to the defendant requiring a severance is when the prosecution intends to introduce as evidence the out of court confession of one of the defendants that also incriminates the other defendant.

The leading case on this subject is *Bruton v. U.S.* (S.Ct.1968). In that case, Bruton and Evans were tried together for the robbery of a post office. Evans had made an out of court confession, in which he stated that he and Bruton had committed the robbery together. The prosecution introduced the confession *against* Evans under the "party admission" exception to the hearsay rule. Because the evidence was inadmissible hearsay as to Bruton, the trial judge instructed the jury that they should not consider the confession as evidence against Bruton. The Supreme Court held that this limiting instruction was inadequate to protect Bruton's rights to confront his accusers under the Confrontation Clause, and reversed his conviction.

The specific holding of *Bruton* is that a limiting instruction at trial does not adequately protect the confrontation rights of the non-confessing defendant when the "powerfully incriminating" confession of a co-defendant is introduced at their joint trial. The *Bruton* rule does not apply when the out of court confession is admissible against the non-confessing defendant under an exception to the hearsay rule, such as the exception for statements by co-conspirators. (For a time the courts held that the Confrontation Clause is not violated if *both* defendants made confessions and their confessions "interlocked," but the Supreme Court has repudiated that view. *Cruz v. N.Y.* (S.Ct.1987)).

The rule is also inapplicable where the defendant who made the out-of-court confession testifies at trial and is subject to cross-examination by the co-defendant. The courts have reasoned that in those circumstances the confrontation rights of the non-confessing defendant have been satisfied through the opportunity for cross-examination. However, because the prosecution will not know in advance of the trial whether the confessing defendant will testify, this possibility cannot be relied upon to solve the potential Confrontation Clause problem.

However, the use of confessions have been further curtailed under *Crawford v. Washington* (S.Ct. 2004). The *Crawford* Court decided testimonial evidence includes, at a minimum, prior grand jury, preliminary hearing or trial testimony, or police interrogations. The confrontation clause is violated and the testimony is inadmissible hearsay when testimonial evidence is offered and the defense has not had an opportunity to cross-examine a currently unavailable witness.

The prosecutor, therefore, must decide how to proceed before trial to avoid a certain reversal of a conviction of the non-confessing defendant. There are four options. First, the prosecutor can try the defendants together, but not introduce the confession into evidence. This course will be chosen only when the prosecutor has a very strong case against the non-confessing defendant without the confession.

Second, the prosecutor can try the defendants together, but edit or "redact" the confession so that it implicates only the defendant who made the confession. This is usually the most appealing option for the prosecutor but, for reasons explained below, it is not always possible.

Third, the prosecutor can try the defendants in one trial but with two juries. The jury considering the case against the non-confessing defendant will then be removed from the courtroom when the evidence concerning the confession is introduced, and therefore this jury will never learn of the confession.

Finally, the prosecutor must often simply forego the benefits of a joint trial and try the defendants separately.

Redaction of the confession often presents the most appealing option for prosecutors faced with a joint trial in which one or more of the defendants have made confessions that also implicate other defendants. This course is permissible, however, only if the confession can be edited in a way that safeguards the rights of both the defendant who confessed and the defendant who did not. The confessor-defendant can object to a redaction that changes the meaning of the confession in a way that prejudices her.

The leading cases addressing the non-confessing defendant's interests when redacted confessions are introduced are *Richardson v. Marsh* (S.Ct.1987) and *Gray v. Maryland* (S.Ct.1998). In *Marsh* the confession introduced at a joint murder trial had been redacted to eliminate all reference to the co-defendant. As presented to the jury, the confession indicated that the confessing defendant, Williams, and a third person, who was not on trial, had discussed the murder in the front seat of a car as they drove to the victim's house. The confession gave no indication that the non-confessing defendant, Marsh, was in the car. Although Marsh subsequently testified that she was in the car when the conversation occurred, which supplied the link that made the confession inculpatory as to her, the court held that no *Bruton* violation occurs where the co-defendant's confession is not on its face incriminating, but inculpates the non-confessing defendant only when linked with evidence introduced later in the trial.

In *Gray v. Maryland*, the co-defendant's confession that named the defendant was redacted by substituting the word "deletion" for the defendant's name in the oral version read to the jury, and a blank space appeared where the defendant was named in the written version given to the jury. Thus, while the defendant's name was not mentioned, the confession presented to the jury in *Gray* referred to the *existence* of another participant in the crime. The Court reasoned that because the jury will often realize that a confession redacted in this way refers specifically to the defendant, it held that a redaction that simply eliminates the defendant's name does not adequately protect the non-confessing defendant's confrontation rights, and therefore cannot be introduced at a joint trial.

A showing of prejudice warranting a severance of defendants can also result from the joined defendants' planned presentation of "mutually antagonistic" defenses. Defenses are mutually antagonistic or "irreconcilable" when acceptance of one defendant's defense precludes the acquittal of the other defendant, as when each defendant seeks to shift the blame for the crime to the other defendant.

The Supreme Court has held, however, that the fact that defenses are antagonistic in this sense is not in itself enough to require a severance. In *Zafiro v. U.S.* (S.Ct.1993), two of the four defendants, Garcia and Soto, were confronted by police as they carried a box into an apartment. They dropped the box and ran into the apartment. The police followed and found the other two defendants, Zafiro and Martinez, inside. The dropped box was discovered to contain cocaine, and additional drugs and a large amount of cash were found in and around a suitcase inside the apartment. At trial, Garcia and Soto each claimed that the box they were carrying belonged to the other, and denied any knowledge of the contents of the box. Martinez claimed that he was a visitor to the apartment, and was unaware of the drugs. Zafiro, who occupied the apartment, claimed that the suitcase in which the drugs were found belonged to Martinez, and that she had no knowledge that it contained drugs.

In response to the defendants' appellate claim that the trial court abused its discretion in denying their severance motion, the Supreme Court first rejected the contention that a severance is required whenever joined defendants assert mutually antagonistic defenses. The Court then held that "a district court should grant a severance under Rule 14 only if there is a serious risk that a joint trial would compromise a specific trial right of one of the defendants, or prevent the jury from making a reliable judgment about guilt or innocence." Because the defendants did not articulate any specific instance of prejudice, but claimed instead that they were prejudiced by the antagonistic nature of the defenses, the trial court's denial of the severance motion was not an abuse of discretion.

A defendant is also entitled to a severance if she can demonstrate that a joint trial would prevent her from obtaining favorable testimony from her co-defendant. An accused cannot compel a co-defendant to testify at a joint trial, and there are sound reasons why the co-defendant would be reluctant to testify voluntarily. Nevertheless, severances on the ground that one defendant will exculpate the other if the cases are tried separately are rarely granted because it is usually impossible to demonstrate that granting the severance will in fact lead to one of the defendant's testifying for the other.

D. FAILURE TO PROVE FACTS WARRANTING JOINDER

It sometimes happens that the prosecution's evidence at trial fails to establish the factual allegations that are the basis for the joinder of the defendants in the indictment or information. The general rule is that a failure to prove facts warranting joinder does not preclude continuation of the joint trial. The leading case on the issue in the federal system is *Schaffer v. U.S.* (S.Ct.1960). That case involved four separate indictments against four groups of defendants. Count 1 charged the two Schaffers and three Stracuzzas with interstate transportation of stolen property from New York to Pennsylvania. Count 2 charged Marco and the Stracuzzas with transporting different stolen property from New York to West Virginia. Count 3 charged Karp and the Stracuzzas with transporting a third shipment of stolen property to Massachusetts. Although there was no allegation that the Schaffers, Marco and Karp in any way cooperated in committing these substantive crimes, a fourth count charged all of the defendants with conspiring to commit the substantive offenses charged in Counts 1 through 3.

On the basis of the conspiracy charge, the defendants were joined for trial under Rule 8(b) authorizing joinder of defendants alleged to have participated in the same act or transaction. At the trial, the court dismissed the conspiracy charge at the conclusion of the prosecution's case on the ground that the prosecution's evidence was legally insufficient to support that charge. The court denied the defendants' motion to dismiss the substantive charges, and the defendants were convicted. On appeal, the defendants argued that the continuation of their joint trial following the dismissal of the charge that was the sole basis for the joinder was improper.

The Court rejected the contention that a severance is required whenever the prosecution's evidence fails to prove the facts that are the basis for the initial joinder, holding instead that the decision whether to sever in such a case is controlled by the prejudice standard contained in Rule 14. The Court stressed that when the charge which originally justified the joinder turns out to lack the support of sufficient evidence, the judge should be particularly sensitive to the possibility of prejudice. Applying those principles to the case before it, the Court concluded that the defendants in *Schaffer* had not suffered prejudice warranting severance because the proof with respect to the various defendants had been "carefully compartmentalized," and because the trial judge in its charge had meticulously set out separately the evidence as to each defendant, and had admonished the jury not to consider the proof against one defendant against any other defendant.

The approach endorsed in *Schaffer* has the advantage of avoiding the possible delay and duplication of effort that results from a severance when the joinder does not cause actual prejudice to the accused. On the other hand, the *Schaffer* rule has been criticized on the ground that it might tempt an unprincipled prosecutor to add a baseless charge to the indictment for the sole purpose of joining defendants for trial.

CHAPTER 9

DOUBLE JEOPARDY

A. PURPOSES AND BASIC STRUCTURE OF DOUBLE JEOPARDY PROTECTION

The Double Jeopardy Clause of the Fifth Amendment provides that no person "shall ... be subject for the same offense to be twice put in jeopardy of life or limb." The core purpose of the clause is the same as the *res judicata* doctrine applied in civil cases. The clause protects the finality of criminal judgments by requiring that once a case has been resolved on the merits, through either a conviction or an acquittal, it may not thereafter be reopened for reconsideration.

The Double Jeopardy Clause also serves other purposes as well. The prohibition against retrying an acquitted defendant protects the innocent by preventing the prosecution from rehearsing and improving the presentation of its case through repeated attempts to convict until it eventually achieves success. The clause also protects the accused from having to endure the harassment and ordeal of multiple trials, which produces expense, anxiety and hardship even if the defendant is not convicted. Finally, the Double Jeopardy Clause recognizes the defendant's interest in having her case heard and decided by a particular jury once that jury has been selected and sworn.

The double jeopardy protection comprises a relatively intricate set of rules. Apart from the complexity of double jeopardy doctrine, discussion of the topic is also made difficult by the fact that there is no completely satisfactory and agreed upon method of categorizing the cases. It may be helpful, therefore, to begin with a simplified outline of the major issues that must be resolved in deciding whether the protection against double jeopardy has been violated.

1. The double jeopardy protection applies only in criminal cases. Questions sometimes arise as to whether the case is *criminal* or *civil* for double jeopardy purposes. A double jeopardy violation occurs only if the defendant is subjected to more than one criminal prosecution for the same offense.

2. The protection of the Double Jeopardy Clause applies only after the defendant has been placed in jeopardy. It is therefore necessary to determine whether jeopardy has *attached*. Until jeopardy has attached, the protections of the Double Jeopardy Clause do not come into play.

3. The clause protects the defendant against being placed in jeopardy "twice." Assuming jeopardy has attached and the defendant is asserting double jeopardy as a bar to further prosecution, it must be determined whether there has been a *termination* of the initial jeopardy in order to ascertain whether

the defendant has been placed in jeopardy once or twice. A termination can occur through an acquittal, a conviction, a dismissal, or a mistrial. However, not every acquittal, conviction, dismissal or mistrial presents a bar to further prosecution.

4. In addition to protecting the defendant from being prosecuted twice, the Double Jeopardy Clause also protects the defendant from being *punished* twice for the same offense. The protection against double punishment applies whether the multiple punishments are imposed in one proceeding or several proceedings.

5. The Double Jeopardy Clause protects the defendant from being twice placed in jeopardy for the "same offense." Thus, once it has been determined that the defendant has been placed in jeopardy, the initial jeopardy has been terminated, and the prosecutor is seeking to prosecute the defendant a second time, it still must be determined whether the second prosecution is for the *same offense* as the first. The double jeopardy protection against being punished twice, discussed in the previous paragraph, applies only when the multiple punishments are being imposed for the "same offense." However, the test for when two offenses are the same for purposes of the multiple punishment protection is different from the definition of when two offenses are the same for purposes of the protection against multiple prosecutions. A third context in which double jeopardy protections apply attaches yet another meaning to the same offense limitation. When the defendant's claim is that the second prosecution

is barred under the *collateral estoppel* protection of the Double Jeopardy Clause, the "same offense" limitation has a different meaning from when the defendant claims that she is being prosecuted twice for the same crime.

6. The double jeopardy prohibition does not apply to prosecutions by separate sovereigns. It must therefore be determined whether the two prosecutions for the same offense are being pursued by the same or different sovereigns. A prosecution of the defendant for the same offense by different sovereigns is not prohibited by the Double Jeopardy Clause.

The Supreme Court has held that the protections of the Double Jeopardy Clause are binding against the states. *Benton v. Maryland* (S.Ct.1969).

B. WHEN JEOPARDY ATTACHES

1. CRIMINAL CASES

The literal language of the Fifth Amendment, which guarantees against being "twice put in jeopardy of *life or limb*," suggests that its protections apply only to crimes that are punished by death or corporeal punishment. The Supreme Court has held, however, that the protections of the Double Jeopardy Clause apply to all crimes, regardless of either the type or severity of punishment. The Double Jeopardy Clause does not apply to civil cases.

The protections of the Double Jeopardy Clause do not become applicable until jeopardy has "attached." In a case that is being tried to a jury, jeopardy attaches at the time the jury is empaneled and sworn. This rule has been held to apply to both federal and state trials. *Crist v. Bretz* (S.Ct.1978). In bench trials tried without a jury, jeopardy attaches when the first witness is sworn. For cases that are resolved by the defendant's plea of guilty, jeopardy attaches when the judge accepts the defendant's plea and enters the conviction.

Prior to the time that jeopardy attaches, the accused has not been subjected to a first jeopardy, and therefore cannot claim that her prosecution constitutes a double jeopardy. If, for example, the charges against the defendant are dismissed during the selection of the jury before the jury has been sworn, the Double Jeopardy Clause does not prevent the prosecution from filing new charges for the same offense and bringing the defendant to trial on those charges so long as it does so within the prescribed statute of limitations period. After jeopardy has attached, the double jeopardy protection bars the prosecution from instituting a "second" prosecution for the same offense, only if there has been a termination of the first jeopardy. A termination of jeopardy can, but does not invariably, occur through an acquittal, conviction, dismissal or mistrial.

2.   CIVIL CASES

The Double Jeopardy Clause cannot be asserted as a bar to a civil suit. This means that the protections of the Double Jeopardy Clause have no application to litigation between private parties, and that the clause cannot be asserted to bar an action instituted by the government if the action is civil in nature. Thus, a defendant who has been tried and acquitted for murder can be sued for wrongful death based on the same conduct without violating double jeopardy, and a party who has been prosecuted for criminal anti-trust violations may also be sued civilly for the same violation.

The Supreme Court's most recent effort to defined the boundary between civil and criminal sanctions for double jeopardy purposes is *Hudson v. U.S.* (S.Ct.1997). In that case the Court repudiated the test that had been established less than a decade earlier in *U.S. v. Halper* (S.Ct.1989), and reaffirmed a narrower test developed in *U.S. v. Ward* (S.Ct.1980). The Court held in *Hudson* that the protections of the Double Jeopardy Clause do not apply to all sanctions that qualify as "punishment" or are in some sense "punitive," but apply only to sanctions that constitute *criminal* punishment. The determination of whether a punishment is criminal for double jeopardy purposes requires a two stage inquiry. The first question is a matter of statutory construction. The court must ask whether the legislature indicated an intention, either expressly or impliedly, that the penalty be criminal or civil. If the legislature intended to impose a criminal sanction, the protections of the Double Jeopardy Clause apply. If the legislature intended a civil penalty, however, the court must proceed to the second stage of the inquiry, and ask whether the statutory scheme is so punitive, either in purpose or effect, as to transform what was clearly intended as a civil remedy into a criminal penalty.

The *Hudson* Court listed seven factors to be used as guideposts in determining whether a sanction that is intended as civil is nonetheless criminal in purpose or effect. Those seven factors, first identified in the 1963 decision in *Kennedy v. Mendoza–Martinez* (S.Ct.1963) are: 1) whether the sanction involves an affirmative disability or restraint; 2) whether it has historically been regarded as a punishment; 3) whether it comes into play only on a finding of *scienter*; 4) whether its operation will promote the traditional aims of punishment—retribution and punishment; 5) whether the behavior to which it applies is already a crime; 6) whether an alternative purpose to which it may rationally be connected is assignable to it; and 7) whether it appears excessive in relation to the alternative purpose assigned. The *Hudson* Court stressed that these factors are to be considered in relation to the statute on its face, rather than as applied to the facts of a particular case. The Court also emphasized that "only the clearest proof" will suffice to override legislative intent and transform what has been denominated a civil remedy into a criminal penalty."

The Court in *Hudson Court found* the defendants were officers and board members of two banks who had arranged loans ostensibly for third parties that in fact benefitted the defendants. In an administrative proceeding, the Office of the Controller of the Currency (OCC) assessed civil penalties of $50,000 and $100,000, eventually settled for smaller sums, and barred the defendants from participation in the conduct of any federally insured depository institution.

The Court applied the two-step *Ward* test, and found that Congress intended the monetary penalties and debarment as civil in nature. The monetary penalty was labeled as "civil" in the statute, and the debarment was carried out under the authority of an administrative agency, which is *prima facie* evidence that Congress intended a civil sanction.

Furthermore, in the second stage of the inquiry, the Court found that only two of the seven *Kennedy* factors were present—the conduct which was the basis for the OCC sanctions is also a crime (factor 5), and the debarment and monetary penalties further the traditional criminal objectives of deterring others from emulating the defendants' conduct (factor 6).

In *Hudson* the Court expressly repudiated the test for whether a sanction is criminal for double jeopardy purposes that had been announced less than a decade earlier in *Halper*. In *Halper* the Court found that the defendant who had been convicted and sentenced to prison and a fine for making false claims against the government totaling less than $600 was subjected to a second "punishment" for double jeopardy purposes when the government also levied a $130,000 civil penalty. The Court held that the civil penalty constituted "punishment" triggering double jeopardy because it was not solely remedial, but could only be explained as also serving the punitive purposes of either retribution or deterrence.

In *Hudson* the Court described the approach taken in *Halper* as flawed in two respects. First, the *Halper* Court's conclusion that double jeopardy protections apply whenever the civil penalty is punitive, because grossly out of proportion to the penalty's remedial purpose, erroneously extended double jeopardy protection to any sanction that constitutes "punishment," rather than limiting double jeopardy protection to *criminal* punishment. Second, the Court in *Halper* applied its analysis to the penalty actually imposed, when it should have limited its inquiry to an examination of the statute on its face.

The Court's decision in *U.S. v. Usery* (S.Ct.1996), though decided after *Halper* and before *Hudson*, is generally consistent with the approach taken in *Hudson*. In *Usery* the Court held that, except perhaps in rare circumstances, civil forfeitures do not constitute punishment for purposes of the Double Jeopardy Clause. The forfeiture statutes at issue in the case authorized the government to forfeit not only the proceeds of crime (e.g., stolen goods) or contraband (e.g., illegal drugs), but also the "instrumentalities" used in the commission of crime. For example, the forfeiture statute relied on in one of the cases authorized the government to confiscate the defendant's house because it had been used to facilitate the unlawful processing and distribution of drugs.

There is some ambiguity over the basis for the Court's holding. At one point the Court declared in seemingly unequivocal terms that "*in rem* civil forfeiture is a remedial civil sanction ... [that] does not constitute punishment under the Double Jeopardy Clause." In another part of the opinion, however, the Court expressly denied that it was holding that *in rem* civil forfeiture is *per se* exempt from the scope of the Double Jeopardy Clause, and engaged in the same two part inquiry established in *Hudson*. With respect to whether Congress intended forfeiture to be civil or criminal, the Court looked to the procedural mechanisms established for enforcing the forfeitures, and concluded that Congress clearly intended a civil sanction. In addition to being *in rem* actions, which are presumed to be civil, the forfeiture statutes included other procedures indicative of their civil character. The statutes provided for seizure without notice to the owner through a summary administrative procedure under some circumstances, and placed the burden of proof on the party claiming the property. In addressing the second stage of the inquiry, the Court identified two non-punitive regulatory goals served by forfeiture: encouraging property owners to manage their property to prevent its use in illegal activity, and abating a nuisance. The fact that forfeiture also serves the purpose of deterrence is not enough to make it criminal. And while the statutes under consideration provide an "innocent owner" exception to the forfeiture requirement, the statutes did not contain a general scienter requirement. Finally, the fact that the forfeiture statutes were tied to criminal activity was insufficient to render the statutes criminal.

In *Kansas v. Hendricks* (S.Ct.1997), the Court determined that civil commitment of persons who, due to a "mental abnormality" or a "personality disorder," are likely to engage in "predatory acts of sexual violence" was not subject to double jeopardy. In reaching its decision, the Court reviewed the *Hudson* factors, finding that the legislature deemed the commitment civil and that deterrence was not intended. The commitment did not make a criminal conviction a prerequisite to confinement nor did it require a finding of scienter. Moreover, commitment was to a mental institution, not a prison. Nonetheless, the Court more recently cautioned, in

Kansas v. Crane (S.Ct.2002) that, in order to retain an involuntary commitment statute as a civil proceeding, "due process requires 'proof of serious difficulty in controlling behavior.'"

C. "SAME OFFENSE"

The Supreme Court has frequently described the Double Jeopardy Clause as consisting of three separate protections: It protects against 1) a second prosecution for the same offense after acquittal; 2) a second prosecution for the same offense after conviction; and 3) multiple punishments for the same offense. *N.C. v. Pearce* (S.Ct.1969). As this statement indicates, the protections of the Double Jeopardy Clause come into play only when the successive prosecutions (protections 1 and 2 above) or multiple punishments (protection 3 above) are for the "same offense."

There is a disagreement within the current Supreme Court over whether the standard for determining when two offenses are the same or different in the successive prosecution context should be the same as the standard for when two offenses are the same or different in the multiple punishment context. In its most recent case addressing the same offense limitation of the Double Jeopardy Clause, five Justices apparently agreed that the definition of "same offense" should be identical in the two contexts, although no opinion commanded a majority of the Court. *U.S. v. Dixon* (S.Ct.1993). A dissenting opinion in the case, by contrast, expressed the view that a different definition of same offense should be applied in the two contexts because the protection against successive prosecutions serves different purposes from the protection against multiple punishments. But while the Court majority in *Dixon* rejected the view that the term "same offense" could have two different meanings, the Court's decisions on the issue have developed clearly different tests for when two offenses are the same when the protection against successive prosecution is being asserted from the test that governs when the protection against multiple punishments is being asserted.

1.   SUCCESSIVE PROSECUTIONS

a.   The *Blockburger/Brown* Same Elements Test

The determination of whether two offenses are the same or different for double jeopardy purposes requires evaluation of both the legal definition of the crime as set forth in the statute and the factual conduct that is the basis for the charge.

The basic test for determining when two statutes define the "same offense" when a double jeopardy bar to successive prosecutions is being asserted was taken from *Blockburger v. U.S.* (S.Ct.1932), a case raising a multiple punishment claim. The test established in that case requires a comparison of the statutory elements of the two offenses. In order to constitute the "same offense," the two statutes need not have identical elements. Under the *Blockburger* test or the *Blockburger-Brown* test (derived from the later case of *Brown v. Ohio* (S.Ct.1977), two statutes are the same offense for double jeopardy purposes unless each statutory provision requires proof of a fact which the other does not. Thus, a crime which consists of elements A and B ("Crime 1") is the same offense as a crime that consists of elements A, B, and C ("Crime 2"), since Crime 1 does not contain any element that is not also an element of Crime 2. However, a crime that consists of elements B, C, and D (Crime 3) is different from both Crime 1 and 2, since those crimes each contain element A that is not required for Crime 3, but Crime 3 requires proof of D, which not an element of either Crime 1 or Crime 2.

In order to assert double jeopardy as a bar to prosecution, the defendant must show not only that she is being prosecuted under statutes that define the same offense, but also that those statutes are being applied to the same conduct. Even if two statutes define the same offense, double jeopardy is not violated if they are being used to prosecute the defendant for different incidents or different victims. For example, a defendant has not been twice placed in jeopardy for the same offense if she is prosecuted separately for two robberies committed against different victims, even if the two prosecutions are based on the same statutory provision. (As will be discussed below, prosecuting the two robberies separately may in some circumstances be barred by the collateral estoppel doctrine.)

Both aspects of the same offense rule, the requirements that the statutory provisions define the same crime and that those statutes are being applied to the same conduct, are illustrated by the facts of *Brown v. Ohio* (S.Ct.1977). The defendant in *Brown* stole a car in East Cleveland, Ohio and was arrested driving the car in Wickliffe, Ohio nine days later. He was charged in Wickliffe with the crime of "joyriding," pleaded guilty to the charge, and was sentenced to a month in jail and a $100 fine. Following his release from jail on that conviction, the defendant was charged in East Cleveland with car theft.

The Supreme Court held that the East Cleveland car theft prosecution was barred by the Double Jeopardy Clause as a second prosecution for the same offense. Under Ohio law, the crime of joyriding consisted of taking or operating a vehicle without the owner's consent. The crime of auto theft consisted of joyriding with the intent permanently to deprive the owner of possession of the car. Joyriding, therefore, is a lesser included offense of car theft, since as all of the elements of joyriding are also elements of auto theft. Because joyriding does not require proof of any element not also required for auto theft, the two crimes are the "same offense" for purposes of the Double Jeopardy Clause. Indeed, two statutes define the same offense for double jeopardy purposes whenever 1) the two statutes have identical elements or 2) one statute defines a crime that is a lesser included offense of the crime defined in the other statute.

Having concluded that the two statutes under which Brown was prosecuted defined the same offense, the Court next addressed the question whether the East Cleveland and Wickliffe charges applied to one criminal act or two for double jeopardy purposes. The determination of whether a course of conduct is one offense or more than one depends on how the crimes are defined. The Court concluded that Ohio law treated the theft and operation of a single car as a single offense. The case would be different, the Court stated, if the Ohio legislature had provided that joyriding is a separate offense for each day in which a motor vehicle is operated without the owner's consent, but it had not. Therefore, the second prosecution was barred by the Double Jeopardy Clause.

As the Court stated in *Brown,* the Double Jeopardy Clause operates to bar a second prosecution for the same offense regardless of the sequence in which the two prosecutions occur. Thus, taking the facts of Brown as an illustration, it is irrelevant for double jeopardy purposes whether the defendant had first been convicted of joyriding and then prosecuted for auto theft, or first convicted of auto theft and then prosecuted for joyriding. In either situation, the subsequent prosecution is barred.

b. Beyond *Blockburger & Brown*

In *Harris v. Oklahoma* (S.Ct.1977), a brief *per curiam* opinion decided the same term as *Brown,* the Court broadened the "same offense" doctrine originally in *Brown*. After the defendant was first convicted of felony murder, the State then attempted to bring an armed robbery prosecution, which also was the predicate for the felony murder charge. In holding that the armed robbery prosecution was barred by the Double Jeopardy Clause, the Court stated simply that "[w]hen, as here, conviction of a greater crime, murder, cannot be had without conviction of the lesser crime, robbery with firearms, the Double Jeopardy Clause bars prosecution for the lesser crime, after conviction of the greater one."

Harris represents a broadening of the test for "same offense" from *Brown*, since armed robbery is not a lesser included offense of felony murder in the same way joyriding is a lesser included offense of auto theft. The felony murder statute that was applied in *Harris*, however, did not necessarily require proof of an armed robbery, but armed robbery was one of several felonies that could form the basis for a felony murder charge. In determining the elements of felony murder for purposes of deciding whether felony murder constitutes the "same offense" as armed robbery, the Supreme Court looked beyond the definition of felony murder as set forth in the statute, and treated the crime of felony murder as consisting of those elements that the prosecution must prove *in the particular case before it*. In *Harris*, the felony murder charges were based on his having committed an armed robbery in which the murder victim was killed. Even though felony murder does not require proof of armed robbery in every case, felony murder did require proof of armed robbery as applied to the facts of Harris' case. Under these circumstances, the predicate felony is "a species of lesser included offense" of felony murder, and constitutes the same offense as felony murder for purposes of the Double Jeopardy Clause.

In *Grady v. Corbin* (S.Ct.1990) the Court extended the principle underlying *Harris* a step further. The defendant in *Corbin* was involved in a traffic accident in which an occupant of the other car was killed. After the defendant had already been convicted of the crimes of driving while intoxicated and crossing the median line, the state charged him with criminally negligent homicide and reckless assault based on the same incident. The prosecution filed a bill of particulars in which it identified three reckless or negligent acts that it would rely upon to establish the homicide and assault charges: 1) driving while intoxicated; 2) failing to keep right of the median; and 3) driving too fast for conditions. Even though the second prosecution was clearly not barred under the *Blockburger–Brown* same elements test, the Supreme Court held that the Double Jeopardy Clause prohibited the state from pursuing the assault and homicide prosecutions after having already prosecuted the defendant for driving while intoxicated and crossing the median. The Court held that a prosecution is barred by double jeopardy if, to establish an essential element of the offense charged in that prosecution, the government will prove *conduct* that constitutes an offense for which the defendant has already been prosecuted. Since the prosecution's bill of particulars indicated that it would prove the conduct that constituted the crimes of crossing the median and driving while intoxicated to prove elements of the crimes of reckless assault and negligent homicide, the assault and homicide charges were barred by double jeopardy.

In *U.S. v. Dixon* (S.Ct.1993), decided just three years after *Corbin*, the Court overruled *Corbin*. In *Dixon* the Court decided consolidated cases involving two defendants. Both defendants claimed that they were being prosecuted in violation of double jeopardy because they had already been convicted of criminal contempt for the same conduct that was the basis of the pending prosecutions. One of the defendants, Dixon, had been released on bail pending his trial with the condition that he not commit any crime while on bail. The pre-trial release statute provided that a violation of the conditions of release constituted contempt of court. While on bail awaiting trial, Dixon was arrested and indicted for a drug crime. After being convicted of contempt for violating the release order, he moved to dismiss the drug charges on double jeopardy grounds.

The other defendant, Foster, was under a civil protection order that prohibited him from molesting, assaulting, or in any manner threatening or physically abusing his estranged wife. Violation of the order subjected Foster to punishment for criminal contempt. After a hearing on alleged violations of the order, Foster was convicted of three counts of contempt for three incidents that constituted violations of the order, but acquitted of alleged violations on several other occasions. Foster was then charged in a five count indictment with one count of simple assault, three counts of threatening to injure, and one count of assault with intent to kill. The charges in the indictment were all based on conduct for which Foster had either been convicted or acquitted in the contempt proceedings. He claimed that the indictment constituted an impermissible second prosecution for the same offenses for which he had already been prosecuted.

The Supreme Court was in agreement (with one exception) that all of the charges against both defendants would be barred under the test of *Corbin*. To prove an essential element of the contempt charge against Dixon, the prosecution was required to prove conduct that constituted the drug possession charge, since Dixon's possession of drugs was the conduct that violated the pretrial release order. Similarly proof of the contempt charges against Foster required proof of conduct that constituted the assault and threaten to injure charges, since Foster violated the protective order by assaulting and threatening his wife.

A majority of the Court held that *Corbin* should be overruled, declaring it "wrong in principle [and]

unstable in application." The five Justice majority
that agreed to overrule *Corbin* were in agreement
that, absent *Corbin*, four of the five counts against
Foster—the counts alleging threatening to injure
and assault with intent to kill—were not barred by
the Double Jeopardy Clause, and the prosecution
for those crimes could proceed. Applying the same
elements test of *Blockburger–Brown*, the Court concluded that the threatening to injure charges and
the assault with intent to kill charge required proof
of an element not required to prove the contempt
charge, and the contempt of court charge required
proof of an element not required for any of substantive offenses. The indictment for assault with intent
to kill required proof of an intent to kill, whereas
proof of violation of the protective order did not
require proof of such an intent. Likewise, the three
charges for threatening to injure required proof of
specific types of threats—a threat to kidnap or to
injure another person or to damage property—
whereas the protective order provided only that
Foster not "in any manner" threaten his wife.
Contempt of court required proof of an element not
required for any of the substantive offenses, name-
ly, knowledge and a wilful violation of the protective order.

The five Justice majority in *Dixon* that agreed to
overrule *Corbin* could not agree on the correct interpretation of *Harris v. Oklahoma*, or on the disposition of the drug charge against Dixon or the
simple assault charges against Foster. In an opinion
joined by only one other member of the Court,

Justice Scalia concluded that, notwithstanding the overruling of *Corbin*, the drug charges against Dixon and the simple assault charges against Foster were barred under the rule of *Harris*. According to Justice Scalia, the pre-trial release order that prohibited Dixon from committing any crime while awaiting trial incorporated the entire governing criminal code in the same way the felony murder statute in *Harris* incorporated the felonies that could serve as the basis for a felony murder charge. As in *Harris*, the underlying drug offense was "a species of lesser included offense" of the contempt charge. In much the same way, the protective order that ordered Foster not to assault his wife incorporated the crime of simple assault as an element that must be proven in order to establish a violation of the order.

Three of the four Justices who agreed with Scalia to overrule *Corbin* disagreed with his interpretation of *Harris* and his conclusion that *Harris* barred the drug charge against Dixon or the simple assault charge against Foster. In an opinion by Chief Justice Rehnquist, these Justices would have limited *Harris* to the context in which it arose, and would have held that, without *Corbin*, double jeopardy did not prevent the drug or simple assault prosecutions. They argued that the *Blockburger–Brown* same elements test requires that the court focus on the statutory elements of contempt of court, rather than on the terms of the particular court orders involved. Under this approach, contempt of court is not the same offense as either drug possession or assault, since there is no overlap between the elements of contempt of court (which consist of a court order made known to the defendant and a wilful violation of that order) and either drug possession or assault. Rehnquist distinguished the felony murder situation presented in *Harris* on the ground that armed robbery is in fact a lesser included offense of felony murder in the sense that a person who commits armed robbery has necessarily satisfied one of the elements of felony murder. (Armed robbery is not, however, a lesser included offense in the more usual sense of that term, which requires that the commission of the greater offense, felony murder, necessarily involves the commission of the lesser offense, armed robbery.)

Although the five Justice majority in *Dixon* voting to overrule *Corbin* could not agree on the interpretation of *Harris* or the disposition of the drug and simple assault charges, three of the four Justices who opposed overruling *Corbin* agreed with Justice Scalia that the drug and simple assault charges were barred by the Double Jeopardy Clause. But while these Justices voted with Scalia to bar those charges, they did not agree with Justice Scalia's interpretation of the same elements test of *Blockburger–Brown*. In an opinion joined by one other member of the Court, Justice White criticized Scalia's interpretation of *Blockburger–Brown* as too narrow because it focused exclusively on the formal elements of the relevant crimes. This type of technical comparison of the elements of the two crimes might be adequate to serve the purpose of protecting against multiple punishments imposed in a single proceeding (See Part D below), but a broader test was necessary to protect against successive prosecutions, which was the interest at stake in the cases of Dixon and Foster. Under Justice White's broader interpretation of the same elements test, all of the charges against both defendants were barred, without resort to the same conduct test of *Corbin*.

The Supreme Court in *Dixon* appears to have returned to the "same offense" test that governed before the decision in *Corbin*. The Court repudiated the same conduct test of *Corbin*, and restored the *Blockburger–Brown* same elements test as the standard for when two offenses are the same in successive prosecution cases. Although no five justices could agree on what it means, the Court appears to have left the rule of *Harris* intact. Indeed, *Dixon* arguably represents a broadening of *Harris*. Under Justice Scalia's interpretation of *Harris*, which is the most generous version of the rule commanding majority approval, two crimes constitute the same offense whenever one is a lesser included offense of the other in the broad sense that, under the circumstances of the particular case, commission of one crime necessarily involves the commission of the other.

c. Incomplete and Ongoing Crimes

In *Brown v. Ohio* the Supreme Court stated that "an exception to the ban against successive prosecutions for the same offense may exist where the state is unable to proceed on the more serious charge at the outset because the additional facts necessary to sustain that charge have not occurred or have not been discovered despite due diligence." As an illustration of a factual scenario that would satisfy this exception, the Court cited a 1912 case involving an initial prosecution for assault and battery followed by a murder prosecution after the assault victim died. *Diaz v. U.S.* (S.Ct.1912).

In *Garrett v. U.S.* (S.Ct.1985), the Supreme Court applied this exception to a case involving an ongoing complex crime. The defendant was first charged and convicted of the crime of importing marijuana. Two months later he was charged with the crime of continuing criminal enterprise (CCE), which requires proof, among other things, that the defendant engaged in a continuing series of violations of specified felonies from which the defendant obtained substantial income or resources. One of the violations alleged against the defendant in the CCE indictment was the importation of marijuana, that was the basis for the prior conviction.

In rejecting the defendant's claim that the CCE charges constituted a second prosecution for the same offense in violation of the Double Jeopardy Clause, the Supreme Court first expressed doubt whether the marijuana crime was a lesser included offense of the CCE crime so as to bar separate prosecutions of the two charges under the test of *Blockburger–Brown*. But the Court went on to hold that, even if the marijuana charge was a lesser included offense of the CCE charge, separate prosecutions were nonetheless permissible because the continuing criminal enterprise had not been completed at the time that the defendant was indicted for the marijuana offense. The indictment charging the CCE offense alleged that the continuing criminal enterprise extended over a period of more than five years, and lasted for several months after the defendant had been indicted and convicted of the marijuana offense.

At the defendant's trial on the CCE charges, the government introduced evidence tending to show that the defendant was still engaged in the criminal enterprise after his conviction on the marijuana offense while free on bail awaiting sentencing. Given the fact that the continuing criminal enterprise that was actually charged against the defendant was still in progress after the point at which he was indicted for the underlying marijuana offense, the Supreme Court concluded that the two charges could be prosecuted separately, even though the government might have been able to charge the defendant with a different continuing criminal enterprise—one that ended on the date of the indictment on the marijuana charges—at the same time he was charged with the marijuana offense.

The general prohibition against re-prosecution for the same offense does *not* apply when the defendant is solely responsible for the separate prosecutions. The Supreme Court has applied this principle to permit a second prosecution in three different contexts. The defendant may be retried for the same offense if she obtains a reversal of her conviction on appeal. *See Montana v. Hall* (S.Ct.1987). The defendant may also be subjected to separate prosecutions if she is responsible for separate trials because she successfully objected to the prosecution's motion to join the charges for trial. *Jeffers v. U.S.* (S.Ct.1977).

Finally, the Court held in *Ohio v. Johnson* (S.Ct. 1984) that a defendant who pleads guilty to a lesser included offense over the objection of the prosecution cannot assert double jeopardy as a bar to a prosecution for the greater offense. In *Johnson* the defendant had been charged in a single indictment with murder and manslaughter. The Supreme Court held that the prosecution was not precluded from trying him for murder after the trial court had accepted his guilty plea to manslaughter, because the defendant had offered only to resolve part of the charges against him, and the state had objected to the disposition of any of the counts without a trial.

2. MULTIPLE PUNISHMENTS IN THE SAME PROCEEDING

The Double Jeopardy Clause prohibits successive or separate prosecutions for two crimes that are the "same offense." It does not prohibit prosecuting two crimes that qualify as the same offense if the charges are joined in a single prosecution. Indeed, one consequence of the Fifth Amendment double jeopardy protection is to require prosecutors to join offenses that are the same for double jeopardy purposes in a single prosecution or forego prosecuting one of the crimes.

Although the Double Jeopardy Clause does not prohibit prosecution of two crimes that are the same offense in a single proceeding, it does prohibit the imposition of multiple or cumulative punishments for the same offense, even if the two crimes are prosecuted together. However, the definition of when two crimes are the same offense for purposes of the protection against multiple punishments differs from the definition that applies in the successive prosecution context.

The question whether cumulative punishments are permitted under the Double Jeopardy Clause arises most often when the defendant is convicted in a single proceeding of two crimes based on the same conduct. This happens very frequently as, for example, when the defendant is charged with both theft and robbery (which is simply theft accomplished through fear or force) for having stolen the victim's purse at knife-point. The issue also sometimes arises when successive prosecutions for the same offense are permitted as, for example, when the defendant who has already been convicted of attempted murder is subsequently convicted of murder after the victim dies. If cumulative punishments are allowed, the defendant may be punished for both convictions. Otherwise, the prosecutor is limited to seeking the stiffest penalty available for either of the two offenses.

The exclusive test for whether the Double Jeopardy Clause prohibits cumulative punishments for two offenses is whether the legislature that created the offenses intended that the two crimes be punished cumulatively. In the multiple punishment context, the Double Jeopardy Clause does no more than prevent the sentencing court from prescribing greater punishment than the legislature intended. If the legislature intended cumulative punishments, then the defendant may receive separate punishments for the two convictions, even if they are for the same offense under the *Blockburger–Brown* test. If the legislature intended that the two crimes not be punished cumulatively, then the imposition of separate punishments violates the Fifth Amendment Double Jeopardy Clause, even if the separate sentences run "concurrently" rather than consecutively.

The *Blockburger–Brown* test requiring a comparison of the statutory elements of the two crimes is used in the multiple punishments context only as an indication of legislative intent. In the absence of other evidence of the legislature's intent, it is assumed that two statutes defining the same offense under *Blockburger–Brown* are not intended to be subject to cumulative punishments. Where, however, the legislature has indicated its intention that each of two statutes creates a distinct crime subject to separate punishment, the two crimes may be punished cumulatively, even if they have identical elements or one is a lesser included offense of the other.

The test that governs the determination whether cumulative punishments are permitted is illustrated by the facts of *Missouri v. Hunter* (S.Ct.1983), the case in which the Court first definitively adopted the test. In *Hunter* the defendant was convicted in a single proceeding of both armed robbery and armed criminal action. As the two crimes were defined under Missouri law, armed criminal action was a lesser included offense of armed robbery, and therefore the two statutes defined the "same offense" under the *Blockburger* test. In enacting the armed criminal action statute, however, the Missouri legislature had expressly provided that the punishment imposed for that crime "shall be in addition to any punishment provided by law for the crime committed ... with ... a dangerous or deadly weapon." In rejecting the defendant's Double Jeopardy challenge to cumulative punishments for the two convictions, the Court stated that "[w]here ... the legislature specifically authorizes cumulative punishment under two statutes, regardless of whether those two statutes prescribe the 'same' conduct under *Block-burger*, a court's task of statutory construction is at an end and the prosecutor may seek and trial court or jury may impose cumulative punishment under such statutes in a single trial."

The Double Jeopardy Clause also limits the punishment that can be meted out on a single conviction. The test for when the punishment for a single conviction violates double jeopardy is the same as the test for when the punishment imposed for multiple convictions violates double jeopardy: The punishment meted out by the sentencing court on a single conviction violates the Fifth Amendment double jeopardy protection if it exceeds what is authorized or intended by the legislature. Thus, if the legislature establishes a prison term of one year as the maximum penalty for a given offense, a defendant who has been sentenced to two years imprisonment has a valid challenge to that sentence under the Double Jeopardy Clause.

D. COLLATERAL ESTOPPEL

In general, the Double Jeopardy Clause prohibits a second prosecution following a conviction or an acquittal only if the second prosecution is for the "same offense" as the first prosecution. In one situation, however, an acquittal serves as a bar to a subsequent prosecution, even though the second prosecution is not for the same offense as the first prosecution that resulted in an acquittal. The Supreme Court has held that the Double Jeopardy Clause includes a collateral estoppel rule similar to the collateral estoppel doctrine applied in civil cases. The criminal collateral estoppel rule, however, is significantly narrower than the civil counterpart.

The Supreme Court first recognized a collateral estoppel component to the Double Jeopardy Clause in *Ashe v. Swenson* (S.Ct.1970). The defendant in the case, Ashe, was one of four men suspected of having participated in the robbery of six poker players. Each of the four suspects was charged with seven separate offenses—six counts of robbery for robbery of the six poker players and a seventh charge based on the theft of a car belonging to one of the victims. Ashe was first brought to trial on the charge that he robbed Knight, one of the poker players. The prosecution's evidence that a robbery had occurred and that Knight was a victim was described by the Supreme Court as unassailable.

The prosecution's evidence identifying Ashe as one of the robbers was, however, weak. The defense did not contest the evidence that Knight had been robbed, but focused its efforts on undermining the evidence of Ashe's involvement. The jury was instructed that if they found that Ashe was one of the robbers, he was guilty of the charge, even if he had not personally taken the money from Knight. The jury found Ashe not guilty.

Six weeks later Ashe was tried for the robbery of Roberts, another of the six poker players. The same witnesses who had been hesitant in their testimony identifying Ashe as one of the robbers at the first trial testified with greater assurance at the second trial, and Ashe was convicted.

The Supreme Court held that the prosecution of Ashe for the robbery of Roberts violated the collateral estoppel doctrine of the Double Jeopardy Clause. Because the two prosecutions involved different victims, they were not for the "same offense," and neither a second prosecution nor multiple punishments would have been barred but for collateral estoppel. As described by the Court, collateral estoppel "means simply that when an issue of ultimate fact has once been determined by a valid and final judgment, that issue cannot again be litigated between the same parties in any future lawsuit." Thus, when an ultimate issue has been resolved in the accused's favor in one trial, the state is precluded from bringing further charges against the accused that require proof of that issue. In *Ashe* the jury in the first trial made a final and valid determination that Ashe was not a participant in the robbery of the six poker players. The state, therefore, was precluded from attempting to prove that fact in a subsequent prosecution by charging him with the robbery of Roberts.

Although important in principle, the collateral estoppel doctrine has a relatively narrow application in practice. This is because in the vast majority of criminal cases, the jury announces its decision through a "general verdict" of either guilty or not guilty, and therefore does not disclose the reasons for its decision. Since most cases require the jury to decide several ultimate issues of fact, in most cases it is impossible to determine from a general "not guilty" verdict what issues have been finally and validly determined.

For example, if the prosecution's case requires proof of A, B, and C, and the defendant asserts complete defenses Y and Z, a not guilty verdict conclusively establishes that the jury resolved one or more of A, B, C, Y, and Z favorably to the accused, but does not reveal which among those five issues was the basis for the decision. Recognizing the inherent difficulty of applying a doctrine of issue preclusion to general verdicts, the Supreme Court in *Ashe* instructed courts applying collateral estoppel "to examine the record of the prior proceeding, taking into account the pleadings, evidence, charge, and other relevant matter" to determine what issues were finally and validly determined by the jury. In most cases, the results of such an inquiry will be inconclusive. The collateral estoppel doctrine comes into play only if the examination of the record leads to the conclusion that "a rational jury could [not] have grounded its verdict upon an issue other than that which the defendant seeks to foreclose from consideration."

The facts of *Ashe* illustrate how the inquiry prescribed by the Court can in some circumstances identify the basis for the jury's decision with sufficient precision to apply collateral estoppel. The prosecution's robbery case against Ashe required proof of several ultimate issues of fact. As the case was actually tried, however, the single real issue for the jury to decide was whether Ashe was one of the robbers. Because of the posture of the case as presented to the jury, it was possible to deduce from the jury's not guilty verdict that the jury concluded that Ashe was not among those involved in the robbery. Because the jury in the prosecution for the Knight robbery had finally and validly concluded that Ashe was not a participant in the robbery of the six poker players, the state was precluded from attempting to prove in a second trial that he was involved in the robbery.

In analyzing any case to determine whether the jury resolved a particular factual issue in the defendant's favor, the jury is presumed to have followed the judge's instructions on the law. That principle is illustrated by the case of *Turner v. Arkansas* (S.Ct.

1972). The defendant, Turner, was first tried and acquitted of felony murder that was alleged to have been committed in the course of a robbery. The state then charged Turner with robbery based on the same events that were the subject of the felony murder charge. The prosecution argued that the robbery charges were not barred by collateral estoppel, because the jury at the felony murder trial might have acquitted the defendant on the ground that, while the defendant was involved in the robbery, the murder was committed by the defendant's accomplice, and not the defendant, in the commission of the robbery. The Supreme Court rejected this argument on the ground that, under the trial court's instructions at the felony murder trial, the jury was obligated to find Turner guilty of murder if he was present at the robbery, regardless of who actually committed the homicide.

In *Schiro v. Farley* (S.Ct.1994) the Court established that "the failure to return a verdict does not have collateral estoppel effect ... unless the record establishes that the issue was actually and necessarily decided in the defendant's favor." In *Schiro* the trial court provided the jury with ten guilty verdict forms. Each form provided a different way to find the defendant guilty of murder. The jury completed and returned the form for felony murder (rape) and left the remaining nine forms blank. The defendant sought to preclude introduction of evidence of an intentional killing to support a request for a death sentence because the "intentional killing form" was left blank. This blank form, according to the defendant, demonstrated that the jury implicitly found against that charge. The *Schiro* Court ruled that there was no collateral estoppel because there were no explicit findings, only blank forms.

The doctrine of collateral estoppel in criminal cases operates in one direction only. The accused may assert collateral estoppel as a bar to the prosecution, but the government cannot use collateral estoppel against the accused. *See Simpson v. Florida* (S.Ct.1971). Thus, in *Ashe*, the prosecution could not have used a jury verdict finding Ashe guilty of robbing Knight to establish conclusively that he was involved in the robbery of Roberts, and Ashe would have been free to contest the prosecution's proof that he was involved in the robbery at the second trial even if he had been convicted at the first trial. (Whether a prior conviction may be used as *evidence* to prove facts determined in that conviction, as opposed to being given preclusive effect under the doctrine of collateral estoppel, depends on whether it is relevant and admissible under the rules of evidence.)

Collateral estoppel does not apply when the two prosecutions involve different defendants. Thus, the acquittal of A for a crime alleged to have been committed with B does not prevent the prosecution of B for that crime, even if the prosecution of the two defendants presented the very same issue.

One effect of the collateral estoppel doctrine is to require the prosecution either to join charges that raise the same issues or to risk the possibility that some of the charges may be precluded if facts that are crucial to later prosecutions are resolved against the government in earlier trials. The doctrine does not apply when the defendant is responsible for separate trials, such as when a severance of parties or charges is granted at the request of the accused.

Collateral estoppel applies only to factual issues that have been finally resolved through adjudication; it does not apply to facts that are resolved through the defendant's plea of guilty. The doctrine does apply, however, to an acquittal that is "implied" by a jury verdict convicting the defendant of a lesser included offense. (See Section G3 below discussing implied acquittals.)

Finally, the doctrine does not apply if the government's standard of proof on the issue that the defendant seeks to preclude was higher at the first trial than at the second trial. As a matter of simple logic, the fact that the prosecution failed to prove fact A beyond a reasonable doubt does not mean that it failed to prove fact A by a preponderance of the evidence. Thus, even if the jury found fact A in the defendant's favor at the first trial where the prosecution's standard was proof beyond a reasonable doubt, the prosecution is not precluded from re-litigating fact A at a subsequent trial where its standard of proof is lower. Based on this principle, the Supreme Court has held that an acquittal on criminal charges does not bar the government from instituting a civil forfeiture action at which the government must prove the commission of the crime by a preponderance of the evidence. *U.S. v.*

One Assortment of 89 Firearms (S.Ct.1984). For the same reason, collateral estoppel does not bar the admission of evidence that the defendant committed a crime for which she had previously been acquitted, if evidence of the previous crime is relevant to some issue at the later trial. For instance, in *Dowling v. U.S.* (S.Ct.1990), the defendant was first tried and acquitted for a burglary that was committed by a person wearing a mask. At a second trial of the defendant for a bank robbery that was also committed by a masked man, the government was permitted to introduce evidence that the defendant committed the burglary, notwithstanding the acquittal, to prove that both crimes were committed by the same person, and that person was the defendant. The reason collateral estoppel did not bar evidence that the defendant committed the burglary at his trial for bank robbery is because evidence of the burglary was relevant and admissible at the bank robbery trial based on proof by a preponderance of the evidence, whereas conviction at the first trial required proof beyond a reasonable doubt.

E. RE-PROSECUTION FOLLOWING ACQUITTAL OR DISMISSAL

1. ACQUITTAL BY JURY OR JUDGE

The prohibition against re-prosecution of the accused for the same offense following an acquittal is probably closest to the core values of the Double Jeopardy Clause. Accordingly, the Double Jeopardy Clause attaches greater finality to an acquittal than to a conviction or other disposition.

The Double Jeopardy Clause presents an absolute bar to re-prosecution of the accused by the same sovereign for the same offense following an acquittal. The prosecution cannot file new charges against the accused for the same offense, nor can the prosecution appeal the judgment of acquittal for any reason. This rule applies whether the acquittal results from a not guilty verdict by a jury, a not guilty verdict by a judge sitting in a bench trial, an acquittal that is "implicit" in a conviction by either judge or jury for a lesser included offense (See Section G3, below), or a ruling by the judge based on an evaluation of the evidence that there is insufficient evidence to support a conviction (See Section G2, below).

As will be discussed below, the prosecution may appeal an acquittal, though not re-try the defendant, if the acquittal was entered after the defendant has already been found guilty. This may occur when, for example, the jury returns a verdict of guilty, that is set aside by the trial judge on the ground that the trial evidence is legally insufficient to establish the defendant's guilt beyond a reasonable doubt.

The Supreme Court has held that an acquittal must be given double jeopardy effect even if the trial judge's action granting the acquittal was a clear violation of proper procedures, as when the trial judge directed a verdict of acquittal before the prosecution had completed its case. *Fong Foo v. U.S.* (S.Ct.1962). Therefore, an acquittal stands as an absolute bar to further prosecution even if the acquittal is demonstrably erroneous, corrupt, or legally unauthorized. For example, an accused who has been acquitted cannot be re-tried for that offense even if incontrovertible evidence shows after the trial that the acquittal was mistaken on the facts or the law and that the defendant is actually guilty. Nor can a defendant be subjected to a second trial for the same offense if the not guilty verdict was motivated by patently improper considerations. For example, a defendant could not be re-tried even if she obtained the acquittal by paying bribes to the entire jury panel (though she could presumably be tried for crimes related to the bribery).

The Supreme Court has said that the rule that the government may not secure a new trial through appeal of an acquittal, no matter how mistaken the decision or serious the trial error, is one of the "elemental principles" of American criminal law. However, the justification for the rule, and for attaching a different significance to an acquittal than a conviction, is uncertain. It may be that an acquittal is given complete finality in order to avoid the risk that the government, possessed of vastly superior resources, will eventually wear down the defendant and convict the innocent. But this rationale does not justify the scope of the protection given to acquittals, which immunizes acquittals that are egregiously erroneous, and rests on the questionable assumption that a defendant who has been convicted through flawed procedures is more likely guilty than a defendant who has been wrongly acquitted.

It has also been suggested that the prohibition against re-trial following an acquittal is necessary to protect the jury's "nullification" power—the power to acquit defendants who are guilty under the law and the facts when justice requires. While this argument is persuasive as applied to jury verdicts, it does not explain why the same finality attaches to acquittals entered by judges, who are not commonly regarded as possessing the power to nullify.

A third argument explains the different treatment accorded convictions and acquittals as reflecting a societal judgment that the accused should be permitted to disturb the finality of a final judgment (by appealing a conviction) but the government should not possess that right.

2. DISTINGUISHING ACQUITTALS AND DISMISSALS

An acquittal creates an absolute bar to the re-trial of the accused for the same offense. It is not the case, however, that every termination of the trial in the defendant's favor constitutes an "acquittal." First, a judge who declares a "mistrial" probably anticipates that the defendant can be re-tried on the same charges. As will be discussed below, that intention is not controlling, and in some circumstances double jeopardy bars re-trial following a mistrial. A judge who orders a "dismissal," by contrast, presumably intends that the proceedings will terminate then and there in favor of the defendant. Not every dismissal, however, constitutes an acquittal that bars re-prosecution. In order to apply the double jeopardy rules, therefore, it is necessary to define what constitutes an acquittal for double jeopardy purposes.

The Supreme Court defined when a dismissal qualifies as an acquittal for double jeopardy purposes in *U.S. v. Scott* (S.Ct.1978). The trial judge in that case had granted the defendant's motion to dismiss the charges on the grounds of prejudicial pre-indictment delay. The dismissal was ordered after the jury had been sworn (and therefore jeopardy had attached) but before the jury had returned a verdict. When the prosecution sought to appeal the trial judge's dismissal order, the defendant argued that double jeopardy barred further prosecution following the dismissal, and the government's appeal therefore should be rejected.

Under the standard for what constitutes an acquittal that had been established just three years
earlier in *U.S. v. Jenkins* (S.Ct.1975) re-prosecution
following the dismissal in *Scott* was clearly not
permitted. The approach that had been endorsed by
the Court in *Jenkins* treated a dismissal as a termination of jeopardy (and therefore a bar to a re-
prosecution) whenever a successful appeal of the
dismissal by the prosecution would result in further
proceedings (typically a second trial) to determine
guilt or innocence. Thus, based on existing law, the
dismissal before verdict in *Scott* was a bar to re-
prosecution, since a successful appeal of the dismissal order by the prosecution would have necessitated a new trial.

In its opinion in *Scott*, the Supreme Court repudiated this approach and overruled *Jenkins*. The
Court stated that the *Jenkins* approach of focusing
on the consequences of the dismissal for the defendant overlooked the fact that, when the defendant
requests or consents to the dismissal, the defendant
rather than the government has created the necessity for a second trial. When the defendant is responsible for the second prosecution, her double
jeopardy interests in avoiding the anxiety and expense of multiple trials and in having her guilt
decided by the first jury empaneled to try the case
must give way to the public's interest in "one
complete opportunity to convict those who have
violated its laws." The Court held that a dismissal
ordered at the request of the defendant should
treated as a termination of jeopardy only if it repre-

sents a resolution of the case on the merits. Quoting from an earlier decision, the Court held that a dismissal constitutes an acquittal for double jeopardy purposes only when "the ruling of the judge, whatever its label, actually represents a resolution [in the defendant's favor], correct or not, of some or all of the factual elements of the offense charged." The Court emphasized that the trial court's characterization of its action is not determinative of the double jeopardy issue. The Court also stated that "the fact that the acquittal may result from erroneous evidentiary rulings or flawed interpretations of governing legal principles affects the accuracy of that determination, but does not alter its essential character [as an acquittal]."

The Court explained the distinction underlying its definition of an acquittal as based on whether the dismissal, however denominated by the court, represents a factual determination that the defendant is not culpable. Applying this standard to the facts of the case before it, the Court concluded that the dismissal in *Scott* did not constitute an acquittal for double jeopardy purposes, since the dismissal had been granted on a basis which did not depend on guilt or innocence. By contrast, according to the Court, a determination that the prosecution has not submitted sufficient evidence to rebut a defense of insanity constitutes a determination that the defendant lacks criminal culpability, and therefore qualifies as an acquittal.

In a subsequent decision, the Court made clear that the dismissal decision need not involve an evaluation of the credibility of the evidence in order to qualify as an acquittal. In *Smalis v. Pennsylvania* (S.Ct.1986), the Court held that a trial court ruling dismissing the charges at the close of the prosecution's case on the ground that the evidence presented was *legally* insufficient to support a conviction was an acquittal, even though the state characterized the ruling as a purely legal question, rather than a factual determination.

The Court's opinion in *Scott* creates some uncertainty regarding the double jeopardy consequences of a dismissal that is ordered without the defendant's consent. In holding that a dismissal granted at the defendant's request does not bar a re-trial, the Court placed heavy emphasis on the fact that the defendant rather than the prosecution has created the need for the second trial. When a dismissal is ordered on the judge's own motion, however, it cannot be said that the defendant is responsible for the second trial, and therefore the rationale for requiring the defendant to submit to another trial is arguably not present. In a more recent case, *Sattazahn v. Pennsylvania* (S.Ct.2003), the defendant gained a reversal of a murder conviction after the trial court imposed a sentence of life imprisonment. On retrial, the prosecution sought the death penalty. The reason that the original life sentence had been imposed was because the jury, in the penalty phase, was hung and, under Pennsylvania law, the trial judge was, in such circumstance, required to impose the life sentence. The Supreme Court held that the judge's decision in imposing the life sentence did not bar reprosecution seeking the death penalty, reaffirming the principles of *Scott*.

3.   ACQUITTAL AFTER CONVICTION

The double jeopardy prohibition against *re-trial* following an acquittal is absolute. The prosecution may, however, *appeal* an acquittal (but not subject the defendant to a second trial) in one situation— when the acquittal is entered after the defendant has already been convicted. A post-conviction acquittal occurs when either the trial court or an appeals court enters an acquittal after the fact finder, which may be either judge or jury, finds the defendant guilty.

Post-conviction acquittals are treated differently from acquittals that are not preceded by a finding of guilt because the Double Jeopardy Clause protects against multiple trials. If a post-conviction acquittal is appealed and found to be erroneous, the error can be corrected without subjecting the defendant to a second trial by simply re-instating the conviction. That option is obviously not available if there is no conviction to be re-instated. In the absence of a conviction, a reversal of the acquittal would necessitate a second prosecution, and the appeal itself is therefore forbidden.

As will be discussed below, the Double Jeopardy Clause does not prohibit a re-trial following reversal of a conviction if the reversal is based on any ground other than the insufficiency of the evidence.

F. RE-PROSECUTION FOLLOWING A MISTRIAL

A "mistrial" is a termination of the trial by the judge before the judge or jury has reached a verdict. A mistrial may be declared at the request of either the prosecution or the defendant, or on the court's own motion.

In characterizing her action as a mistrial, rather than a dismissal, the judge ordinarily intends that her action will not prevent the prosecution from re-trying the defendant on the same indictment or information. It is not the case, however, that a re-trial is invariably permitted following the declaration of a mistrial. Whether the prosecution may re-try the defendant after a mistrial depends, in the first instance, on whether the defendant acquiesced in the decision to declare a mistrial. If the defendant opposed the declaration of a mistrial, then a re-trial is permitted only if the judge's decision to order a mistrial meets the "manifest necessity" standard. If the defendant either requested the mistrial or consented to it, then she may be re-tried, unless the prosecution goaded or provoked the defendant into seeking a mistrial.

A judge who orders a dismissal, as opposed to a mistrial, may or may not intend that the dismissal create a permanent bar to further prosecution, but that intention does not affect the double jeopardy consequences of the judge's action. As discussed above, a dismissal that constitutes a resolution in the defendant's favor of some or all of the factual questions bearing on the defendant's guilt or innocence qualifies as an acquittal, and bars further prosecution. But where the dismissal does not qualify as an acquittal, and when it is ordered at the request or with the consent of the defendant, the permissibility of a re-trial is governed by the same standard that governs re-trial following a mistrial ordered with the defendant's acquiescence. See Subsections 1 and 2 below.

1. MANIFEST NECESSITY

The termination of the trial through a mistrial, rather than through a dismissal, represents a decision by the trial court to permit the prosecution to try the defendant again on the same charge. Under the standard first announced in *U.S. v. Perez* (S.Ct. 1824) a mistrial declared without the defendant's consent is proper under the Double Jeopardy Clause only if there existed a "manifest necessity" for the mistrial. In recent cases, the Court has stressed that the manifest necessity standard does not provide a "mechanical formula" for evaluating the propriety of declaring a mistrial, and has acknowledged that the mistrial need not be "necessary" in a literal sense for a re-trial to be permissible.

The Court has stated that there are in fact degrees of necessity, and that a mistrial should be declared only when the prosecutor has carried the burden of establishing a "high degree" of necessity for terminating the proceeding without a verdict. Ultimately, the determination of whether double jeopardy bars a re-trial declared over the defendant's opposition requires a balancing of competing interests. On the one hand are the defendant's interests in obtaining a resolution of the charges by bringing the trial to completion, preserving the possibility of an acquittal by this judge or jury, and having the case decided by the particular tribunal that has been selected to try it. These interests must be weighed against the considerations which lead to the declaration of a mistrial. The Supreme Court has emphasized that appeals courts reviewing whether the declaration of a mistrial was warranted should accord broad deference to the judgment of the trial court.

Although the Supreme Court has stated that the determination whether manifest necessity exists turns on the facts of the particular case, and that prior decisions on that question escape meaningful categorization, the Court's decisions have established guidelines to be applied in evaluating the propriety of a mistrial declaration. The two leading cases are *Illinois v. Somerville* (S.Ct.1973) and *Arizona v. Washington* (S.Ct.1978). In *Somerville*, the trial judge had declared a mistrial, over the defendant's objection, when it was discovered early in the trial that the indictment on which the defendant was being tried was fatally defective. Under state law, the defect in the indictment could not be remedied through an amendment, and the defendant was entitled to an automatic reversal for any conviction rendered on the indictment. If the trial had proceeded and the defendant had been acquitted, however, retrial would have been barred, notwithstanding the defective indictment.

Based on its review of prior decisions on the question, the Supreme Court declared that there exists a manifest necessity for a mistrial and reprosecution is permitted if either 1) an impartial verdict cannot be reached or 2) a verdict of conviction could be reached but would have to be reversed on appeal due to an obvious procedural error in the trial. The clearest example of a case in which retrial is permitted because an impartial verdict is not possible is when the jury is unable to reach any verdict because they are deadlocked. As another example of a case where an impartial verdict could not be reached, the Court cited its decision in a case in which a mistrial was granted because one of the jurors was acquainted with the defendant and therefore probably prejudiced against the government. Examples of prior cases in which mistrials were properly declared because a verdict of guilty would have to be reversed on appeal included one case in which one of the trial jurors was not qualified to serve, and a case in which it was discovered after jeopardy had attached that the defendant had not entered a plea to the charge. The facts of *Somerville*, the Court held, also fell into this category, and re-trial of the defendant after the mistrial was therefore permissible.

A mistrial declared in a case that did not meet either of the general requirements stated in *Somerville* is presumably improper, and re-trial of the defendant would not be permitted. It is clear, how-

ever, both from the opinion in *Somerville* and especially from the Court's subsequent decision in *Arizona v. Washington*, that the determination of
whether manifest necessity exists requires consideration of additional factors beyond whether an impartial verdict is possible or a verdict of guilty will
be subject to certain reversal. One factor that is
plainly relevant but clearly not determinative is
whether the government or the defendant is responsible for the problem that gave rise to the motion
for a mistrial. When the prosecution is the cause of
the difficulty that led to the mistrial, its claim that
it should be allowed to re-try the defendant is less
compelling. As the facts in *Somerville* demonstrate,
however, this factor will not by itself bar a re-trial,
particularly if the government gains no special advantage from being able to convene a second trial.

In assessing whether the declaration of a mistrial
was proper, consideration should also be given to
whether the trial court considered less drastic alternatives to a mistrial, such as a curative jury instruction or a trial continuance. The relevance of this
factor is illustrated by the Supreme Court's decision
in *U.S. v. Jorn* (S.Ct.1971). In *Jorn* the trial court
had declared a mistrial in order to give prosecution
witnesses an opportunity to consult with their attorneys to protect their Fifth Amendment right
against self-incrimination. In holding that there was
not a manifest necessity for the mistrial, the Court
in *Jorn* stressed that the trial judge had not considered the option of granting a continuance to allow
the witnesses to consult as an alternative to a

mistrial. Although the Court's later opinions in *Somerville* and *Washington* do not support a conclusion that a trial court's failure to consider alternatives to a mistrial will by itself render the decision to order a mistrial improper, the availability of alternatives remains a relevant consideration in determining whether the justification for the mistrial outweighs the defendant's interests in proceeding to a verdict.

Another highly important consideration is whether the grounds that are asserted for the declaration of a mistrial lend themselves to manipulation by the prosecutor as a means of harassing or gaining advantage over the defendant. Of particular concern is the possibility that the prosecution will manipulate the justification for a mistrial in order to gain more time to strengthen its case. That is the concern that the Court in *Somerville* identified as underlying its decision in the earlier case of *Downum v. U.S.* (S.Ct.1963). In *Downum*, the trial court granted the prosecution's request for a mistrial when the prosecution failed to secure the attendance of a critical witness. The prosecution was aware when the trial began that the witness had not been located or subpoenaed, but proceeded with jury selection anyway. Without the witness's testimony, the prosecution would be unable to sustain its burden of proof. On review of the trial court's mistrial order, the Supreme Court held that the trial court's decision to permit the prosecution to re-try the case was improper.

In its opinion in *Somerville*, the Supreme Court distinguished the facts in *Downum* from the case before it. In both cases, the prosecution had been responsible for the problem that led to the mistrials: in *Somerville* the prosecutor failed to allege a necessary element of the offense in the indictment; whereas in *Downum* the prosecutor did not secure the attendance at trial of a necessary witness. The critical difference between the two cases, according to the Court, is that the *Downum* situation lent itself to prosecutorial manipulation, whereas the *Somerville* facts did not. The Court's concern is that the prosecution will seek a mistrial in cases where its evidence is weak or the trial is not going well in order to bolster its evidence or improve its presentation at a second trial. The Court in *Somerville* regarded this as at least a possibility in the situation presented in *Downum*, stating that the mistrial granted in that case operated as a post-jeopardy continuance to enable the prosecution to strengthen its case. The facts of *Somerville*, by contrast, did not present a risk of prosecutorial manipulation, since the ground for seeking a mistrial—a formal defect in the indictment—was unrelated to the strength of the prosecution's evidence.

Another factor that may be relevant to whether a mistrial declaration was proper is whether the trial court's decision to terminate the proceedings was motivated by a desire to protect the defendant's interest in a fair trial. That factor is illustrated by the facts of *Gori v. U.S.* (S.Ct.1961), though the status of that decision is questionable in light of subsequent cases. The trial judge in *Gori* declared a mistrial, without consulting the defendant, when the judge became concerned that prosecutor's questioning of a witness would lead to the presentation of evidence prejudicial to the defendant. In upholding the trial court's decision to grant a mistrial, the Supreme Court deemed it significant that the mistrial had been granted in the sole interest of the defendant.

In *Washington*, the Supreme Court emphasized that the trial court's assessment of the necessity for declaring a mistrial is entitled to considerable deference on appeal. The Court further held that the precise degree of appellate scrutiny of trial court decisions to declare a mistrial varies depending on the reason for the mistrial. The trial court's discretion is narrowest and the appellate court's scrutiny is strictest when the mistrial is declared because of the unavailability of critical prosecution evidence, or when there is reason to believe that the prosecutor is using the superior resources of the state to harass or gain tactical advantage over the accused. The strict scrutiny applied in such circumstances reflects the concern expressed in *Somerville* that the prosecution not be permitted to use a mistrial to buy time to strengthen its case or to subject the defendant to a second trial unnecessarily. At the other end of the spectrum, the trial judge exercises the broadest discretion when a mistrial is premised on the trial judge's belief that the jury is unable to reach a verdict. If a mistrial declared because of a deadlocked jury were treated as a bar to further prosecution, trial judges might be tempted to employ coercive means to break the deadlock in order to vindicate society's interest in giving the prosecution one complete opportunity to convict those who have violated its laws.

The Court in *Washington* held that a trial court finding of manifest necessity for a mistrial based on the trial judge's conclusion that the impartiality of the jury may have been compromised, as occurred in *Washington*, is also entitled to special respect on appeal. Deference to trial court assessments of possible juror bias is called for because the trial judge, who observed the events giving rise to the mistrial motion, is uniquely situated to assess their likely impact on the jury. In *Washington* the trial court granted the prosecution's mistrial motion after defense counsel told the jury in opening statement that the prosecutor had hidden and suppressed evidence. This comment, which was found to be improper, may have prejudiced the jury against the prosecution. The Supreme Court acknowledged that a mistrial under these circumstances was not "necessary" in a strict, literal sense. The Court agreed with the evaluation of a lower federal court that some trial judges would have proceeded with the trial after instructing the jury to disregard the comment. Nevertheless, according to the Court, to ensure the evenhanded administration of justice and protect the integrity of the trial, the highest degree of respect must be given to a trial judge's assessment of the likelihood that the impartiality of the jury has been affected by the improper comment or other events occurring during the trial. Although the trial judge in *Washington* had not expressly found "manifest necessity" for a mistrial in those words, the Supreme Court held that such an express finding is not invariably necessary, and the trial judge had not abused his discretion in declaring a mistrial.

2.   WITH THE DEFENDANT'S CONSENT

In *U.S. v. Dinitz* (S.Ct.1976) the Court held that the manifest necessity standard does not apply when the mistrial is declared at the request or with the consent of the accused. Except in cases of judicial or prosecutorial overreaching, discussed below, "a motion by the defendant for a mistrial is ordinarily assumed to remove any barrier to re-prosecution." This is so even if the mistrial motion is necessitated by judicial or prosecutorial error.

The reason for routinely permitting re-trial when the defendant acquiesces in the mistrial is because the defendant's mistrial request has objectives similar to the interests that underlie the Double Jeopardy Clause. Part of the purpose of the Double Jeopardy Clause is to protect the defendant against the anxiety, expense, and delay resulting from multiple prosecutions. A defendant who has been prejudiced by judicial or prosecutorial error may conclude that continuing the present trial would result in a conviction followed by a long appellate process and a second trial. Faced with such a prospect, the defendant may have little interest in completing the trial and obtaining a verdict with the first jury, but prefer instead to terminate the tainted proceedings and submit to a second trial as the best available means of obtaining a speedy and final resolution of the charges. The defendant may also, of course, choose not to request a mistrial, notwithstanding seriously prejudicial error. By not seeking a mistrial the defendant is able to preserve her chances of winning an acquittal from the first jury, failing which she can still pursue an appeal and perhaps secure a second chance for an acquittal at a second trial. "The important consideration," according to the Court, "is that the defendant retain primary control over the course to be followed," since granting the accused the choice of whether to terminate the trial or proceed to a verdict best accommodates the interests of the Double Jeopardy Clause.

In *Dinitz* the defendant had expressly requested a mistrial. A defendant who, though not actively seeking a mistrial, expresses agreement with the court's decision to declare a mistrial, may also be re-tried, even if there is no manifest necessity for terminating the trial before verdict.

3. PROSECUTORIAL OR JUDICIAL OVERREACHING

It has long been recognized that the rule permitting re-prosecution following a mistrial granted with the consent of the defendant cannot be absolute. Some limitations on the rule are necessary to prevent abuse by the prosecution. For instance, in the absence of such limitations, a prosecutor could deliberately commit error warranting a mistrial whenever it developed during the trial that the prosecution's evidence was deficient or its presentation flawed in order to provoke the defendant into requesting a mistrial. Relying on the fact that the defendant had requested the mistrial, the prosecution could then obtain a second and more promising opportunity to prove the defendant's guilt. More broadly, if the prosecution were able to provoke a mistrial and then re-try the defendant, the defendant's right to complete her trial before the first jury would be significantly undermined.

In *Dinitz* the Court recognized the need for an exception to the general rule permitting re-trial following defense requested mistrials to protect the defendant against governmental action intended to provoke mistrial requests and thereby subject the defendant to multiple prosecutions. As explained in *Dinitz*, the Double Jeopardy Clause "bars re-trials where 'bad-faith conduct by judge or prosecutor' . . . threatens the '[h]arassment of an accused by successive prosecutions or declaration of a mistrial so as to afford the prosecution a more favorable opportunity to convict.' "

The Supreme Court defined the scope of the exception to the rule that re-trial is permitted following a defense requested mistrial in *Oregon v. Kennedy* (S.Ct.1982). The prosecutor in that case had asked a trial witness whether his reason for not doing business with the defendant was because the defendant "is a crook." The defendant requested a mistrial on the basis that the question had prejudiced the jury against the defendant. The court granted the mistrial, and the defendant then sought to bar re-trial. At a hearing on that issue the trial court found as a matter of fact that it was not the intention of the prosecutor to cause a mistrial. Lower courts nonetheless found that re-trial was impermissible under Supreme Court precedents suggesting that re-trial is barred under the Double Jeopardy Clause whenever the judge or prosecutor acts in "bad faith" or "overreaches" in causing a mistrial.

The Supreme Court rejected the bad faith standard, holding that a defendant may raise the bar of double jeopardy to a second trial after having succeeded in aborting the first on his own motion *only where the governmental conduct in question is intended to "goad" the defendant into moving for a mistrial.* In explanation of the requirement of proof of intent to provoke a mistrial before re-trial will be barred, the Court emphasized the difficulty of administering a rule prohibiting retrial when the prosecutor acts in bad faith or overreaches. Unlike a test that looks to whether the prosecutor's actions amounted to overreaching, which the Court characterized as an "essentially standardless rule," a test based on the prosecutor's intent turns on a question of fact. The Court also argued that a broader rule might work to the ultimate detriment of defendants, since a trial judge might be reluctant to grant a mistrial if the court knew that the defendant would also attempt to bar a re-trial. Since the trial court had expressly found that the prosecutor in *Kennedy* had not intended to provoke a mistrial, retrial of the case was not barred by the Double Jeopardy Clause.

G.   RE-PROSECUTION FOLLOWING CONVICTION

The Double Jeopardy Clause prohibits re-prosecution of the defendant for the same offense following a conviction. In *Brown v. Ohio* (S.Ct.1977), for example, the Court held that the defendant's prosecution for car theft was barred by his prior conviction for joyriding, since joyriding and car theft are the "same offense" for double jeopardy purposes.

1.   RE–PROSECUTION FOLLOWING REVERSAL OF CONVICTION

In the early case of *Ball v. U.S.* (S.Ct.1896), the Court recognized an exception to the general prohibition against re-prosecution following a conviction. The bar against re-prosecution does not apply and the prosecution may re-try the defendant for the same offense when the defendant has obtained a reversal of her conviction on the basis of some error in the proceedings leading to the conviction. The *Ball* exception to the double jeopardy bar applies to a reversal based on erroneous evidentiary rulings, incorrect instructions on the law, or any ground other than the insufficiency of the trial evidence. When a conviction is reversed based on insufficient evidence, re-trial is prohibited.

The Supreme Court has identified several considerations underlying the rule permitting re-trial of a defendant who has won a reversal on appeal. First, permitting a second trial is necessary to the sound administration of justice, since placing the defendant beyond the reach of further prosecution because of any defect sufficient to warrant reversal is too high a price for granting the defendant the right to vindicate her fair trial rights. *U.S. v. Tateo* (S.Ct.1964). The Court has also argued that permitting a second trial following a successful appeal may ultimately work to the benefit of the defendant, since appeals courts might be reluctant to reverse convictions if the courts knew that reversal would totally immunize the defendant from further prosecution. Finally, the Court has stated that re-trial after reversal of a conviction is not the type of governmental oppression prohibited by the Double Jeopardy Clause.

2. RE–PROSECUTION FOLLOWING REVERSAL FOR INSUFFICIENT EVIDENCE

In *Burks v. U.S.* (S.Ct.1978) the Court recognized an exception to the general rule that double jeopardy is not a bar a re-trial of a convicted defendant following reversal on appeal. *Burks* held that when the reversal is based on the reviewing court's determination that the trial evidence is not sufficient to support the conviction, the Double Jeopardy Clause bars a retrial on the same charge. The Court reasoned that an appellate reversal for insufficient evidence is indistinguishable in substance from an acquittal at trial, and therefore should be given the same effect. Reversal on appeal based on lack of evidence to support the verdict represents a finding that the prosecution has failed to prove the defendant's guilt. Indeed, a post-conviction ruling that the trial evidence does not support conviction means that the prosecution's case was so lacking that it should not have even been submitted to the jury. The fact that the determination is made by an appellate court rather than at trial should not affect its double jeopardy consequences. Because the Double Jeopardy Clause affords absolute immunity from further prosecution to a defendant who obtains an acquittal at trial, the same consequences should attach to an appellate ruling, and re-trial for the same offense is not allowed. By contrast, an appellate reversal based on a finding of trial error implies nothing with respect to the guilt or innocence of the defendant, and does not bar re-prosecution.

In *Tibbs v. Florida* (S.Ct.1982) the Court distinguished *Burks*, which involved a reversal for insufficient evidence, from a reversal based on a finding that the verdict is against the *weight* of the evidence. The prosecution's evidence is legally insufficient under *Burks* when, viewing the evidence in the light most favorable to the prosecution, no rational juror could find the defendant guilty. In evaluating the legal sufficiency of the evidence, the reviewing court does not assess the credibility of the evidence, but determines whether the evidence is sufficient to support a conviction if it is believed. By contrast, a finding that the verdict is against the weight of the evidence involves an evaluation of credibility. In making such a finding, the appellate court sits, in effect, as a "thirteenth juror" and disagrees with the jury's resolution of conflicting testimony.

A finding that the evidence is legally insufficient, whether entered at trial or on appeal, represents a determination that an acquittal is the only proper verdict, and therefore must be given absolute finality. The Court in *Tibbs* stated, however, that a reversal based on a finding that the guilty verdict is against the weight of the evidence is not equivalent to an acquittal. Such a finding does not require the special deference that is accorded acquittals, but simply affords the defendant a second opportunity to seek a favorable judgment at trial. This granting of the defendant a second chance to prevail at trial, even though the evidence presented at the first trial was legally sufficient to convict, "does not create 'an unacceptably high risk that the Government, with its superior resources, [will] wear down [the] defendant' and obtain a conviction through persistence."

In *Lockhart v. Nelson* (S.Ct.1988) the Court addressed the question whether a defendant may be re-tried when critical evidence necessary to support the defendant's conviction is determined on appeal to have been improperly admitted. The defendant in *Nelson* won a reversal of his conviction on appeal on the ground that evidence had been erroneously admitted at trial. The appeals court also concluded that, while the evidence actually admitted at trial was legally sufficient, in the absence of the erroneously admitted evidence, the remaining evidence was not sufficient to support the conviction.

The Supreme Court held that double jeopardy does not bar retrial under the circumstances presented in *Nelson*. Under *Burks*, according to the Court, the reviewing court must consider all of the evidence admitted by the trial court in deciding whether retrial is permissible. So long as the evidence offered by the state and admitted by the court—whether erroneously or not—would have supported the conviction, a second prosecution is not barred. According to the Court, permitting a second trial at which the prosecution can seek to supply additional evidence in place of that which was held inadmissible simply recreates the situation that would have obtained had the problem with the evidence been perceived at trial, since the prosecution would presumably have been given the chance to make up the deficiency in its evidence at that point.

3. CONVICTION AS IMPLIED ACQUITTAL

In *Green v. U.S.* (S.Ct.1957), the Court held that a conviction for a lesser included offense results in an "implied acquittal" of the more serious offense. The jury at Green's trial had been instructed that they could find the defendant guilty of either first or second degree murder. Under the law of the jurisdiction, second degree murder was a lesser included offense of murder in the first degree. The jury returned a verdict of guilty of second degree murder, and was silent with respect to the more serious charge. The Supreme Court held that the jury's conviction of Green for second degree murder was an implied acquittal of first degree murder, and should be given the same effect for double jeopardy purposes as if the jury had expressly found the defendant not guilty on that charge. As a result, a defendant, such as Green, who has been acquitted of the greater offense through a conviction for a lesser offense may not thereafter be prosecuted for the greater offense. Additionally, if the defendant successfully appeals the conviction for the lesser offense, the prosecution may re-try the defendant for that offense, but may not make a second attempt to convict the defendant for the greater offense. Thus, under the facts of *Green*, the prosecution is limited at the re-trial to seeking to convict the defendant of second degree murder.

A defendant who pleads guilty to a lesser included offense may not assert double jeopardy as a bar to prosecution on the greater offense. The taking of a guilty plea to a lesser included offense does not imply a finding of not guilty on the greater charge. In addition, the entry of the guilty plea does not cause jeopardy to attach on the greater offense.

4. SENTENCING AS ACQUITTAL

The Supreme Court has held that the Double Jeopardy Clause does not attach the same finality to sentencing decisions as is given to determinations of guilt or innocence. Except in the case of capital sentencing, which is discussed below, double jeopardy is not an impediment either to prosecution appeals of sentencing decisions or to re-sentencing. The imposition of one sentence, a one year prison term, for example, is not an "implied acquittal" of a sentence to a longer term. Although the defendant cannot be punished twice for one conviction, the defendant cannot assert double jeopardy as a bar to the imposition of an increased sentence on re-sentencing. This rule applies whether the re-sentencing occurs following a government appeal of the initial sentence, or after a re-trial occasioned by the defendant's successful appeal of her conviction.

The basic reason for treating sentencing decisions differently from determinations of guilt or innocence is that re-sentencing does not implicate the concerns of the Double Jeopardy Clause to the same extent as re-trial. Sentencing decisions do not ordinarily create as much anxiety for the accused as the basic determination of guilt or innocence, and re-sentencing does not subject the defendant to the risk of being harassed and eventually convicted even though innocent. Sentencing proceedings, which are often based on information developed outside the courtroom, do not approximate the ordeal of a trial.

The Supreme Court has held that double jeopardy consequences do attach to capital sentencing decisions. A decision to impose a non-capital sentence, whether entered by a judge or a jury, constitutes an acquittal of a death sentence. The reason capital sentencing is treated differently is because death penalty sentencing involves more formal procedures and a more structured decision making process than non-capital sentencing. A capital sentencing proceeding typically involves a separate hearing, at which the prosecution must prove the existence of certain statutory aggravating circumstances. The decision maker is authorized to impose a death sentence only if it finds from the evidence presented at the hearing that required aggravating factors have been proven. Because capital sentencing involves the resolution of specific factual questions on the basis of evidence presented at a formal hearing, it more nearly approximates the procedures for adjudicating guilt, and is entitled to a similar finality under the Double Jeopardy Clause.

H. DUAL SOVEREIGNTY DOCTRINE

The Supreme Court has long held that the Double Jeopardy Clause has no application to prosecutions that are instituted by different sovereign authorities. Under what is known as the dual sovereignty doctrine, two crimes can never be the "same offense" if they are being prosecuted by different sovereigns, even if the crimes have identical statutory elements. Because the two crime are not the same offense, the Double Jeopardy Clause is not a bar to either successive prosecutions or multiple punishments.

In determining whether successive prosecutions or multiple punishments are permitted under the dual sovereignty doctrine, the only issue is whether the prosecuting authorities are in fact different sovereignties. For purposes of the Double Jeopardy Clause, the federal government and each of the states are separate sovereignties. Thus, a prosecution by a state for a state crime does not bar a subsequent or concurrent prosecution by the federal government for a federal offense. Nor does a prior federal prosecution bar a state prosecution. Although rare, the same conduct could also be prosecuted by two different states. For instance, if the conduct constituting a murder occurred in two different states, the defendant could be charged, tried, convicted, and punished for murder in both states. Native American Indian tribes exercise independent sovereign power, and can therefore pursue prosecutions regardless of what the federal or state governments might also undertake. By contrast, municipalities and other administrative subdivisions of the states are not separate sovereignties, but exercise the sovereign authority of the state. Thus, a prosecution for a state crime bars a prosecution for a violation of a municipal law, and vice versa.

The rationale for the dual sovereignty doctrine is rooted in the assumptions underlying our federal system of government. Under American federalism, the states are not simply administrative divisions of a unitary sovereign power, but exercise governmental power in their own right. From this it is thought to follow that state and federal criminal statutes serve different interests even though the two statutes address the very same conduct.

CHAPTER 10

GUILTY PLEAS AND PLEA BARGAINING

A. PLEAS AND PLEA BARGAINING

1. TYPES OF PLEAS

Every person who is charged with a crime is required to respond to the charge by entering a formal plea. This occurs first at a proceeding known as "arraignment," at which the defendant is informed of the charge and requested to plead. It is not uncommon, however, for defendants to plead not guilty at arraignment and then change their plea at a later date.

In most jurisdictions the defendant may enter one of three pleas: not guilty, guilty, or nolo contendere. A nolo contendere or "nolo" plea, which in many places is available only with the approval of the court, is like a guilty plea, except that it does not entail a formal admission of guilt, and therefore cannot be used as proof that the defendant committed the crime in a subsequent civil case.

The constitution guarantees the accused an absolute right to plead not guilty, and thereby require the state to prove the defendant's guilt at trial. Nevertheless, the great majority of criminal convictions result from the entry of a guilty plea by the defendant rather than a verdict of guilty at trial. By pleading guilty the defendant relinquishes her right to a trial, admits guilt, and consents to a judgment of conviction and the imposition of sentence.

2. TYPES OF PLEA BARGAINS

A plea bargain involves a guilty plea by the defendant in exchange for concessions or benefits from the prosecution. Not all guilty pleas are the result of a bargain. In many situations the defendant enters a guilty plea without having received any formal concessions from the prosecution.

All guilty pleas, whether the result of plea bargain or not, must satisfy certain statutory and constitutional requirements to be valid. When the plea is based on a bargain, however, the existence of an agreement between the prosecution and the defense raises additional concerns and brings new rules into play.

Prosecutors and defendants enter into plea bargains because both sides perceive a benefit in the bargain. The prosecutor benefits by obtaining a certain conviction and avoiding the expenditure of time and other resources required by a trial. But in order to induce the defendant to give up the possibility of winning an acquittal at trial, the prosecutor must offer the defendant some benefit in return. The benefit for the defendant is typically in the form of concessions on the charges or concessions on the punishment or both. The prosecutor can grant concessions on the charge in two different ways. First, the prosecutor may agree to accept a plea of guilty to a reduced charge. Thus, a prosecutor may accept the defendant's plea of guilty to manslaughter in satisfaction of an indictment for murder. Second, the prosecutor may agree to dismiss some charges in exchange for the defendant's pleading "on the nose" to other charges. For example, a defendant charged with a string of burglaries may be permitted to plead guilty to one burglary in exchange for the dismissal of the others.

In principle, the prosecutor's ability to offer a reduced sentence as an incentive to plead guilty is more limited, since the sentencing power belongs to the judge rather than the prosecutor. But because judges often give considerable weight to prosecutors' sentencing recommendations, prosecutors frequently use their power to influence sentencing decisions to persuade defendants to plead guilty.

Sentence bargains are typically based on one of two types of promises. In some cases the prosecutor promises only to recommend to the judge an agreed upon sentence, or not to oppose the recommendation by defense counsel. Even though such recommendations are not binding, because judges in many places routinely follow prosecutors' sentencing recommendations, such promises can bring substantial benefits to the defendant. In other cases the prosecutor promises a specific sentence in return for the defendant's guilty plea. The judge is not obligated to impose the sentence agreed upon by the prosecution and defense, though in practice judges very often do. If the sentence actually imposed is harsher than what the defendant had bargained for, the defendant will often be entitled to withdraw her guilty plea and proceed to trial.

3.   THE DEBATE OVER PLEA BARGAINING

Approximately ninety percent of all convictions in the US are the result of a guilty plea by the defendant rather than a verdict of guilty at trial. The Supreme Court has recognized the importance of plea bargaining, declaring it an "essential component of the administration of justice" which, if properly administered, is to be encouraged. *Santobello v. N.Y.* (S.Ct.1971).

Although plea bargaining is a deeply entrenched part of the criminal justice system, the practice of plea bargaining remains controversial, and critics continue to advocate that the practice be abolished. The policy debate over plea bargaining raises two closely related questions: First, is plea bargaining a desirable method for resolving criminal cases, and second, even if undesirable, are we, as a society, willing to bear the cost of operating a criminal justice system without it?

The question whether plea bargaining is good or bad has many facets, and the discussion here will touch on only some of them. One frequent criticism of plea bargaining is that it results in differential treatment of offenders who, according to the critics, should be treated the same. There is ample evidence that defendants who plead guilty receive more lenient sentences than defendants who are convicted at trial. This sentencing disparity has its source in the plea bargaining process itself. In the absence of some benefit to the defendant for pleading guilty, most defendants would presumably contest their guilt at trial, since there is always a possibility, however slim, of an acquittal. The sentencing disparity reflects the necessity of offering defendants an inducement to forego the possibility of an acquittal and plead guilty.

The critics who regard the sentencing disparity as bad disagree over why it is bad. The lenient treatment accorded defendants who plead guilty is viewed by some as a failure of the legal system to fully enforce the criminal law. A defendant who receives charge or sentencing concessions in exchange for her guilty plea, according to this argument, is being punished less than the law demands. From another perspective, the harsher sentences meted out to defendants who are convicted at trial is regarded as an unjust punishment for the exercise of the right to a trial.

Plea bargaining is also criticized on the ground that it results in the conviction of the innocent. Prosecutors exert powerful pressure on defendants to plead guilty by offering substantially reduced punishment for entering a plea. For example, it is not uncommon for prosecutors to offer deals that allow defendants to avoid incarceration only if they agree to plead guilty. Moreover, the sentencing differential between pleading guilty and going to trial is likely to be greater (and the pressure to plead

guilty more intense) in cases where the prosecution's case is weak (and the defendant's innocence
more likely), since a defendant who rates her
chances of acquittal high can demand more concessions for pleading guilty.

There is no question that the prosecutor's plea
negotiation strategies cause some innocent defendants to plead guilty. On the other hand, it is also
true that innocent defendants are sometimes convicted at trial.

Another argument against plea bargaining is that
it adversely affects the quality of legal representation defense attorneys provide for their clients. Defense counsel often have a personal financial incentive to encourage their clients to plead guilty rather
than go to trial. The conflict of interest created by
this financial incentive may color the attorney's
evaluation of whether pleading guilty is the best
course for the client.

In addition, the plea bargaining system requires
that defense counsel maintain good long term relations with the prosecutor. In order not to jeopardize
that relationship, defense counsel sometimes feel
pressure to accept a plea offer to avoid antagonizing
the prosecutor.

Defense attorneys may also feel tempted to recommend pleading guilty because it involves less risk
to the lawyer's reputation. Predictions about the
outcome of a trial can prove wrong, but pleading
guilty involves less uncertainty than trial, and
therefore less risk of error.

Probably the most common defense of plea bargaining focuses not on supposed virtues of plea bargaining as such, but on the costs of operating a system without plea bargaining, in which all criminal cases are resolved through a trial. The effect of the elimination of plea bargaining on the criminal justice system cannot be predicted with certainty, but it would probably be profound. At present, only about ten percent of criminal cases go to trial. If prosecutors were prevented from rewarding defendants who plead guilty, the number of trials would presumably increase dramatically. Unless significant changes were made in trial procedures to make trials shorter and simpler, the increase in trials as a result of the elimination of plea bargaining might well overwhelm the system completely.

Plea bargaining can also be defended as a response to the uncertainties of the adjudicatory process. Evidence about past events is rarely clear or certain, yet criminal verdicts must be stated in absolute and unqualified terms of guilty or not guilty. Plea bargaining permits the uncertainty associated with adjudication to be factored into the verdict. On this view, the negotiation of criminal sanctions through plea bargaining serves roughly the same function as the negotiation of damage settlements in civil litigation. A civil litigant who believes she has a fifty percent chance of winning a claim worth $100,000 should be willing to settle the claim for $50,000 (putting aside the costs of litigating the claim). The discount or bargain simply represents the uncertainty of the outcome. Similarly, a prosecutor who believes she has a fifty percent chance of winning a first degree murder conviction should be willing to accept a guilty plea to a reduced charge.

Another argument in defense of plea bargaining is that it enables prosecutors to better tailor the punishment to fit the crime and the offender, and facilitates the purposes of the criminal law by ensuring the prompt imposition of criminal sanctions.

Finally, plea bargaining can be seen as the cost and consequence of our exceptionally complex trial procedures. This view asserts that because American criminal trials are so long and complex, the system can afford to try only a small percentage of defendants; the rest must be pressured into pleading guilty. The relationship between plea bargaining and the complexity of the trial process is borne out by a comparison of the US criminal justice system with systems operating in much of Europe, where trials are shorter and less complex, and plea bargaining is less common.

B. PLEA BARGAINING: CONSTITUTIONAL ISSUES

1. VOLUNTARINESS

Due process requires that every guilty plea, whether based on a bargain or not, must satisfy constitutional standards of voluntariness to be valid. Problems of voluntariness arise most often, however, when the plea is entered pursuant to a bargain.

The plea bargaining system depends on the existence of inducements for the defendant to plead guilty. In the absence of some benefit in pleading guilty, many defendants would presumably not give up the possibility of winning an acquittal at trial. The inducements to forego trial and plead guilty can come from three different sources.

First, some statutes create an incentive for defendants to plead guilty by providing for a different sentence for defendants who plead guilty and those who are convicted at trial. Second and more commonly, prosecutors provide inducements for defendants to plead guilty by offering concessions on either the sentence or the charge for those defendants who plead. Third, in some jurisdictions judges participate in plea negotiations, and can therefore influence the defendant's decision to plead guilty through threats or promises of a harsher sentence if the defendant goes to trial.

The use of inducements to encourage guilty pleas gives rise to different types of constitutional challenges depending on whether the inducement is effective in persuading the defendant to plead guilty. If the defendant *does not* plead guilty and is therefore denied the benefit that was offered in exchange for a plea, the defendant may claim that she has been punished for exercising her constitutional rights, or that the harsher sentence or charge is vindictive. On the other hand, if the defendant *does* plead guilty and receives the offered benefit, she may argue that the inducement offered in exchange for her plea coerced her into waiving her constitutional rights, and that her plea is therefore constitutionally involuntary.

U.S. v. Jackson (S.Ct.1968) involved a claim that a statutory inducement to plead guilty had the effect of punishing those defendants who rejected the offered benefit and went to trial. The federal kidnapping statute at issue in *Jackson* authorized a death penalty for defendants convicted after a jury trial, but set a maximum penalty of life in prison for defendants who either pled guilty or waived the right to a jury and were convicted by a judge. The defendant in the case had elected trial by jury and was sentenced to death after the jury convicted him. The Supreme Court held that because the statute made the risk of a death sentence the price for receiving a jury trial, the death penalty provision of the statute imposed an "impermissible burden" on the exercise of a constitutional right, and was therefore unconstitutional.

Although the limits of the *Jackson* holding are uncertain, both the Court's opinion and later decisions clearly demonstrate that the constitution does not impose a blanket prohibition against statutory inducements to plead guilty, or against differential treatment of defendants who plead guilty and those who go to trial. One factor that may have influenced the outcome in *Jackson* is the fact that the case involved a death sentence, and therefore may have been subjected to closer constitutional scrutiny than would have been the case if the defendant's life had not hung in the balance. Indeed, in the subsequent case of *Corbitt v. N.J.* (S.Ct.1978) the Court declined to follow *Jackson*, relying in part on the fact that the statute at issue in *Corbitt* did not involve the death penalty.

The Court in *Jackson* may have also been influenced by a belief that statutory inducements to plead guilty should be judged more strictly than inducements that are part of the plea bargaining process. This is because statutes that provide differential sentences for defendants who plead and defendants who do not, preclude consideration of the facts of the individual case or defendant.

It is clear, however, that the constitution does not prohibit all statutory inducements to plead guilty. The Court in *Jackson* emphasized that the statute at issue in that case was unconstitutional because it burdened the defendant's right to trial "unnecessarily"; the state's legitimate interest in limiting death sentences to cases in which the jury recommends it could be accomplished without penalizing those who assert their right to jury trial. By contrast, as will be discussed below, inducements to plead guilty offered by the prosecutor as part of the plea bargaining process are not regarded as "unnecessary," since they serve the legitimate purpose of encouraging guilty pleas. *See Bordenkircher v. Hayes* (S.Ct.1978). Moreover, in *Corbitt*, the Court upheld a statute that required a mandatory life term for those convicted of first degree murder at trial, but authorized the judge to impose *either* life or 30 years for those who pleaded guilty. The Court distinguished *Jackson* in that under the scheme challenged in *Corbitt* the more severe punishment was not reserved exclusively for those defendants who go to trial, and, therefore the statute in *Corbitt* did not make the defendant's choice between pleading guilty and going to trial the sole determinant of the ultimate punishment.

Because the defendants in *Jackson* were sentenced to death after having been found guilty at trial, the Court had no occasion in that case to address whether a guilty plea entered under the statute could be challenged as involuntary. That very question, however, was presented to the Court two years later in *Brady v. U.S.* (S.Ct.1970).

The defendant in *Brady* pled guilty to kidnapping under the same statute that was at issue in *Jackson*, but his plea was entered before the Supreme Court declared the death penalty provision of that statute unconstitutional. After the Court decided *Jackson*, Brady sought to vacate his guilty plea on the ground that it was coerced by the threat of a death sentence if he contested his guilt before a jury.

In rejecting Brady's argument the Supreme Court first affirmed that a guilty plea entails a waiver of constitutional rights, and therefore must be a voluntary expression of the defendant's own choice. The Court held, however, that the defendant's plea is not rendered involuntary in the constitutional sense merely because the threat of a death sentence "caused" the plea in the sense that the defendant would not have pled guilty but for the death penalty provision of the statute. The Court perceived no significant difference between Brady's situation and the defendant who pleads guilty because her lawyer advises her that the judge is normally more lenient with defendants who plead guilty, or the defendant who pleads guilty on the understanding that other charges will be dropped in exchange for the plea. In all of those situations, the Court stated, the defendant might never plead guilty absent the possibility or certainty that the plea would result in a lesser penalty than the sentence that could be imposed after a trial, yet the plea is nonetheless voluntary.

The defendant in *Brady* was induced to plead guilty because of a sentencing differential contained in a statute, and did not involve a plea bargain. The later case of *Bordenkircher v. Hayes* makes clear that a plea is not rendered involuntary because it was induced by threats or promises from the prosecutor during plea negotiations. The defendant in *Hayes* was charged with uttering a forged instrument in the amount of $88.30, an offense that was punishable by a term of two to ten years in prison. During plea negotiations, the prosecutor offered to recommend a sentence of five years in prison if the defendant would plead guilty to the indictment. The prosecutor also stated that if the defendant did not plead guilty to the charge, he would return to the grand jury and seek an indictment under the state's habitual criminal statute, which would subject the defendant to a mandatory life sentence. The defendant refused the prosecutor's offer, the prosecutor obtained the habitual criminal indictment, and the defendant was convicted of the charge at trial and sentenced to life in prison.

Because the defendant in *Hayes* was convicted at trial rather than by a plea of guilty, the Supreme Court was not called on to decide directly whether a guilty plea to the original indictment entered in response to the threat of prosecution on the more serious charge could be attacked as involuntary. But, in rejecting the defendant's argument that the conviction should be invalidated because the prosecutor's actions in seeking the new indictment was vindictive, the Court clearly approved the prosecutor's threat to indict on the higher charge as a permissible method of encouraging the defendant to plead guilty.

Brady, *Hayes* and other cases make clear that the constitution does not prevent the state from encouraging guilty pleas by providing differential treatment to defendants who plead guilty and defendants who are found guilty at trial. As the Court has recognized, to hold otherwise would seriously disrupt the system of plea bargaining. The Court has also recognized, however, that the power to encourage guilty pleas has a potential for abuse and is subject to constitutional limitations. In *Brady* the Court qualified its decision by stating that a guilty plea that is induced by threats or promises that are *improper* is invalid. Although the Court did not elaborate on the issue, the Court stated that an inducement is improper if it is based on a misrepresentation, an unfulfilled or unfulfillable promise, or a threat or promise that is by its nature improper as having no relationship to the prosecutor's business. A prosecutor cannot, of course, extract a guilty plea through actual or threatened physical harm or through mental coercion that overbears the defendant's will. Although the Court has not expressly said so, there is a strong argument that it is improper for the prosecutor to threaten charges which are not supported by available evidence.

The approval of guilty pleas that are induced by proper threats or promises, and the disapproval of pleas obtained by improper inducements, leaves open the question of what if any latitude exists for the defendant to argue that her plea is invalid because the inducements offered by the prosecutor, although proper, were so overpowering as to render the plea involuntary. Although such a claim is in principle possible, the Court's opinion in *Bordenkircher v. Hayes* suggests that the chances of succeeding are not good.

Although the Supreme Court has not addressed the issue, a defendant probably has a stronger argument that her plea is involuntary if the plea was induced by threats or promises by the judge. The reason for treating inducements by the judge differently from inducements by the prosecutor is a fear that threats or promises from the judge, who has the power actually to decide on the sentence, will more easily overpower the defendant's will than similar entreaties by the prosecutor. Because of this fear, the Federal Rules of Criminal Procedure prohibit the judge from participating in plea bargaining.

2. VINDICTIVENESS AND PLEA BARGAINING

The use of inducements to plead guilty creates potential problems of voluntariness if the defendant succumbs to the inducements and pleads guilty. If the defendant does not plead guilty but is convicted at trial, the resulting sentence or conviction may be subject to challenge on the ground that the defendant is being punished with a harsher penalty for the exercise of her constitutional right to be tried on the charge.

What has come to be known as the vindictiveness doctrine has its source in the Supreme Court's decision in *N.C. v. Pearce* (S.Ct.1969). The defendant in that case obtained a reversal of his conviction for sexual assault on the ground that his confession was improperly admitted at trial. Following a second trial and conviction for the same offense, the defendant received a harsher sentence than had been imposed after the first trial. The Supreme Court then held that the imposition of the longer sentence following the defendant's successful appeal violated his due process rights, stating that "vindictiveness against a defendant for having successfully attacked his conviction must play no part in the sentence he receives after a new trial."

In *Blackledge v. Perry* (S.Ct.1974) the Court made clear that the *Pearce* principle prohibiting vindictive sentencing also has application to the prosecutor's charging decisions. In *Perry* the prosecutor charged the defendant with a more serious crime after the defendant exercised his right under state law to a *de novo* appeal of his conviction for misdemeanor assault. Applying the rationale of *Pearce*, the Court held that a defendant is entitled to pursue her statutory right to a *de novo* appeal without apprehension that the state will retaliate by substituting a more serious charge. The Court established what amounts to a presumption of vindictiveness when the prosecutor "ups the ante" as occurred in *Perry*, holding that a prosecutor in such a case must be able to identify specific reasons for increasing the charge.

In *Bordenkircher v. Hayes*, the Court held that the presumption of vindictiveness established in *Perry* does not apply to a prosecutor's decision to up the ante if it is presented to the defendant as an encouragement to plead guilty during the "give and take" of plea negotiations. In *Hayes* the prosecutor threatened the defendant with a significantly more serious charge if the defendant rejected the prosecutor's plea offer. When the defendant refused the offer and was convicted on the more serious charge, the defendant appealed claiming that the rule against vindictive prosecution prohibited conviction on the higher charge. The Supreme Court rejected that argument, holding that there is no element of punishment or retaliation provided the choice between pleading guilty on the lower charge and being tried on a higher one is openly presented to the defendant during plea negotiations, and the defendant is free to accept or reject the prosecution's offer.

In approving the prosecutor's plea bargaining tactics in *Hayes*, the Court acknowledged that requiring the defendant to choose between pleading guilty on the lesser charge and facing more serious punishment may have a discouraging effect on the defendant's assertion of trial rights. The Court also stated, however, that the imposition of these difficult choices is an inevitable and permissible attribute of the plea bargaining system. If the prosecutor were prohibited from raising the ante during plea negotiations, she could presumably apply the same pressure on the defendant to plead guilty by simply filing the more serious charge at the outset, and then offer to reduce the charges during the negotiation process.

3. EFFECTIVE ASSISTANCE OF COUNSEL

The Sixth Amendment right to counsel has been interpreted as guaranteeing a right to the assistance of counsel during "critical stages" of the criminal process. The plea negotiation process is a critical stage to which the Sixth Amendment right applies. Although the Supreme Court has not yet ruled on the issue, a defendant can presumably waive her right to counsel and represent herself during plea negotiations.

The Sixth Amendment right includes the right to assistance of counsel that is *effective*. The test for effective assistance of counsel in the plea bargaining context is the same two part test that is applied for effective assistance of counsel at trial or other evidentiary proceedings. *See Strickland v. Washington* (S.Ct. 1984). In order to establish a deprivation of the right to effective assistance of counsel, the defendant must show, first, that counsel's representation fell below an objective standard of "reasonableness" and second, that the defendant suffered actual prejudice as a result of counsel's deficiencies. Both prongs of the test must be satisfied to make out an ineffective assistance of counsel claim.

The first prong of the test—the "performance" prong—looks to whether the attorney's representation was within the range of competence demanded of attorneys in criminal cases. This evaluation is made difficult by the fact that the courts have not spelled out what is required of defense attorneys representing defendants in plea negotiations. It is uncertain, for example, what obligation the attorney has to investigate the case before recommending a guilty plea. One point is clear, however. Because an attorney's advice to a defendant contemplating a guilty plea entails a complex assessment of the strength of the prosecution's case, courts do not require that the attorney's predictions or advice be accurate or "withstand retrospective examination in a post-conviction hearing."

In *McMann v. Richardson* (S.Ct.1970) for example, the Court held that an attorney's advice to the defendant to plead guilty was not constitutionally deficient, even though it was later determined that the defendant's pre-trial confession was involuntary, and therefore could not have been used as evidence if the defendant had gone to trial. As the Court stated, "[t]hat this Court might hold a defendant's confession inadmissible in evidence, possibly by a divided vote, hardly justifies a conclusion that the defendant's attorney was incompetent or ineffective when he thought the admissibility of the confession sufficiently probable to advise a plea of guilty."

In order to satisfy the second "prejudice" prong the defendant must show that there is a reasonable probability that, but for counsel's errors, she would not have pleaded guilty and would have insisted on going to trial. In *Hill v. Lockhart* (S.Ct.1985) the Court relied on this requirement in holding that the defendant had not shown a deprivation of his right to effective assistance of counsel. The defendant based his ineffective assistance claim on his attorney's failure to inform him that under state law he was required to serve one-half of his sentence before he would become eligible for parole. The Court held that it was unnecessary to assess whether this failure was sufficient to satisfy the performance prong, since Hill's claim failed to satisfy the prejudice prong. First, the defendant had not alleged that he would have pleaded not guilty and insisted on a trial if his counsel had correctly informed him about the parole eligibility date. But the Court also suggested that even if such an allegation had been made, failure to inform the defendant of the parole terms did not create a reasonable probability that the defendant would have rejected the plea, since the same parole conditions would have been applicable had the defendant been convicted at trial.

An ineffective assistance of counsel claim can also be framed as a challenge to the knowing and intelligent character of the plea. See Section C1 below. When presented in this way, the defendant argues that the advise she received from her lawyer was so defective that her plea was not in fact knowing and intelligent. However, the result will be the same whether the defendant's challenge to the conviction is based on a claim of ineffective assistance or based on a claim that the plea was not intelligently entered. Regardless of how the claim is presented, the question is whether the advice of the attorney "was within the range of competence demanded of attorneys in criminal cases." *McMann v. Richardson.*

C. RECEIVING THE PLEA

The defendant's plea of guilty carries the same legal consequences as a verdict of guilty following a full adversarial trial. Because a guilty plea serves as the foundation for conviction and punishment, safeguards are required to ensure that the defendant's constitutional rights have been honored and that the plea establishes a valid basis for conviction.

The procedures for entry of guilty pleas are now generally regulated by statutes which set forth in detail the requirements for a valid plea. Rule 11 of the Federal Rules of Criminal Procedure governs the taking of guilty pleas in federal court. Like similar state provisions, Rule 11 requires a hearing or "plea colloquy" at which the judge must address the defendant personally in order to ensure that the requirements for a valid plea are satisfied.

1.   ASSURING A KNOWING AND INTELLIGENT PLEA

a.   Understanding the Charge

Because a conviction entered pursuant to a guilty plea rests on the defendant's admission of guilt, a valid plea requires that the defendant understand the charge to which she is pleading. Rule 11 requires the judge to "address the defendant in open court and inform him, and determine that he understands, . . . the nature of the charge to which the plea is offered."

The leading Supreme Court case on the requirement that the defendant understand the nature of the charge is *Henderson v. Morgan* (S.Ct.1976). The defendant in *Henderson*, a 19 year old of substantially below average intelligence, had been indicted for first degree murder, and pled guilty to second degree murder after his attorneys unsuccessfully sought to reduce the charge to manslaughter. The Supreme Court invalidated the defendant's plea because he was not informed that second degree murder requires an intent to kill.

The Supreme Court in *Henderson* held that due process requires that the defendant receive "real notice of the true nature of the charge against him." But the Court's opinion also assumed without deciding that a description of every element of the offense is not required for a valid plea, and explained the result in the case before it on the basis that "intent is such a critical element of second degree murder that notice of that element is required." This statement suggests that due process does not require invalidation of the plea based on a failure to inform the defendant of an element which is not "critical." The characterization of intent to kill as critical to second degree murder was apparently based on the fact that such element distinguishes the crime from manslaughter.

Another crucial factor in the *Henderson* decision was the fact that the trial judge had found as a fact that the intent element of the charge had not been explained to the defendant. But in most cases, the Court stated, it can be presumed that defense counsel routinely explain the nature of the charge in sufficient detail to give the accused notice of what she is pleading guilty to. Lower courts have relied on this presumption to reject *Henderson* claims where the record contained no evidence that either the judge or defense counsel had informed the accused of a critical element of the offense.

b. Understanding the Penalty

Rule 11 requires that the defendant be informed of and understand certain consequences of pleading guilty. Specifically, the judge must inform the defendant of 1) any mandatory minimum penalty; 2) the maximum possible penalty, including the effect of any supervised release term; 3) the applicability of sentencing guidelines in determining sentence; and 4) any possibility that the court will order the defendant to make restitution to the victim.

State requirements concerning what the defendant must be told regarding the consequences of pleading guilty are often less demanding than the federal rule. Disclosure of the maximum penalty is deemed most important, though an argument can be made that it is also critical that the accused be informed of any required minimum sentence. Neither Rule 11 nor the states require that the defendant be informed of "collateral" consequences of conviction. These may include loss of the right to vote or serve as a juror, loss of drivers license, or deportation.

The Supreme Court has held that failure to inform the accused of a release supervision requirement as required by Rule 11 did not violate the defendant's due process rights. *U.S. v. Timmreck* (S.Ct.1979). Whether the constitution requires that the defendant be informed of maximum or mandatory minimum sentences is uncertain. Even if due process does require that the defendant be aware of these consequences, a plea is presumably valid if the defendant received the information from her attorney or in some other way.

c. Understanding the Rights Waived

In *Boykin v. Alabama* (S.Ct.1969) the defendant pleaded guilty to five counts of armed robbery just three days after the appointment of his court-appointed lawyer. He was later sentenced to death on all five counts. The record of the plea showed that at the time the defendant pled guilty the trial judge asked him no questions concerning his plea, and the defendant did not address the court.

The Supreme Court invalidated Boykin's plea on the ground that it was not shown to be intelligent and voluntary as required by the constitution. The Court identified three constitutional rights that the defendant gives up by pleading guilty: the Fifth Amendment right against compulsory self-incrimination; the right to trial by jury; and the right to confront one's accusers. The Court stated that it would not presume a waiver of these rights from a silent record.

On its face *Boykin* appears to require invalidation of a guilty plea whenever the record of the plea does not include an express waiver of constitutional rights. Subsequent cases, however, have not applied the *Boykin* rule in this unqualified fashion. Courts have upheld guilty pleas over a constitutional challenge in the absence of an express waiver provided the plea is found to be intelligent and voluntary.

Rule 11 and comparable state statutes also require that the accused be informed of her constitutional rights and execute a valid waiver. Failure to comply with these statutory requirements can constitute a distinct ground for challenging the validity of the plea.

d. Effect of Inaccurate Legal Advice

Challenges to the knowing and intelligent character of the plea are sometimes based on a claim that the defendant entered the plea in reliance on incorrect advise from her attorney. In *Brady v. U.S.*, for example, the defendant claimed that his plea was not intelligent and knowing because, as a result of his lawyer's failure to anticipate the Supreme Court's decision invalidating the penalty provision of the statute he was charged under, the defendant entered his plea under the mistaken belief that he could be sentenced to death if he went to trial.

The Supreme Court rejected the challenge, stating that the decision to plead guilty will often be influenced by the defendant's assessment of questions for which there are no certain answers, such as the strength of the prosecution's case and the likelihood of leniency if a plea of guilty is accepted. But, according to the Court, "[t]he rule that a plea must be intelligently made does not require that a plea be vulnerable to later attack if the defendant did not correctly assess every relevant factor entering into his decision." More specifically, "a voluntary plea of guilty intelligently made in light of the then applicable law does not become vulnerable because later judicial decisions indicate that the plea rested on a faulty premise." Instead, the test used to determine whether the attorney's advice rendered the plea unintelligent is the same test that is used to determine whether the defendant was denied effective assistance of counsel—was the attorney's advice "within the range of competence demanded of attorneys in criminal cases." *McMann v. Richardson* (S.Ct.1970).

2. ASSURING VOLUNTARINESS OF THE PLEA AND COMPETENCY OF THE ACCUSED

Rule 11 states that the judge shall not accept a guilty plea without first addressing the defendant personally in open court and determining that the plea is voluntary and not the result of force, threats, or promises, apart from any promises that make up the plea agreement. The standard for the voluntariness of a guilty plea was developed by the Court in its cases involving plea bargaining, as discussed above.

Rule 11 does not expressly require an inquiry into the defendant's mental competency as part of the process of receiving the defendant's plea. But in order to make a meaningful choice to relinquish her right to a trial and plead guilty, the defendant must possess a certain level of mental competence. Moreover, due process prohibits conviction of a defendant who is incompetent.

It has been argued that the standard for competency to plead guilty should be higher than the standard of competency to stand trial. Competency to stand trial requires only that the defendant have "sufficient present ability to consult with his lawyer with a reasonable degree of rational understanding" and have "a rational as well as factual understanding of the proceedings against him." *Dusky v. U.S.*

(S.Ct.1960). Competency to plead guilty, it is argued, should require an ability to understand the rights being waived and an ability to make a reasoned choice between pleading guilty and going to trial. It is further argued that a higher standard is appropriate because, when the conviction is based on a guilty plea, the determination of guilt is based on the defendant's plea, rather than the verdict of a judge or jury.

In *Godinez v. Moran* (S.Ct.1993), however, the Court expressly rejected the contention that the standard of competency required for the entry of a valid guilty plea differs from the standard of competency required for a defendant to be tried. The decision to plead guilty, the Court reasoned, "is no more complicated than the sum of total of decisions that a defendant may be called upon to make during the course of the trial." Accordingly, the Court held that there is no basis for demanding a higher standard of competence for those defendants who choose to plead guilty.

3. DISCLOSURE AND/OR ACCEPTANCE OF THE PLEA AGREEMENT

As late as the 1960s, the practice of plea bargaining was largely unacknowledged and unregulated. Before plea bargaining was brought into the open, defendants routinely denied during the plea colloquy that they had been promised anything in return for their guilty plea, even though judge, prosecutor, and defense counsel all knew this to be false.

With a series of decisions beginning in the 1970s, the Supreme Court made clear that plea bargaining is not prohibited by the constitution, and established some constitutional parameters for the practice. Plea bargaining is now conducted openly, and plea agreements are generally subject to the scrutiny and approval of the court.

Rule 11(e) of the Federal Rules of Criminal Procedure requires that the existence of any plea agreement be disclosed to the court at the time the defendant enters her plea. The rule authorizes three types of plea agreements. In exchange for the defendant's plea of guilty or nolo contendere, the prosecutor may 1) move for dismissal of other charges; 2) agree that a specific sentence is appropriate; or 3) recommend a particular sentence or agree not to oppose a recommendation by the defense.

If the agreement is for dismissal of charges or for a specific sentence (Types 1 or 2), the court must decide whether to accept or reject the agreement of the parties. If the court accepts the agreement, the defendant must be informed that the disposition provided for in the plea agreement will be embodied in the judgment of conviction and sentence. If the court rejects the agreement, the defendant must be given the opportunity to withdraw her guilty plea, and must be informed that if she pleads guilty the sentence may be less favorable than that contemplated in the agreement. If the only agreement is for a recommendation of a particular sentence (Type 3), the defendant has no assurance that the ultimate disposition will conform to the recommendation, and the defendant does not have a right to withdraw the plea if the court declines to follow the recommendation.

The standards by which the judge is to decide whether to accept or reject a plea agreement are not well settled. In one often cited case, *U.S. v. Ammidown* (D.C.Cir.1972), the trial judge rejected a plea agreement which involved a reduction from first to second degree murder in exchange for the defendant's promise to cooperate in the prosecution of a co-defendant. The defendant was then tried and convicted on the first degree murder charge, and then appealed the conviction on the ground that the trial judge had improperly rejected the plea agreement.

In reversing the conviction and ordering reinstatement of the plea agreement, the appeals court defined a trial judge's authority to reject plea agreements involving charge reductions narrowly. The court held that, because the prosecutor rather than the judge has primary responsibility for charging decisions, the trial judge may not reject a charge agreement on the basis that the court's conception of the public interest differs from the prosecution. "The question is not what the judge would do if he were the prosecuting attorney, but whether he can say that the action of the prosecuting attorney is such a departure from sound prosecutorial principle as to mark it an abuse of prosecutorial discretion."

Some courts have defined the trial judge's authority to reject a proposed charge bargain more broadly than *Ammidown*. Moreover, the restrictive rule stated in *Ammidown* applies only to plea agreements that involve a reduction in the charge. Judges generally have greater authority to disapprove sentence agreements, since the sentencing authority belongs to the judge. It has been argued that applying different standards to judicial review of charge agreements and sentence agreements is unjustified, since a reduction in the charge is in many cases simply another way of ensuring a shorter sentence.

4. FACTUAL BASIS FOR A PLEA

Rule 11 requires the trial judge to determine that there is a factual basis for the defendant's guilty plea before entering judgment on the plea. The factual basis requirement helps ensure that the defendant is in fact guilty, and provides the judge with information about the offense that can be useful in imposing an appropriate sentence. Creating a record of the existence of a factual basis also discourages later efforts to challenge the plea.

The factual basis requirement is not intended as "proof" that the defendant committed the crime, and the information on which the court bases its determination need not satisfy the requirements for admissibility at trial. Typically the court bases its finding on information from the defendant, the prosecutor, or the pre-sentence report.

The requirement of a judicial determination of a factual basis for the plea is not constitutionally required except in one circumstance—when the defendant denies guilt but pleads guilty. In *N.C. v. Alford* (S.Ct.1970) the Court held that the constitution does not prohibit the acceptance of a guilty plea from a defendant who asserts that she is innocent of the charge, but stated that pleas coupled with claims of innocence should not be accepted unless there is a factual basis for the plea. The defendant in that case denied having committed the crime, but stated that he was pleading guilty to a reduced charge to avoid the possibility of a death sentence if he went to trial for first degree murder.

In upholding the defendant's plea, the Court observed that, as a constitutional matter, a guilty plea by a defendant who denies guilt is no different from a plea of nolo contendere, since both involve the defendant's consent to conviction and punishment without an admission of guilt. Although the Court did not specify what factual showing is required when the defendant offers to plead guilty while asserting innocence, the Court's emphasis on the "overwhelming" evidence of Alford's guilt has been interpreted to mean that a stronger factual basis is required when the defendant denies guilt than in other situations.

D. RESPECTING THE BARGAIN

The practice of plea bargaining inevitably gives rise to claims that the bargain has been broken.

The enforcement of plea agreements requires consideration of three questions: 1) what were the terms of the agreement; 2) has the agreement been breached; and 3) what is the appropriate remedy.

1. BREACHES BY THE PROSECUTOR

In *Santobello v. N.Y.* (S.Ct.1971) the Court held that the accused has a constitutional right to the enforcement of promises made by the prosecutor as part of a plea agreement. The defendant in *Santobello* agreed to plead guilty to a reduced charge in return for the prosecutor's promise to make no recommendation as to sentence. By the time of the sentencing hearing, the prosecutor who had negotiated the plea had been replaced. The prosecutor who appeared at the sentencing hearing was not aware of the plea agreement, and recommended the maximum allowable sentence, which the judge imposed. In response to the defendant's claim that the failure to abide by the plea agreement violated his constitutional rights, the Supreme Court held that "when a plea rests in any significant degree on a promise or agreement of the prosecutor, so that it can be said to be part of the inducement or consideration, such promise must be fulfilled."

It is occasionally difficult to determine whether the terms of a plea agreement have been violated. In *U.S. v. Benchimol* (S.Ct.1985) the defendant pleaded guilty pursuant to a plea agreement whereby the prosecutor agreed to recommend probation on the condition that the defendant make restitution. At sentencing defense counsel informed the judge that the pre-sentence report erroneously stated that the prosecution would stand silent, and that the prosecution in fact recommended a sentence of probation with restitution. The prosecutor responded to defense counsel's statement with the comment "that is an accurate representation."

The Court of Appeals held that the prosecution had breached the plea agreement because it did not explain its reasons for recommending a lenient sentence, but left the impression of less-than-enthusiastic support for leniency. The Supreme Court disagreed. While a defendant is free to bargain for an enthusiastic recommendation, the Court stated, no such promise had been made by the prosecutor, and the Court refused to read such a term into the bargain that was actually agreed upon. The Court suggested that a prosecutor would be in breach of the plea agreement if at the time of sentencing the prosecutor expressed personal reservations about the agreement to which the government had committed itself.

Plea agreements that involve charge reductions present fewer problems of interpretation than sentence agreements, since the prosecutor's promise to dismiss charges is typically carried out at the time the plea is entered.

In *Santobello* the Supreme Court declined to specify the appropriate remedy for a violation by the prosecutor of the plea agreement. Upon finding that the prosecutor's misstatement of the terms of the agreement constituted a breach, the Court remanded the case to the state court to decide whether the defendant should be entitled to 1) withdraw his guilty plea, or 2) specific performance of the bargain, which in Santobello's case would mean resentencing before a different judge based on an accurate statement of the plea agreement. In most cases the defendant would prefer specific performance. The Supreme Court has declined, however, to endorse a rule granting the defendant a choice of remedies.

a. Withdrawn Offers

The terms of a plea agreement become enforceable only after the defendant has pleaded guilty. The constitution does not prevent the prosecutor from withdrawing a plea *offer*, even after it has been accepted by the defendant, if the offer is withdrawn before the plea is entered.

In *Mabry v. Johnson* (S.Ct.1984) the defendant had already accepted the prosecutor's offer of a 21 year concurrent sentence when the prosecutor withdrew the offer as a "mistake." The defendant pled guilty pursuant to a less favorable agreement, then sought to compel the prosecutor to comply with the original offer. The Court held that a plea agreement, standing alone, is without constitutional significance, and gives rise to no right to enforcement by the defendant. Because the withdrawn offer did not in any way coerce the defendant's guilty plea, and the plea was otherwise voluntary and intelligent, it was valid.

Notwithstanding the Court's decision in *Mabry v. Johnson*, the defendant may be able to compel the prosecutor to comply with a withdrawn offer if the defendant has detrimentally relied on the offer by, for example, making a confession or foregoing possible challenges to the charge.

2.   BREACHES BY THE DEFENDANT

A defendant who fails to perform her obligations under a plea agreement may lose the benefit of the bargain. The Supreme Court applied that principle in *Ricketts v. Adamson* (S.Ct.1987) in concluding that the defendant's breach of the plea agreement authorized the prosecution to vacate the defendant's conviction under the plea agreement and try the defendant on the pre-plea charge.

The defendant in the case, Adamson, was permitted to plead guilty to second degree murder with a specified prison term in return for his promise to testify against his accomplices. The written plea agreement specified that, in the event the defendant refused to testify, the agreement would be null and void, the original first degree murder charges automatically reinstated, and the parties restored to the same position they were in before the agreement. Adamson entered the plea, was sentenced pursuant to the agreement, and testified against the accomplices, who were convicted of first degree murder.

When the conviction of the accomplices was reversed on appeal, however, Adamson informed the prosecutor that he would not to testify at the re-trial without further concessions, claiming that he had fulfilled his obligation under the plea agreement. The prosecutor then reinstated the first degree murder charges. Adamson challenged the reinstatement in state court as a violation of his double jeopardy rights, but the state supreme court held that Adamson breached the plea agreement by refusing to testify, and that this breach removed the double jeopardy bar to re-prosecution. At this point Adamson offered to testify against the accomplices, but the prosecutor refused the offer. Adamson was tried and convicted of first degree murder, and sentenced to death.

In the Supreme Court, Adamson argued that his double jeopardy rights were violated by his prosecution on the first degree murder charges because there had been no breach of the plea agreement that would remove the double jeopardy bar. He argued that he could not have breached the plea agreement when he expressed his intention not to testify, because at that point his obligations under the plea agreement had not yet been determined, since the state supreme court had not yet decided that the plea agreement required his testimony. He further argued that he did not breach the agreement after the state supreme court decided it obligated him to testify, since at that point he agreed to do so.

The Supreme Court rejected Adamson's arguments. The terms of the plea agreement, according to the Court, could not be clearer. Under the agreement, the defendant's failure to testify would return the parties to the position they were in before the agreement was reached. The consequence of restoring the status quo ante was that defendant could not complain of a *second* prosecution, since as the case stood before the agreement the defendant had not yet been subjected to a *first* prosecution.

E. CHALLENGING THE PLEA

It is not uncommon for a defendant to attempt to invalidate her guilty plea after the plea has been entered. Challenges to guilty pleas are of two basic types: challenges to the plea itself, such as a claim that the plea is not voluntary and intelligent; and challenges that are independent of the plea, such as a claim that the defendant's Sixth Amendment speedy trial right was violated, or that the grand jury that issued the indictment was selected through unlawful procedures.

There are three procedural mechanisms that may be used to attack the plea: 1) a motion to withdraw the plea that is filed in the trial court; 2) an appeal of the plea to an appellate court; or 3) a collateral attack or *habeas corpus* challenge in either a state or federal trial court. The degree of difficulty faced by a defendant seeking to abrogate her plea may depend on which of these mechanisms is used.

1. WITHDRAWAL OF THE PLEA

As discussed in Section C3 above, a federal defendant may automatically withdraw her guilty plea if the judge rejects a plea bargain that involves a dismissal of charges or a specific sentence. After the plea has been accepted, withdrawal is permitted only if the motion to withdraw is filed before sentencing, and only if certain conditions are satisfied.

Under Federal Rule of Criminal Procedure 32(d), withdrawal is permitted upon a showing of "any fair and just reason" why the plea should be withdrawn. In determining whether this standard has been met, the court should consider both the grounds asserted by the defendant for withdrawal and the prejudice to the prosecution if withdrawal is permitted.

Many states permit a motion to withdraw a guilty plea to be filed either before or after sentencing. Typically, however, a defendant who moves to withdraw her plea after sentencing must show that denial of the motion would result in a "manifest injustice," a more demanding test than the "fair and just reason" test applied to pre-sentence withdrawals.

2. CHALLENGES TO THE VALIDITY OF THE PLEA

A commonly asserted basis for challenging the validity of the plea is a claim that the judge who accepted the plea did not fully comply with the requirements for receiving the plea. The defendant's chances of succeeding with such a challenge may depend on whether the claim is made on direct appeal or in a collateral *habeas corpus* proceeding.

In *McCarthy v. U.S.* (S.Ct.1969) the Supreme Court held that a federal defendant attacking his plea on direct appeal for non-compliance with Rule 11 is entitled to a reversal without the necessity of showing that he was prejudiced by the error. The defendant in *McCarthy* appealed his conviction on the ground that the judge who received his guilty plea did not address the defendant personally to determine that his plea was voluntary and intelligent as required by Rule 11. In support of its automatic reversal rule, the Court noted that Rule 11 is designed to facilitate a more accurate determination of the voluntariness of the plea, and that meticulous adherence to Rule 11 will prevent the waste of judicial resources required to process frivolous post-conviction attacks on guilty pleas.

After *McCarthy* was decided, however, Rule 11 was amended to include a harmless error provision. Section 11(h) of the Rule now provides that "any variance from the procedures required by this rule which do not affect substantial rights shall be disregarded." Under this harmless error approach, a violation of the rule will not result in invalidation of the plea if it could not have affected the defendant's decision to plead guilty.

A federal defendant claiming a violation of Rule 11 in a federal habeas corpus proceeding must show considerably more prejudice than is required in a motion to withdraw or on direct appeal. To succeed in a habeas corpus proceeding, a federal defendant must show that the error resulted in a "complete miscarriage of justice" or in a proceeding "inconsistent with the rudimentary demands of fair procedure." Thus, in *U.S. v. Timmreck* (S.Ct.1979) the Court held that the trial judge's failure to inform the defendant of a special parole term that had the effect of adding five years to his sentence did not entitle the defendant to reversal of his plea in the habeas corpus proceeding.

3. EFFECT OF THE PLEA ON ASSERTION OF OTHER RIGHTS

The Supreme Court has held that the entry of a guilty plea forecloses the defendant from asserting in federal court many constitutional challenges to the conviction that do not involve an attack on the plea itself. For example, in *Tollett v. Henderson* (S.Ct.1973) the defendant attacked his murder conviction, which was based on his plea of guilty, on the grounds that the grand jury that indicted him was selected in a racially discriminatory manner in violation of the constitution. The Supreme Court held that an error in the selection of the grand jury, even if proven, is not a basis for invalidating the conviction. The Court stated that a guilty plea represents "a break in the chain of events which has preceded it in the criminal process," and that a defendant who has admitted guilt "may not thereafter raise independent claims relating to the deprivation of constitutional rights that occurred prior to the entry of the plea."

The principle stated in *Henderson* does not bar all prior constitutional claims. First, the Supreme

Court has held that some types of constitutional challenges survive the defendant's guilty plea, though the Court has not specified precisely which claims fall into this category. One type of challenge which can be asserted notwithstanding a plea of guilty is a due process claim of vindictive prosecution. *Blackledge v. Perry* (S.Ct.1974).

In *Blackledge*, where this was decided, the defendant was initially charged with misdemeanor assault based on a prison altercation. Under applicable state procedure, such crimes were tried before a judge without a jury, but, if convicted, the defendant had an absolute right to a trial *de novo* in another court. The defendant was convicted of the misdemeanor, and gave notice of his intention to exercise his right to a re-trial. Before the re-trial, however, the prosecutor obtained a felony indictment against the defendant for the same conduct covered in the misdemeanor charge. The defendant pled guilty to the felony, then challenged his conviction as a violation of his due process right against vindictive prosecution, claiming that he was being punished for exercising his right to appeal.

The Supreme Court agreed with the defendant that his prosecution for the felony was unconstitutionally vindictive, and rejected the state's argument that the defendant was foreclosed from asserting that claim under the principle of *Tollett v. Henderson*. The Court reasoned that, unlike the jury selection claim in *Henderson*, the vindictive prosecution claim established in *Perry* "went to the very power of the State to bring the defendant into court to answer the charge." And whereas the jury selection violation in *Henderson* could be "cured" through a new indictment by a properly selected grand jury, that was not true of the vindictive prosecution violation, since the very initiation of the felony charge operated to deny the defendant due process.

A second type of challenge that has been held to survive the defendant's plea of guilty is a claim that the conviction violates the defendant's rights under the Double Jeopardy Clause of the Fifth Amendment. In *Menna v. N.Y.* (S.Ct.1975) the defendant was indicted for the crime of refusing to answer questions before a grand jury after having already served a 30 day jail sentence under a contempt of court adjudication for the same conduct. The defendant pled guilty to the indictment, and then challenged the conviction as a violation of double jeopardy. The Court held that the defendant's double jeopardy claim was not barred by his plea of guilty.

The Court in *Menna* suggested that the test for whether a claim is forfeit by a guilty plea depends on whether the claim involves a challenge to the defendant's "factual guilt." The defendant's guilty plea, according to the Court, "renders irrelevant those constitutional violations not logically inconsistent with the valid establishment of factual guilt," but does not bar assertion of claims that would prevent conviction regardless of the state's ability to establish the defendant's guilt.

However, this test has been criticized as inconsistent with the result in *Henderson*, since the defendant's jury selection claim in that case was barred even though violation of grand jury selection procedures would prevent conviction regardless of the state's ability to prove the defendant's guilt at trial. The distinction stated in *Perry* between errors that can be cured and those that cannot provides a better basis for distinguishing claims that are forfeit and those that are not. A double jeopardy violation, like a vindictive prosecution, cannot be remedied by the state, but stands as an absolute bar to prosecution, and therefore generally survives the defendant's guilty plea.

In *U.S. v. Broce* (S.Ct.1989) the Court added a qualification to the rule that double jeopardy claims survive the defendant's guilty plea and can be asserted in a federal *habeas corpus* proceeding. The defendants in *Broce* pleaded guilty to two counts of conspiracy. In a post-conviction *habeas corpus* proceeding, the defendants introduced evidence showing that the two conspiracies were actually part of a single larger conspiracy, and argued that they therefore had been twice convicted for what was in fact one offense in violation of the Double Jeopardy Clause. The Supreme Court held that, notwithstanding *Menna*, the defendants' guilty pleas barred them from asserting their double jeopardy claim in a collateral proceeding. The critical difference for the Court between *Menna* and *Broce* was that proof of the double jeopardy violation in *Broce* necessitated consideration of evidence outside the record of the plea proceeding. Because the defendants pled guilty to indictments that, on their face, described separate conspiracies, they could not thereafter seek to show that the facts established a single conspiracy. How far the *Broce* rule applies to other incurable constitutional claims is unclear.

Although most types of antecedent constitutional claims are forfeit by the defendant's plea of guilty, the defendant may nonetheless be able to raise a barred constitutional claim in an indirect fashion by claiming ineffective assistance of counsel. Instead of arguing that the prior claim invalidates her conviction, the defendant argues that her conviction is invalid because her attorney's failure to raise the claim amounted to ineffective assistance. In order to succeed with such course, the defendant must satisfy the two prong test established in *Strickland v. Washington* and applied to the plea bargaining context in *Hill v. Lockhart*.

4. CONDITIONAL PLEAS

The rule that the defendant forfeits most antecedent constitutional claims by pleading guilty may cause some defendants who would otherwise plead guilty to go to trial for the sole purpose of preserving their constitutional claim. This is because, under the forfeiture principle of *Henderson*, insisting on a trial may be the only way the defendant can obtain appellate review of her claim, since the final judgment rule generally prevents the defendant from taking an interlocutory appeal. For example, a defendant charged with a drug crime, who has little hope of successfully contesting the prosecution's proof that she possessed drugs, may nonetheless go to trial as the only way of obtaining appellate review of the denial of her motion to suppress the drugs as the tainted fruit of an unlawful search and seizure.

In order to avoid unnecessary trials, the federal system and many states allow the defendant to enter a conditional plea of guilty. Under Federal Rule of Criminal Procedure 11(a)(2), a defendant may, with the approval of the court and consent of the prosecutor, enter a conditional plea of guilty or nolo contendere, reserving in writing the right to appellate review of the adverse determination of any specified pre-trial motion. The defendant's constitutional claim is then heard on appeal from the judgment of conviction entered on the guilty plea. If the defendant prevails on appeal and the earlier determination of the pre-trial motion is overturned, the defendant is permitted to withdraw the plea.

CHAPTER 11

ASSISTANCE OF COUNSEL

A. RIGHT TO COUNSEL

The Sixth Amendment provides that "in all criminal prosecutions, the accused shall enjoy the right ... to have the assistance of counsel for his defense." It has always been understood that this provision guarantees that a person accused of a crime has the right to secure legal representation by hiring a lawyer. For many years it was not clear, however, whether or to what extent the constitution requires the government to provide a lawyer to an indigent defendant who cannot afford to pay for one.

The Supreme Court first recognized an indigent defendant's constitutional right to appointed counsel in a state criminal prosecution in *Powell v. Alabama* (S.Ct.1932). The right to counsel recognized in *Powell* was based on the Due Process Clause of the Fourteenth Amendment, and applied only to defendants on trial for capital crimes.

Three decades later, in *Gideon v. Wainwright* (S.Ct.1963), the Court held that an indigent defendant has a constitutional right to appointed counsel under the Sixth Amendment. The Court declared that, "in our adversary system of criminal justice, any person haled into court, who is too poor to hire a lawyer, cannot be assured a fair trial unless counsel is provided for him." Observing that both state and federal governments "spend vast sums of money to establish machinery to try defendants accused of crime," and that lawyers are everywhere deemed essential to the prosecution, the Court concluded that "lawyers in criminal courts are necessities, not luxuries."

The Court's opinion in *Gideon* suggested that the right of an indigent defendant to appointed counsel applies whenever the defendant is charged with a felony. In subsequent decisions, however, the Court has made clear that the state is required to provide the defendant with an attorney only if the charges result in actual imprisonment. Because the entitlement to appointed counsel depends on the sentence actually imposed, rather than the penalty authorized by law, the decision whether to provide the accused with a lawyer will limit the court's sentencing options in the event of a conviction.

The Sixth Amendment right to counsel, which applies to "criminal *prosecutions*," does not attach until a person has been formally charged with a crime. For that reason, a person who is the target of a grand jury investigation does not have a right to counsel under the Sixth Amendment. There is also no constitutional right to counsel at a bail hearing. The defendant does, however, have a right to an attorney at the time the defendant is required to enter a plea at arraignment.

As discussed more fully elsewhere, both the preliminary hearing (see Chapter 3) and sentencing (see Chapter 14) are considered "critical stages" of the prosecution for purposes of the Sixth Amendment, and counsel is therefore required. Although the Sixth Amendment is not applicable to the appellate process, the Supreme Court has held that the Due Process and Equal Protection Clauses guarantee a right to counsel in any first appeal as of right. (See Chapter 15.) There is no right to counsel for a second, discretionary appeal. Nor does the defendant have a constitutional right to counsel when attacking the conviction through a collateral proceeding, such as a *habeas corpus* proceeding.

B. WAIVER OF COUNSEL

A defendant may waive her right to be represented by an attorney, but in order for the waiver to be valid it must be "knowing, intelligent, and voluntary." The requirement that the waiver of the right to counsel be knowing has been interpreted to require that the defendant be informed of the right and make an explicit waiver. A waiver will not be inferred from the defendant's silence or from circumstantial evidence. In order for the waiver to be intelligent, it must be shown that the defendant was made aware of what the assistance of counsel entails, and then made a deliberate choice to forego that assistance. Because of the strong presumption against waiver, the judge must undertake a thorough inquiry into the defendant's background and the circumstances of the case before the waiver should be accepted. A decision by the defendant to waive counsel during one stage of the proceeding, the preliminary hearing, for example, does not necessarily result in a waiver of counsel during later stages.

1.   RIGHT TO SELF REPRESENTATION

In *Faretta v. California* (S.Ct.1975) the Supreme Court held that a defendant cannot be *required* to be represented by an attorney. The trial judge in that case initially granted Faretta's request to defend himself, but later reversed that decision and required Faretta to accept the services of a public defender. The defendant appealed his subsequent conviction, claiming that the constitution guaranteed him a right to conduct his own defense.

In upholding Faretta's right to self-representation, the Court relied on the language of the Sixth Amendment, which speaks of a right to "assistance" of counsel, rather than a right to representation by counsel, and English and colonial history, which had recognized a right of the accused to self-representation. The Court acknowledged that recognizing a right to proceed *pro se* is inconsistent with other Sixth Amendment cases stressing that lawyers are indispensable to assuring a fair trial. The Court concluded, however, that the state cannot force counsel on an unwilling defendant. "[A]lthough [the accused] may conduct his defense ultimately to his own detriment, his choice must be honored."

In order to waive counsel and proceed *pro se*, a defendant must possess the level of competency necessary to stand trial, but need not demonstrate an ability to conduct an effective defense. Before accepting a defendant's waiver of counsel and decision to represent herself, the trial judge should make the defendant aware of the dangers and disadvantages of dispensing with the assistance of an attorney. A wrongful denial of the defendant's request to proceed *pro se* is not subject to harmless error analysis; the defendant in such a case is entitled to an automatic reversal. A defendant who elects to represent herself and is convicted cannot thereafter claim that she was denied effective assistance of counsel. Grounds for denying a request to proceed without counsel include when the (1) request is so disruptive of orderly schedule of proceedings as to justify rejection, (2) defendant engages in serious and obstructionist misconduct, or (3) defendant is unable to reach level of appreciation needed for knowing and intelligent waiver.

2. STANDBY COUNSEL

In *Faretta* the Court stated that the trial judge may appoint "standby counsel," even over the defendant's objection, to assist when the defendant requests help. In the subsequent case of *McKaskle v. Wiggins* (S.Ct.1984) the Court held that standby counsel's participation in the trial without a specific request from the defendant does not invariably violate the defendant's right to self-representation. Unsolicited participation by standby counsel does not violate the defendant's right of self representation provided that, 1) the defendant is not deprived of "actual control over the case he chooses to present to the jury," and 2) "participation by standby counsel without the defendant's consent should not be allowed to destroy the jury's perception that the defendant is representing himself."

C. CHOICE OF COUNSEL

A defendant who hires an attorney has a right to choose who that attorney shall be. The right of a non-indigent defendant to counsel of her own choosing is not, however, unlimited. A defendant does not have a right to be represented by an attorney who has a conflict of interest, even if the defendant prefers the risks of an attorney with potentially conflicting loyalties over other alternatives. In addition, the Court has held that a defendant's Sixth Amendment right to counsel is not violated by the government's use of forfeiture statutes to confiscate assets that might be used to hire a lawyer. The Court has reasoned that, while such forfeitures may limit the defendant's ability to hire the attorney of choice, the right to choose one's attorney does not include the right to an attorney paid for from assets lawfully acquired by the government.

The constitution guarantees an indigent defendant a right to competent counsel, but apparently does not guarantee a right to counsel of choice. In *Morris v. Slappy* (S.Ct.1983) the defendant was assigned a new public defender when the first attorney assigned to represent him was hospitalized. The trial judge denied the defendant's request for a continuance to permit the first attorney to return to the case, and the defendant proceeded to trial with the replacement. The Court of Appeals reversed the defendant's subsequent conviction on the ground that the denial of the continuance deprived the defendant of "a meaningful attorney-client relationship," but the Supreme Court reversed the Court of Appeals. The Court stated that "[n]o court could possibly guarantee the kind of rapport with his attorney—privately retained or provided by the public—that the Court of Appeals thought part of the Sixth Amendment guarantee of counsel."

D. EFFECTIVE ASSISTANCE OF COUNSEL

The Supreme Court has held that the constitution guarantees not simply a right to counsel but a right to the assistance of counsel that is in some measure "effective." This right to effective assistance of counsel extends to the plea negotiation process, the trial, capital sentencing proceedings, and a first appeal as of right. The right is equally applicable to retained and appointed counsel. Because the right to effective assistance of counsel fulfils the constitutional right to counsel, the right to legal representation that is effective applies only in those situations in which the constitution guarantees a right to an attorney.

In its cases discussing what the guarantee of effective assistance of counsel requires, the Court has identified three different ways the right can be violated. First, in *Strickland v. Washington* (S.Ct. 1984) the Court defined the standards for determining when an attorney's performance in representing the client results in "actual" ineffective assistance of counsel. Second, a defendant can be deprived of effective assistance of counsel as a result of certain types of interference with the attorney's representation of the client. And third, a defendant may be denied effective assistance of counsel if the attorney is working under a conflict of interest.

1. THE STRICKLAND RULE

It was not until 1984 in the case of *Strickland v. Washington* that the Supreme Court first definitively set forth the standards for when an attorney's representation is so deficient as to deny the defendant effective assistance of counsel. The Court began by declaring that "[t]he benchmark for judging any claim of ineffectiveness must be whether counsel's conduct so undermined the proper functioning of the adversarial process that the trial cannot be relied on as having produced a just result."

The Court then established a two prong test for determining when this has occurred. In order to establish constitutional ineffective assistance of counsel the defendant must show, first, that the attorney's performance in representing the defendant was constitutionally deficient, and second, that the defendant was prejudiced as a result of the attorney's errors or omissions. In order to establish a deprivation of effective assistance of counsel, the defendant must satisfy both prongs of the test. That is, the defendant must show both that counsel's performance was deficient, and that she was prejudiced by those deficiencies. The Court's opinion in *Strickland* emphasized, and later cases have confirmed, that the requirements for demonstrating ineffective assistance of counsel are demanding, and the defendant must overcome a strong presumption that counsel's performance was within the range of competent representation in order to prevail.

a. The Performance Standard

The first prong of an ineffective assistance of counsel claim—the performance prong—requires the defendant to demonstrate "that counsel made errors so serious that counsel was not functioning as the 'counsel' guaranteed by the Sixth Amendment." In defining what this standard means, the Court expressly declined to adopt specific guidelines or requirements for measuring counsel's performance. The Court stated that "[n]o particular set of detailed rules for counsel's conduct can satisfactorily take account of the variety of circumstances faced by defense counsel or the range of legitimate decisions regarding how best to represent a criminal defendant."

In addition, requiring counsel's representation to conform to some set of rules or guidelines might interfere with counsel's independence, and distract the attorney from the mission of vigorous advocacy of the client's cause. The Court held instead that the Sixth Amendment right must be judged based on the reasonableness of counsel's performance under prevailing professional norms. In order to establish ineffective assistance of counsel, the defendant must show "that counsel's representation fell below an objective standard of reasonableness." The court considering an ineffective assistance of counsel claim must determine whether, "in light of all the circumstances, [the attorney's] acts or omissions were outside the range of professionally competent assistance."

In evaluating whether an attorney's performance is deficient, the reviewing court is to "indulge a strong presumption that counsel's conduct falls within the wide range of reasonable professional assistance." This means that "the defendant must overcome the presumption that, under the circumstances, the challenged action 'might be considered sound trial strategy,' " rather than attorney error.

The facts in *Strickland* illustrate the application of the performance prong of the test. The defendant claimed that he was denied effective assistance of counsel at his capital sentencing hearing. The sentencing hearing followed the defendant's guilty plea, entered against the attorney's advice, to three counts of capital murder and other crimes. At the plea proceeding, the defendant admitted to a string of burglaries, but stated that he had no significant prior criminal record, and that he accepted responsibility for his crimes. In response, the judge said that he had "a great deal of respect" for people who admit responsibility, but that he was making no statement about his likely sentencing decision.

In his *habeas corpus* petition to set aside the death sentence, the defendant alleged various deficiencies in the attorney's preparation for and conduct of the sentencing hearing. Specifically, the defendant claimed his attorney was ineffective because he failed to request either a presentence report or a psychiatric report, to investigate and present character witnesses, to present "meaningful arguments" to the sentencing judge, or to investigate the medical examiner's reports or cross-examine the medical experts.

The Court held that the attorney's performance was not unreasonable, and that the defendant therefore failed to satisfy the first prong of the test. Defense counsel's strategy for avoiding a death sentence, according to the Court, was to rely as fully as possible on the defendant's statements accepting responsibility for the crimes at the plea colloquy, together with the sentencing judge's reputation for attaching significance to an acceptance of responsibility, and to argue that the defendant committed the crimes under extreme emotional disturbance, which qualified as a mitigating circumstance that could avoid imposition of a death sentence.

When viewed from this perspective, the attorney's alleged deficiencies appeared as reasonable strategy choices, rather than errors or neglect. Based on his conversations with the defendant, it was reasonable for defense counsel to conclude that character and psychological evidence would be of little value. The basic facts about the defendant's financial and emotional troubles had been mentioned at the plea colloquy, and relying on the evidence of the defendant's character already presented at the plea proceeding had the advantage of avoiding potentially harmful cross examination. Defense counsel did not request a pre-sentence report, according to the Court, because it would have revealed that the defendant's criminal history was more extensive than appeared from the plea proceedings. Thus, even without applying the presumption of adequate representation, the Court stated, there was "little question ... that trial counsel's defense, though unsuccessful, was the result of reasonable professional judgment."

Kimmelman v. Morrison (S.Ct.1986) provides an example of attorney conduct that was found to be constitutionally deficient. The ineffective assistance claim was based on the attorney's failure to file a motion to suppress evidence within the statutory deadline, which resulted in the court's refusal to address the merits of the claim. The attorney sought to excuse his neglect by claiming that he was unaware that the evidence had been seized. The Supreme Court concluded, however, that the attorney's failure to obtain discovery of the evidence could not be explained as a reasonable strategic decision, but reflected a "startling ignorance" of the law, and placed his conduct outside of prevailing professional norms.

b. The Prejudice Requirement

Errors or omissions by an attorney, however serious, do not constitute ineffective assistance of counsel unless the client suffered "prejudice" as a result of the attorney's deficient performance. Prejudice in this context refers to an actual impairment of the defendant's chances of achieving a favorable outcome.

To demonstrate prejudice constituting ineffective assistance of counsel, the defendant must show that "there is a reasonable probability that, but for counsel's unprofessional errors, the result of the proceeding would have been different." This is the same test that the Court subsequently established for demonstrating the materiality of exculpatory evidence that triggers a requirement of disclosure to the defense under the Due Process Clause. As the Court emphasized in applying this standard to discovery claims, a "reasonable probability" of a different outcome does not mean that it must be shown that the outcome would probably have been different. *Kyles v. Whitley* (S.Ct.1995). Rather, according to the Court in *Strickland*, "[a] reasonable probability is a probability sufficient to undermine confidence in the outcome."

Hill v. Lockhart (S.Ct.1985), discussed in Chapter 10, involved a denial of an ineffective assistance claim for failure to demonstrate prejudice. The defendant in that case claimed that his attorney provided inadequate advice regarding his guilty plea because the attorney did not inform the defendant that under state law he would be required to serve one-half of his sentence before becoming eligible for parole. The Court held that it was not necessary to decide whether a failure to inform the client of this requirement was unreasonable, since the defendant had not alleged that he would not have pleaded guilty even if the information had been provided.

There is some uncertainty whether a defendant has suffered the kind of prejudice required to establish ineffective assistance of counsel if the attorney's errors or omissions create a reasonable likelihood of a different outcome, but do not call into question the reliability or fairness of the trial in determining guilt or innocence. That issue was presented, but not necessarily settled, in *Kimmelman v. Morrison* (S.Ct.1986). The error in that case involved the attorney's unexcused failure to seek suppression of evidence alleged to have been obtained in violation of the Fourth Amendment right against unreasonable search and seizure. After determining that the attorney's performance was constitutionally deficient, the Supreme Court remanded the case for a determination of whether the defendant was prejudiced by the attorney's error. In its remand, the Supreme Court instructed the lower court to determine whether the Fourth Amendment claim had merit, and, if so, whether exclusion of the improperly obtained evidence would have affected

the result. This approach to the prejudice requirement suggests prejudice exists even if the attorney's
incompetent representation did not undermine the
reliability of the trial in determining guilt or innocence. For while a successful motion to exclude the
evidence in *Kimmelman* might have resulted in the
defendant's acquittal, the conviction that actually
resulted was not necessarily rendered unreliable by
the admission of the evidence, since the evidence,
even if subject to suppression, was logically probative of the defendant's guilt.

A differently composed majority of the Court suggested a different interpretation of the prejudice
requirement in *Lockhart v. Fretwell* (S.Ct.1993),
though the unusual facts of that case raise questions as to its applicability to other circumstances.
The ineffective assistance claim in that case was
based on the attorney's failure at the defendant's
capital sentencing hearing to object to the state's
attempt to secure a death sentence by proving as an
aggravating circumstance a fact that duplicated an
element of the offense. Under the prevailing interpretation of capital sentencing law at the time of
the sentencing hearing, reliance for capital sentencing purposes on a fact that duplicated an essential
element was improper, and an objection to the
state's submission of that fact as an aggravating
circumstance would probably have been sustained.
The interpretation of the law changed, however, as
a result of a Supreme Court decision rendered *after*
the defendant was sentenced to death. Under the
law as it existed *at the time the defendant chal-*

lenged his death sentence, the use of an aggravating circumstance that duplicated an element of the offense was proper. Thus, as the Supreme Court perceived the issue, the question in *Lockhart* was whether a defendant is prejudiced by attorney error which, though creating a reasonable probability of a different outcome, does not place the reliability or fairness of that outcome in doubt.

The Supreme Court held that the defendant in *Lockhart v. Fretwell* was not prejudiced by his attorney's failure to raise an objection which, though valid at the time of the sentencing hearing, did not result in an unreliable sentencing decision judged according to the law at the time the attorney's conduct was challenged. The Court stated that an analysis of the question of prejudice that focuses "solely on mere outcome determination, without attention to whether the result of the proceeding was fundamentally unfair or unreliable, is defective." And in language intimating that the approach in *Lockhart* may be applied outside the narrow context of that case, the Court stated that "[t]o set aside a conviction or sentence solely because the outcome would have been different but for counsel's error may grant the defendant a windfall to which the law does not entitle him."

Two cases since *Lockhart* are noteworthy. First, is *Glover v. United States* (S.Ct.2001) where the Court held that trial counsel's failure to argue for defendant's sentencing structure under the guidelines in a proper and effective manner, causing a sentence imposition of 6 to 21 months more than deserved, constituted prejudice under the first prong of *Strickland*. The second case is *Bell v. Cone* (S.Ct. 2002) is a complex case in which the defendant, convicted in state court of brutal murders, was sentenced to death. His state court appeals of his conviction and sentence failed and he filed a federal writ of *habeas corpus*, which was granted by a federal appeals court. The basis for the defendant's claim of ineffective assistance of counsel was that defense counsel made decisions leading to a failure to rebut state evidence and argument at the death penalty phase, which defendant claimed prejudiced him. The Supreme Court applied the *Strickland* test for prejudice and rejected the *Cronic* presumption of prejudice standard (see the next section). Moreover, the Court reversed the grant of the writ, finding that the application of *Strickland* was proper and not inconsistent with established federal law as required by the Antiterrorism and Death Penalty Act's amendments to the federal *habeas corpus* statute.

2. STATE INTERFERENCE WITH REPRESENTATION

The approach to ineffective assistance of counsel claims set forth in *Strickland v. Washington*, which requires a showing of both inadequate representation and prejudice to the accused, is premised on the view that "the right to effective assistance of counsel is recognized not for its own sake, but because of the effect it has on the ability of the accused to receive a fair trial." *U.S. v. Cronic* (S.Ct. 1984). The Supreme Court has also recognized, however, that there are some circumstances in which the likelihood that the defendant was deprived of effective assistance of counsel is so great that a denial of the right will be found without any inquiry into the attorney's actual performance or possible prejudice to the accused that resulted.

The Supreme Court's fullest statement of the principles that govern when a denial of effective assistance of counsel will be presumed is *U.S. v. Cronic* (S.Ct.1984). The defendant in *Cronic* claimed that he was denied effective assistance of counsel because the attorney assigned to represent him on charges arising out of a complicated "check kiting" scheme had been assigned to the case just 25 days before the trial began, and was a real estate lawyer who had never before tried a criminal case. The defendant did not allege any specific errors or omissions in the attorney's preparation for or conduct of the trial, but argued instead that the circumstances of counsel's appointment compelled the conclusion that the representation he received was deficient.

The Court began its analysis by stating that the Sixth Amendment right to effective assistance of counsel is generally not implicated in the absence of some effect of counsel's representation on the reliability of the trial process. The Court acknowledged, however, that there are "circumstances that are so likely to prejudice the accused that the cost of litigating their effect in a particular case is unjustified," and prejudice is therefore presumed. Most obviously, a defendant need not demonstrate prejudice when there has been a complete denial of counsel. Short of that, there are circumstances when, "although counsel is available to assist the accused during trial, the likelihood that any lawyer ... could provide effective representation is so small that a presumption of prejudice is appropriate." As an example of such a circumstance, the Court cited *Powell v. Alabama* (S.Ct.1932) where, six days before trial, the judge purported to appoint "all the members of the bar" to represent a group of young black defendants charged with a capital crime. On the day the trial was to begin, a lawyer from another jurisdiction appeared on behalf of persons "interested" in the defendants.

The Court in *Powell* held that "such designation of counsel ... was either so indefinite or close upon the trial as to amount to a denial of effective and substantial aid in that regard." However, the Court in *Cronic* also cited another case in which the defendant was not deprived of effective assistance of counsel, even though the attorney had been assigned to try the capital case just three days before the trial began. *Avery v. Alabama* (1940).

The *Cronic* Court also observed that in another case it had refused to create a *per se* rule requiring reversal because of late appointment of counsel. It is only "when the surrounding circumstances justify a presumption of ineffectiveness can a Sixth Amendment claim be sufficient without inquiry into counsel's actual performance at trial." Because the facts in *Cronic* did not warrant such a presumption, the defendant's ineffective assistance claim was denied.

The Supreme Court has on several occasions found a denial of effective assistance of counsel without a demonstration of actual prejudice based, not on the circumstances of appointment of counsel, but on interference with the attorney's conduct of the defense. In its opinion in *Strickland v. Washington*, the Court mentioned several such cases, including *Geders v. U.S.* (S.Ct.1976), which involved a ban on attorney-client consultation during an overnight recess; *Herring v. N.Y.* (S.Ct.1975) in which the attorney was not allowed to present a summation at a bench trial; *Brooks v. Tennessee* (S.Ct.1972) involving a state requirement that a defendant wishing to testify must do so before any other defense witnesses; and *Ferguson v. Georgia* (S.Ct.1961) which involved a rule limiting the defendant to presenting an unsworn statement to the jury, and therefore prevented counsel from conducting direct examination of the client.

Bell v. Cone (S.Ct.2002), discussed in the prior section, must be considered again here. The Court, in *Cone*, warned against expansion of the *Cronic* exception. A presumption of prejudice was permissible, the Court noted, only where the "failure is complete," and not where counsel simply failed to take particular steps (important though they might well be) in challenging the prosecution's case. Because counsel had challenged the state's case in some respects, the claims that the attorney did not do specific things, such as present a closing argument, constituted no more than claims of "specific attorney error," which were "subject to Strickland's performance and prejudice components."

3. ATTORNEY CONFLICT OF INTEREST

An attorney has an ethical obligation of loyalty to her client. A conflict of interest that compromises the attorney's duty of loyalty can interfere with the representation provided by the attorney, and in some circumstances constitutes ineffective assistance of counsel within the meaning of the Sixth Amendment.

Conflicts of interest can arise for a variety of reasons, but the circumstance that has been addressed most fully in judicial decisions dealing with the right to effective assistance of counsel is that in which one attorney or one firm represents multiple clients.

The test for whether a defendant has been deprived of effective assistance of counsel because of attorney conflict of interest has two parts. *Cuyler v. Sullivan* (S.Ct.1980). First, the defendant must show that the attorney was operating under an actual conflict of interest. Second, the defendant must show that this conflict adversely affected the attorney's performance. The defendant is not required to establish that she suffered prejudice as a result of the effect that the conflict had on the attorney's representation.

The facts of *Glasser v. U.S.* (S.Ct.1942) illustrate the application of this test. The Court in *Glasser* found that an attorney's representation of two co-defendants in a single trial deprived defendant Glasser of effective assistance of counsel because the attorney declined to cross-examine a key government witness, and did not challenge potentially inadmissible evidence. The attorney's apparent reason for not taking these steps was to minimize the jury's perception of the co-defendant's guilt.

In addition to defining the requirements for ineffective assistance based on conflicts of interest, the Supreme Court has also held that in some circumstances the trial judge has a constitutional duty to inquire into possible conflicts of interest before the trial begins. Whenever an attorney representing multiple clients makes a timely pretrial objection to joint representation, the trial judge must either, 1) appoint separate counsel for the defendants, or 2) conduct an inquiry sufficient to ensure that the risk of actual conflict of interest is "too remote to warrant separate counsel." *Holloway v. Arkansas* (S.Ct. 1978). Failure to follow these procedures constitutes a deprivation of the right to counsel requiring an automatic reversal.

The Supreme Court has held that a trial judge is not required to undertake a *sua sponte* inquiry into possible conflict of interest in all cases of multiple representation. Relying on the ethical obligation of lawyers to avoid conflicts of interest and to inform the judge if one arises, the Supreme Court has held that, where the attorney has not raised an objection, the trial judge may assume "either that multiple representation entails no conflict or that the lawyer and his clients knowingly accept such a risk of conflict as may exist." *Cuyler v. Sullivan* (S.Ct. 1980)

E. THE ROLE OF APPOINTED COUNSEL

Defense counsel sometimes file a timely notice of appeal, but then decide after studying the trial record that there are no non-frivolous claims worth presenting to the appellate court. This situation poses no special difficulty if the attorney is hired and paid by the client; the attorney simply withdraws from representing the client, who is then free to retain a different lawyer if she wishes. But switching lawyers is not an option for an indigent defendant, who is represented by an attorney appointed by the government.

As a protection to the indigent defendant against the risk that appointed defense counsel will overlook or forego meritorious appellate issues, the Supreme Court held in *Anders v. California* (S.Ct. 1967) that appellate counsel seeking to withdraw from the case on the grounds that there is nothing worth appealing must file a brief (called an *Anders* brief) with the appellate court that refers to anything in the record "that might arguably support an appeal." The defendant must be given an opportunity to add to this brief, and counsel will be permitted to withdraw only after the appeals court decides that an appeal would be "wholly frivolous."

In two cases decided after *Anders* the Supreme Court approved state procedures different from those at issue in the *Anders* case. In *McCoy v. Court of Appeals of Wisconsin* (S.Ct.1988) the Court considered the constitutionality of a state procedure that required appointed counsel to include in a no-merit brief an explanation of *why* the issues that might be raised on appeal lack merit. The Court rejected an argument that this requirement forced counsel to violate her ethical obligations to the defendant by requiring defense counsel to take a position in opposition to the attorney's client. The Court held instead that the explanation required by the Wisconsin procedure furthered the basic purpose of the *Anders* rule by encouraging a careful consideration of the issues.

In its most recent decision on the obligations of appointed counsel in cases lacking meritorious appellate claims the Court approved procedures that fell short of those required in *Anders*. In *Smith v. Robbins* (S.Ct.2000) the Court rejected a challenge to a California procedure (called the *Wende* procedure) that did not require either an explicit statement from counsel that the appeal lacks merit or a brief identifying issues that might arguably support an appeal. Instead, upon concluding that an appeal would be frivolous, counsel is required to file a brief with the appellate court summarizing the procedural and factual history of the case, including citations to the record. Counsel must also affirm that counsel has reviewed the record and explained her evaluation to the client, provided the client with a copy of the brief, and informed the client of the right to file a *pro se* supplemental brief. The procedure requires the court to review the entire record, and authorizes the court to affirm the conviction if it finds the appeal to be frivolous. Emphasizing that the constitution does not mandate any specific method for satisfying constitutional standards, the Court held that the *Wende* procedure is adequate to guarantee an indigent defendant the appellate rights guaranteed by the Fourteenth Amendment.

CHAPTER 12

THE TRIBUNAL: IMPARTIAL JUDGE AND JURY

A. RIGHT TO JURY TRIAL

The Sixth Amendment to the constitution guarantees the accused the right to trial "by an impartial jury of the State and district wherein the crime shall have been committed." The right to trial by jury is also guaranteed by all state constitutions, and by state and federal statute. These guarantees may be more or less broad than the Sixth Amendment right.

In *Duncan v. Louisiana* (S.Ct.1968), the Court held that the Sixth Amendment right to trial by jury is binding on the states. In reaching that conclusion, the Court stated that Fifth and Sixth Amendment rights applicable to federal criminal proceedings are also applicable to state prosecutions if they are "basic in our system of jurisprudence." The Court reviewed the long history of the use of juries in Anglo–American law, and the universal recognition of the right to jury trial in serious criminal cases in the laws of the states. Given this evidence of the country's commitment to the use of juries, the Court had little difficulty concluding that trial by jury in criminal cases is "fundamental to the American scheme of justice."

The Court stated that the right to trial by jury is granted to criminal defendants to protect against oppression by the government. Providing the accused the right to be tried by a jury constitutes "an inestimable safeguard against the corrupt or over-zealous prosecutor and against the compliant, biased, or eccentric judge." The Court acknowledged that the jury has its weaknesses and has been criticized as "unpredictable, quixotic, and little better than a roll of the dice," but concluded that in most cases juries do understand the evidence and come to sound conclusions.

The Sixth Amendment guarantee encompasses the right to a jury determination of guilt or innocence; it does not guarantee a right to a jury determination of the sentence. This is true even in cases in which the prosecution is seeking the death penalty. Thus, the Supreme Court has held that the constitution is not violated by a state sentencing scheme in which the trial judge can override a jury recommendation of a life sentence and impose a death sentence. *Spaziano v. Florida* (S.Ct.1984).

1. PROCEEDINGS TO WHICH THE CONSTITUTIONAL RIGHT APPLIES

a. Sentence Enhancement

The Supreme Court has held that the right to a trial by jury extends to factors used to enhance the severity of punishment imposed upon an accused. In *Apprendi v. New Jersey* (S.Ct.2000) the Court held that any fact other than that of prior conviction that increases penalty for crime beyond a prescribed statutory maximum is an element of a crime and must be submitted to the jury and proved beyond reasonable doubt. In *Ring v. Arizona* (S.Ct.2002), the Court held that the Sixth h Amendment requires a jury to determine enumerated aggravating factors where death penalty may be imposed only upon finding of such factors as functional equivalent of element of greater offense. And, in *Blakely v. Washington* (S.Ct.2004) the Court held that where a sentencing guidelines system allows an enhanced sentence based on facts other than those used in computing a standard range sentence, the existence of those facts must be found by jury if not admitted by defendant.

b. Petty Offenses

In *Duncan v. Louisiana* the Court recognized that there is a category of "petty" offenses which is not subject to the Sixth Amendment jury trial requirement, but expressly declined to settle the exact location of the line between petty offenses and serious crimes. Two years later in *Baldwin v. N.Y.* (S.Ct.1970), the Court held that any crime that is *punishable* by more than six months imprisonment is not "petty" for purposes of the Sixth Amendment, and therefore the defendant is entitled to trial by jury.

The Court explained that the line between serious and non-serious crimes should be drawn based on the punishment that is authorized by the legislature, rather than the punishment actually imposed on the defendant, because the maximum authorized penalty is the most reliable indicator of society's appraisal of the gravity of the crime. For crimes as to which the legislature has not established a maximum punishment, such as criminal contempt, the determination of whether the crime is "petty" is made based on the penalty actually imposed.

The Supreme Court has recognized the possibility that monetary penalties alone or a sentencing scheme that combined incarceration of six months or less with other penalties could move the crime into the serious category giving rise to a right to trial by jury. The Court has held, however, that a crime punishable by incarceration of six months or less is presumed to be petty, and the defendant is entitled to a jury trial under the Sixth Amendment only if she can demonstrate that any additional statutory penalties, viewed in conjunction with the maximum authorized period of incarceration, "are so severe that they clearly reflect a legislative determination that the offense in question is a 'serious' one." *Blanton v. North Las Vegas* (S.Ct.1989).

Applying this standard, the Court has found that a crime that carried a maximum six months imprisonment plus a $5000 fine was nonetheless "petty." *U.S. v. Nachtigal* (S.Ct.1993). The Court has also held that a $10,000 fine imposed against a labor union for contempt of court did not make the crime a serious one, noting that the $10,000 fined added up to less than one dollar per person as applied against the 13,000 member union. *Muniz v. Hoffman* (S.Ct.1975). When several crimes are tried together in a single proceeding, the availability of a Sixth Amendment right to trial by jury depends on whether any of the individual charges is for a nonpetty crime, not on whether the imposition of consecutive sentences for the various offenses could add up to more than six months. *Lewis v. U.S.* (1996).

c. Juvenile Proceedings

The Sixth Amendment right to trial by jury does not apply to the adjudicative phase of a state juvenile court delinquency proceeding. *McKeiver v. Pennsylvania* (S.Ct.1971). The language of the Sixth Amendment, which applies to "criminal prosecutions," does not by its express terms extend to juvenile adjudications, which have traditionally been regarded as civil. In holding that juries are not required for juvenile proceedings, however, the Court did not rely on this narrow linguistic analysis of the issues. Instead the Court focused on the likely consequences of using juries in juvenile proceedings, stating that requiring juries risks transforming the juvenile proceeding "into a fully adversary process," and putting "an effective end to what has been the idealistic prospect of an intimate, informal protective proceeding."

2. WAIVER OF JURY TRIAL

In some cases the defendant may wish to waive trial by jury because she believes she stands a better chance of an acquittal if she is tried before a judge. It is now commonly assumed that the right to trial by jury is primarily, if not solely, for the benefit of the accused, to be invoked or waived as she sees fit. In fact, however, it was not until the Supreme Court's decision in *Patton v. U.S.* (S.Ct. 1930) that the permissibility of a waiver of jury trial was clearly settled. In that case the Court rejected the view that the accused did not possess the power to waive trial by jury because federal courts lacked jurisdiction to try a criminal case in the absence of a jury. The Court concluded instead that the constitutional right to trial by jury is intended primarily for the protection of the accused, and therefore waiver of a jury by the party principally benefitted should be possible. The Court stressed that to be effective a waiver of jury trial by the accused must be both express—waiver will not be presumed from a silent record—and intelligent.

In the federal system and a majority of states, the defendant may waive trial by jury only with the approval of the court and the consent of the prosecution. *See* Fed. R. Crim. Pro. 23(a). In *Singer v. U.S.* (S.Ct.1965), the Court upheld this requirement. The Court held that the defendant does not have a constitutional right to be tried by a judge without a jury, and that there is no constitutional impediment to conditioning a defendant's attempted waiver of a jury on the consent of the trial judge and the prosecutor. Rule 23(a) of the Federal Rules of Criminal Procedure does not require the prosecution to articulate its reasons for refusing to consent to a waiver of jury trial. The Court in *Singer* acknowledged that there might be some circumstances where the defendant's reasons for wanting to be tried by a judge alone are so compelling that the prosecutor's insistence on trial by jury would result in the denial to the defendant of an impartial trial. Lower courts have not, however, been receptive to claims by defendants that they should be permitted to waive a jury despite the prosecutor's objections, and prosecutors' decisions to block attempted waivers have generally been upheld.

3.   JURY SIZE

The Federal Rules of Criminal Procedure and the laws of most states preserve the common law requirement that the criminal jury consist of twelve persons. In *Williams v. Florida* (S.Ct.1970), however, the Court held that a 12–person panel is not a necessary ingredient of "trial by jury" that is guaranteed by the Sixth Amendment, and that the defendant's Sixth Amendment rights were not violated by his trial in state court before a jury of six. In arriving at this conclusion, the Court first determined that the traditional practice of 12 person juries was a "historical accident" unrelated to the purposes for which trial by jury was established, and that the incorporation of a right to trial by jury in the constitution did not necessarily preserve every feature of the jury as it existed at common law.

The Court then turned to the *purpose* of the jury as the key to determining its essential features. The objective of protecting against government oppression, which the Court identified as the primary purpose of the jury, is accomplished through the interposition between the accused and his accuser of the commonsense judgment of a group of lay persons. To effectively serve this function the jury must be large enough to promote group deliberation free from outside attempts at intimidation, and large enough to provide a fair possibility for obtaining a group that is representative of the community.

The Court found little reason to believe, however, that a six person jury would be less able to achieve these goals than a 12 person jury. The Court also stated that the reliability of jury factfinding is not a function of jury size, and that the fact that smaller juries generally have a lower rate of hung juries is not necessarily a disadvantage to the defendant, since a hung jury is just as likely to block an acquittal (to the disadvantage of the defendant) as a conviction. Finally, the Court stated that reducing the size of the jury from 12 to six would not "significantly diminish" the extent to which the jury was representative of all groups in society, provided that arbitrary exclusions from the jury rolls were forbidden.

The Court in *Williams* cited several social science studies in support of its conclusion that there are "no discernible differences" between the results reached by the two different-sized juries. Following the *Williams* decision, critics argued that the studies cited by the Court did not support the Court's conclusions, and social scientists undertook a more intensive investigation of the effect of size differences on jury performance.

In *Ballew v. Georgia* (S.Ct.1978) the Court relied on some of those later studies in holding that the defendant's trial before a five person jury violated the Sixth Amendment. According to the Court, those empirical studies suggested that progressively smaller juries 1) are less likely to foster effective group deliberation; 2) are less able to achieve accurate results; 3) produce fewer hung juries, which will be detrimental to the defendant; and 4) will not be as truly representative of the community. The Court also observed that there is no significant state advantage in reducing the size of the jury from six to five, since the savings in time and money would be minimal. Although the Court adhered to its holding in *Williams*, and confessed that it could not "discern a clear line between six and five," the Court held that the reduction of the jury below six impairs the purpose and functioning of the criminal jury to a constitutional degree.

4.   AGREEMENT REQUIREMENT

Under the common law and in most jurisdictions today, the unanimous agreement of the entire jury is required for either a conviction or an acquittal. In

Apodaca v. Oregon (S.Ct.1972), however, the Court held that unanimity is not required by the Sixth Amendment. The defendants in that case had been convicted by non-unanimous juries under a state law that permitted conviction by no fewer than 10 of the 12 jurors.

In rejecting the claim that conviction by a non-unanimous jury violated the Sixth Amendment, the Court stated that the relevant question is whether unanimity is required to accomplish the primary purpose of the jury, which is protecting against government oppression. In terms of the jury's ability to fulfil this function, the Court perceived no difference between juries required to act unanimously and those permitted to convict or acquit by votes of 10 to two or 11 to one. The Court deemed it irrelevant that requiring unanimity would produce hung juries in some cases where a non-unanimous jury would either convict or acquit, since the defendant's interest in obtaining the commonsense judgment of a group of lay persons is served whether the jury reaches a verdict or not.

The Court also rejected the contention that unanimity is required to give effect to the requirement that juries be drawn from a group representing a cross section of the community. The fact that minority viewpoints may be outvoted in the final result, according to the Court, does not mean those viewpoints have not been represented in the decision making process.

In *Johnson v. Louisiana* (S.Ct.1972), decided the same day as *Apodaca*, the Court rejected the argument that conviction by a jury vote of nine to three violated the defendant's due process right to proof beyond a reasonable doubt. The premise of the defendant's argument was that the disagreement of three jurors with the majority's decision to convict established that there existed a reasonable doubt as to the defendant's guilt. In rejecting this contention, the Court relied on the fact that the jury's failure to reach unanimous agreement has not traditionally been equated with the existence of reasonable doubt requiring an acquittal, since the defendant can be re-tried following a hung jury.

No state has attempted to reduce the margin required for a conviction below nine to three. Although the Supreme Court did not explicitly address the constitutionality of a voting requirement that permitted conviction by vote of eight to four or seven to five, the opinions in *Apodaca* and *Johnson* suggest that such a weakening of the agreement requirement would not be permitted.

In *Burch v. Louisiana* (S.Ct.1979), the Court addressed the constitutionality of combining the use of a six person jury, permitted by *Williams*, with a non-unanimous voting rule, approved in *Apodaca*. The defendant in *Burch* was convicted by a six person jury that found him guilty by a vote of five to one. For much the same reasons that led the Court to conclude that a five member jury threatened the fairness of the proceeding and the proper role of the jury, the Court held that the constitution requires that six person juries be unanimous.

5.   JURY NULLIFICATION

A jury verdict of acquittal cannot be appealed or otherwise reconsidered for any reason. As a result of that rule, and also because the jury need not disclose the reasons for its decision, the jury has the power to acquit the defendant even if the law and the evidence clearly establish guilt beyond a reasonable doubt. The jury's exercise of this power is commonly referred to as "jury nullification."

Whether it is proper for the jury to acquit a defendant who is legally guilty is the subject of continuing scholarly debate. In support of jury nullification is the argument that the jury's nullification power is necessary to prevent application of unjust laws or the application of good laws to achieve unjust results. Opponents of jury nullification maintain that the practice undermines the rule of law, and that the determination of what laws are just is the responsibility of the legislature, not an unelected group of trial jurors. The Supreme Court has occasionally expressed guarded support for the jury's nullification power.

The jury's nullification *power* is rooted in rules and practices that are probably too firmly established to be open to serious reconsideration. The only real question, which is sometimes cast in terms of whether the jury possesses a *right* to nullify, is whether the jury should be informed of its nullification prerogative by the trial judge. The answer in the federal system and the majority of the states is that the jury should not be told of its power to nullify. Juries are typically informed that it is their duty to apply the law as explained by the judge to the facts as proven by the evidence.

The leading statement on the reasons for not instructing jurors of their nullification power is contained in the majority opinion in the D.C. Circuit's decision in *U.S. v. Dougherty* (D.C.Cir. 1972). The court observed that jurors acquire information about their duties and role from sources other than the instructions of the trial judge, and argued that these other sources adequately convey to jurors an appreciation of their freedom in an appropriate case to depart from what the judge prescribes. Informing the jurors of their power, according to the court, risks overuse of that power. The court also argued that a nullification instruction, which in substance instructs them to follow their conscience, would place an unnecessary burden on jurors by depriving them of the psychological security of simply following the law.

B. JURY SELECTION

1. THE JURY SELECTION PROCESS

The process of selecting a jury proceeds through several stages. The first step is to compile a list of names of potential jurors. This list may be referred to as the "jury list," "source list" or simply the "jury pool." In the federal system and most states, the law requires that the jury list be compiled so as to be as fully representative of the entire population as possible. The primary source of names is voter registration rolls. However, because not all persons eligible for jury service register to vote, voter registration lists are sometimes supplemented with other lists, such as lists of licensed drivers, tax rolls, welfare rolls, and telephone directories. A minority of states continue to rely on the so-called "key man" system to create the jury pool. In these jurisdictions, prominent members of the community (the "key men") are responsible for compiling a list of potential jurors, often based on statutory criteria requiring selection of persons of "integrity" or "honesty and intelligence." Jury lists that are generated by the key man system are often not as representative as those that are compiled by more random methods, and consequently more likely to give rise to legal challenges.

The second step is to assemble a "venire," sometimes also called a "panel," from among the jury pool. The venire consists of those persons who have actually been summoned and appear for jury service. In the federal system and most states, the jurors making up the venire are chosen through a process of random selection from the jury list. Because some proportion of jurors summoned for jury duty will not appear, either because they have a statutory excuse or because they did not receive or ignored the summons, the venire may not be as representative of the community as the jury pool.

In states that continue to use the key man system, the selection of the venire is likely to be less random. In a few places, the composition of the venire is manipulated through a conscious selection from the jury pool to ensure that the venire closely mirrors the larger community.

The final step is to pick from among the venire a group of trial jurors and alternates. This ordinarily begins with the random selection from the venire of several dozen jurors for assignment to a courtroom where a trial is scheduled to begin. In what is referred to as "*voir dire*," this group is then questioned by either the judge or the attorneys or both regarding their suitability to serve as jurors in the case at hand. On the basis of the jurors' responses to *voir dire* questions, the prosecution and defense are permitted to "challenge" jurors, which means to excuse them from serving on this case. The purpose of *voir dire* and juror challenges, at least in theory, is to ensure that the jurors chosen to try the case are impartial.

There are two types of juror challenges. The parties are permitted an unlimited number of "for cause" challenges. However, the exercise of challenges for cause is subject to the strict control of the trial judge, and must be based on legal grounds. In order to challenge a juror for cause, the party exercising the challenge must demonstrate to the satisfaction of the trial court that the juror is either legally disqualified or would be unable to judge the case impartially.

All jurisdictions also grant both the defense and the prosecution a limited number of "peremptory challenges." A peremptory challenge permits the removal of the juror without the necessity of demonstrating bias or any other legal grounds.

2. SELECTING THE VENIRE

a. Constitutional Requirements

Both the Sixth Amendment guarantee of trial by jury and the Equal Protection Clause of the Fourteenth Amendment impose limits on the selection of the jury venire. The jury selection doctrines based on the Equal Protection Clause developed earlier than the Sixth Amendment doctrines, in part because the Sixth Amendment was not held applicable to the states until the Supreme Court's decision in *Duncan v. Louisiana* in 1968. Currently, the Sixth Amendment is the source of the more potent limitations on the selection of the venire, but equal protection doctrine retains significance in the selection of state grand juries, since the Sixth Amendment is not applicable to that process.

b. Equal Protection

In *Strauder v. W.Va.* (S.Ct.1879) decided within a few years after the ratification of the Fourteenth Amendment, the Court struck down as a violation of equal protection a state statute that limited jury service to "white male persons." The following year the Court held that the intentional exclusion of Blacks from jury service through discriminatory application of a facially neutral statute was likewise a denial of equal protection.

The intentional exclusion of African Americans and members of other suspect or quasi suspect classes from jury service implicates the equal protection rights of both the defendant and the excluded jurors. A defendant who is herself a member of a suspect class has an equal protection right to be tried before a jury that is selected in a manner that is free from purposeful discrimination. In addition, the potential jurors have an equal protection right not to be excluded from jury service because of their class membership. The Supreme Court held in *Powers v. Ohio* (S.Ct.1991) that a defendant who is not herself a member of the suspect class may nonetheless raise an equal protection challenge to discriminatory jury selection practices because she has standing to assert the equal protection rights of the excluded jurors.

The Equal Protection Clause does not impose any affirmative requirement that members of protected classes be represented in the jury venire. Rather, the Clause operates as a negative prohibition against purposeful discrimination. What this means is that members of a protected class may not be excluded from jury service *because of* their class membership. In recognition of the difficulty or impossibility of proving intentional discrimination in many cases in which it exists, the Supreme Court held, in *Norris v. Alabama* (S.Ct.1935) that a *prima facie* case of purposeful discrimination can be established with statistical evidence demonstrating that the group is substantially under represented among those called for jury service as measured by the group's numbers in the population.

Thus, in *Castaneda v. Partida* (S.Ct.1977), a case involving selection of grand jurors which is equally applicable to the selection of trial jurors, the Court found that a prima facie case of discrimination had been proven with evidence that 79% of the county were Mexican American, but only 39% of those called for jury service were Mexican American. The Court has rejected the claim that a selection procedure that requires jury selection officials to apply subjective criteria, such as a requirement that prospective jurors be persons of "good character and sound judgment"—is itself a violation of equal protection, though the use of such factors provides an opportunity to discriminate that may support a finding of a *prima facie* case of discrimination.

Once a *prima facie* case of discrimination has been proven, the burden shifts to the state to show that the under representation is not a result of intentional discrimination. Mere denial of an intent to discriminate by jury selection officials is not enough to dispel the presumption of an intent to discriminate. Nor may the *prima facie* case be rebutted by evidence that the statistical disparity could be the result of factors other than intentional discrimination. In *Castenada v. Partida*, for example, the Court dismissed the state's argument that the under representation of Mexican Americans on jury lists might result from the fact that a larger proportion of Mexican Americans did not satisfy legitimate eligibility requirements in the absence of evidence that that was in fact the case.

c. Sixth Amendment Fair Cross Section

The Supreme Court first announced the Sixth Amendment requirement that the jury be drawn from a group that represents a fair cross section of the community in federal cases decided before the Sixth Amendment was held applicable to state trials. The requirement assumed considerably greater importance after the Court extended the rule to the selection of jurors in state criminal trials in *Taylor v. Louisiana* (S.Ct.1975). The defendant in *Taylor* was convicted by a jury that was drawn from a venire made up entirely of men. Under Louisiana law, women were not legally disqualified for jury service, but the number of women actually called as jurors was very small because of a law requiring a woman to file a written declaration of her desire to be subject to jury service in order to be called.

The Court held that the defendant's trial before a jury selected from a group from which women had been systematically excluded violated his Sixth Amendment right to trial by jury. The Court reasoned that the exclusion of large and distinctive groups from the jury pool would impair the jury in its exercise of the common sense judgment of the community, and hamper the performance of the jury's essential purpose of guarding against the exercise of arbitrary government power. Although acknowledging that exclusion of either men or women "might not in a given case make an iota of difference," the Court stated that "a flavor, a distinct quality is lost if either sex is excluded."

In a much later case addressing the Sixth Amendment fair cross section requirement, the Court offered a somewhat different rationale for the rule. In *Holland v. Illinois* (S.Ct.1990) the Court concluded that the requirement that jurors be drawn from a group that is representative of the community is not designed to assure a representative jury, but is imposed as a means of effectuating the constitutional guarantee of an impartial jury. The fair cross section requirement furthers this objective by preventing the state from "stacking" the jury pool with pro-prosecution jurors, and therefore ensures that the prosecution and the defense operate on "a level playing field" in the exercise of their peremptory challenges.

The Sixth Amendment right belongs to all defendants, and is not dependent on a shared identity between the accused and the juror. Thus, in *Taylor*, the Court rejected the contention that the male defendant was ineligible to complain about the absence from the venire of female jurors. The Supreme Court has repeatedly emphasized that the fair cross section requirement applies only to the group from which the jury is drawn—the venire or the panel—and not to the jury itself. The defendant is not entitled to a jury of any particular composition, and the jury itself is often less representative than the venire, either because of its smaller size or because of the effect of for cause and peremptory challenges.

Unlike the equal protection doctrine, the Sixth Amendment fair cross section requirement does not require proof of purposeful exclusion. To demonstrate a Sixth Amendment violation, the defendant must show that the jury selection procedure "systematically exclude[s] distinctive groups in the community, and thereby fail[s] to be reasonably representative [of the community]." As with an equal protection claim, this will ordinarily be proven with a statistical showing of a disparity between the group's representation in the community and its representation among potential jurors. The Sixth Amendment standard, however, focuses less on the reasons for the disparity than does the equal protection standard.

The Sixth Amendment does not require that all groups in society be represented in the jury venire. The Court has stated that the requirement only embraces groups that are both "large" and "distinctive." Most importantly, however, the requirement only extends to groups whose inclusion in the venire furthers the objectives of 1) guarding against government oppression through the exercise of the common sense judgment of the community; 2) preserving public confidence in the fairness of the criminal justice system; and 3) implementing the belief that sharing in the administration of justice is a phase of civic responsibility. *Lockhart v. McCree* (S.Ct.1986).

In addition to women, who were recognized as comprising a distinctive group in *Taylor*, the Court in *Powers v. Ohio* (S.Ct. 1991) has also found racial groups to qualify under the Sixth Amendment standard. In *Powers* the Court held that the defendant could object to the exclusion of a certain race from the jury, even if the defendant was not a member of that race. The Court has rejected the claim that persons opposed to the death penalty are a distinctive group for Sixth Amendment purposes.

3. VOIR DIRE

Voir dire refers to the question and answer session between the court, the parties and the prospective jurors during which the parties exercise their for cause and peremptory challenges. The two basic purposes of *voir dire* are to enable the prosecution and defense to identify jurors who are subject to a challenge for cause and to facilitate the intelligent exercise of peremptory challenges. A third less widely accepted function of *voir dire* is to provide the attorneys with an opportunity to prime the jurors to accept their evidence and arguments in the trial to come.

The former practice of direct attorney *voir dire* questioning of jurors is gradually giving way to judge conducted *voir dire*. In the federal system the judge has the discretion to question the jurors herself or permit the attorneys to do so. The trial judge exercises very broad discretion over the scope of *voir dire* questioning. Appellate courts only rarely find that limitations imposed by the judge on the questions attorneys are permitted to ask on *voir dire* are improper.

The Supreme Court has found a constitutional right to question prospective jurors about specific subjects in only a very small number of situations. In *Ham v. S.C.* (S.Ct.1973), which involved the prosecution of a Black civil rights worker for a marijuana offense, the Court concluded that the defendant's constitutional rights were violated by the trial judge's refusal to question potential jurors about possible racial prejudice. In the subsequent case of *Ristaino v. Ross* (S.Ct.1976), however, the Court construed the *Ham* holding narrowly, finding that the mere fact of a White victim and Black defendants was less likely to distort the trial than the special factors involved in *Ham*. In *Turner v. Murray* (S.Ct.1986) the Court held that the circumstance that the defendant was charged with an interracial crime did give rise to a constitutional right to question potential jurors about race when the charge was for a capital offense.

In *Mu'Min v. Virginia* (S.Ct.1991) the Court addressed the scope of *voir dire* guaranteed by the constitution when the defendant claims that her right to a fair trial may be infringed by the jurors' exposure to pre-trial publicity regarding the crime. In *Mu'Min* a majority of the prospective jurors, including eight of the members of the jury panel, admitted having learned about the case from media reports or other outside sources. The defense requested that those jurors be questioned *in camera* (to avoid contamination of the rest of the panel), and that they be questioned about the *content* of news reports that they had seen or heard. The trial judge denied the request for *in camera* questioning, and refused to ask about the content of the publicity. All of the jurors seated in the case, including those who had read or heard about the case, stated on *voir dire* that they could judge the defendant fairly on the evidence presented at trial.

The issue in the Supreme Court was whether the trial court's refusal to question the potential jurors about the content of adverse publicity deprived the defendant of his constitutional right to an impartial jury and a fair trial. In answering that question, the Court related the constitutional requirements for *voir dire* to the substantive constitutional standard for juror impartiality. The constitution does not require that jurors be totally ignorant of the facts of the case, or completely without preconceptions of the defendant's guilt. A juror is impartial within the meaning of the Sixth Amendment and the Due Process Clause if she is able to put aside her opinions and decide the case on the evidence presented at the trial. The question for the trial court, then, is whether the juror's assertions of impartiality are to be believed.

The Court acknowledged that its prior decisions had established that adverse pretrial publicity can create such a presumption of prejudice in a community that the jurors' claims that they can be impartial should not be credited. But the facts of *Mu'Min*, according to the court, did not present such a case. Had the trial court in *Mu'Min* been confronted with the "wave of public passion" engendered by pretrial publicity that occurred in *Irvin v. Dowd* (S.Ct.1961), the constitution might well have required that the judge undertake a more extensive examination of potential jurors than it had. But, the Court stated, because of differences between the communities where the two cases were tried—*Irvin v. Dowd* was tried in a thinly populated rural area whereas *Mu'Min* was tried in a metropolitan area—and differences in the nature and extent of pretrial publicity, the showings in the two cases were not comparable. Accordingly, the trial court's acceptance of the jurors' assertions of impartiality without subjecting them to inquiry about the content of pre-trial publicity did not deprive the defendant of a fair trial.

4. CHALLENGES FOR CAUSE

The grounds for challenges for cause are typically defined by statute. They ordinarily include a set of specific disqualifications, such as a prohibition against jurors serving in a case in which they also served as a grand juror, a case in which they have an interest, or a case involving a person to whom they are related. The statutes also provide more generally for a challenge for cause against a juror who is biased, typically defined as a juror who has a state of mind that would prevent the juror from acting impartially. A distinction is made between "actual bias," which exists when a juror acknowledges her inability to be impartial, and "implied bias," which is presumed when circumstances are such that the juror's claims of impartiality should not be believed.

The Sixth Amendment also guarantees the defendant the right to an "impartial jury." In a very long line of cases dating from the trial of Aaron Burr in the early part of the 19th century, the Supreme Court has defined the impartiality guaranteed by the constitution in terms similar to those used in statutory formulations. Courts have generally imposed high standards for demonstrating bias sufficient to support a challenge for cause, and the number of jurors excused on that ground is typically small.

a. Pre-trial Publicity

One context in which the constitutional requirement of an impartial jury has been most fully developed is when the defendant claims a denial of a fair trial because of the effects of prejudicial pre-trial publicity. News coverage concerning the crime or the accused can bias potential jurors against the defendant by pre-disposing them to believe the defendant guilty before the trial even begins. *Voir dire* can be used to seek to identify and eliminate jurors who have been exposed to prejudicial publicity, but in some especially notorious cases finding jurors who have heard or read nothing about the case may be impossible. Moreover, removing from the panel all those who are generally well informed has the likely disadvantage of diminishing the representativeness and general intelligence of the jury.

In *Irvin v. Dowd*, the Supreme Court set forth the constitutional framework to be used in determining the adequacy of jury selection procedures when the defendant claims infringement of her fair trial rights because of pre-trial publicity. The Court began by stating that the constitutional guarantee of an impartial juror means "a juror whose verdict is based on the evidence developed at the trial." This standard does not require, however, that the jurors be totally ignorant of the facts and issues involved, or that any juror who has been exposed to pre-trial publicity be automatically excused. Indeed, even a juror who has a "preconceived notion as to the guilt or innocence of an accused" as a result of pre-trial publicity need not necessarily be excluded from the jury panel. It is sufficient, according to the Court, "if the juror can lay aside his impression or opinion and render a verdict based on the evidence presented in court."

In determining whether a juror can put aside her preconceptions and evaluate the case based on the evidence presented at the trial, the juror's own claims of impartiality are not necessarily determinative. In some cases, the nature and extent of pre-trial publicity raise a presumption of juror partiality, notwithstanding the jurors' sincere assertions during *voir dire* of an ability to return an impartial verdict.

In *Dowd* the Court found that the totality of the circumstances compelled a conclusion that the defendant had been denied a fair trial, overriding the trial judge's finding that the jurors were impartial. The record showed that in the months preceding his capital murder trial the defendant had been subjected to a barrage of prejudicial and inflammatory publicity from both print and broadcast media. The news coverage, which blanketed the small community where the case was tried, included reports of the defendant's prior convictions, his confession to six murders and his indictment for four of them, and his offer to plead guilty in exchange for a 99–year prison sentence. During *voir dire* more than half of the 430 potential jurors were excused because they admitted having a fixed opinion of the defendant's guilt, and almost 90 percent of those asked harbored some opinion of his guilt. Eight of the 12 jurors selected stated they believed the defendant was guilty, some going so far as to say that it would take evidence to overcome their belief. Although those jurors also professed an ability to put aside their opinions and judge the case fairly, the Court found that in the circumstances their statements could be given "little weight." The Court concluded that, "[w]ith his life at stake, it is not requiring too much that the petitioner be tried in an atmosphere undisturbed by so huge a wave of public passion and by a jury other than one in which two-thirds of the members admit, before hearing any testimony, to possessing a belief in his guilt."

In *Murphy v. Florida* (S.Ct.1975) the Court concluded that the circumstances of that case did not warrant a conclusion that juror partiality deprived the defendant of a fair trial. Murphy's trial received extensive coverage in the media, but most of the news reports concerning the defendant appeared seven months before jury selection began, and were "largely factual in nature." The proportion of prospective jurors who were dismissed because they indicated an opinion as to the defendant's guilt was considerably smaller in *Murphy* than in *Dowd*, and did not suggest "a community with sentiment so poisoned against [the defendant] as to impeach the indifference of jurors who displayed no animus of their own."

In *Patton v. Yount* (S.Ct.1984) the Court distinguished *Dowd* primarily on the basis that in *Yount* four years had elapsed between the time when the adverse publicity was at its height and the selection of the jury and trial. Yount's first trial, which resulted in a conviction that was reversed on appeal, was preceded by a wave of publicity similar to what occurred in *Dowd*. The publicity that preceded the second trial four years later was much less extensive and also less inflammatory. At the *voir dire* of jurors for the second trial, a large percentage of potential jurors and eight of the 14 ultimately chosen to serve as trial jurors and alternates stated they had at some point held an opinion on the defendant's guilt. The record of the *voir dire* showed, however, that by the time of the second trial many of the potential jurors had let the details of the case slip from their minds, and the passage of time had either weakened or eliminated their earlier opinions of the defendant's guilt. The Court held, therefore, that the trial judge's finding that the jurors were impartial was not manifestly erroneous.

The determination whether pretrial publicity creates a presumption of juror partiality that will override a finding by the trial judge that the jurors are impartial must be based on an evaluation of the totality of the circumstances of the particular case. As summarized by Professors LaFave, Israel and King, the three factors that the Court has found particularly significant in making that evaluation are: "1) the strength of the voir dire responses of the jurors with reference to their previously developed opinions, 2) the nature of the pretrial publicity, and 3) the time elapsed between the height of the publicity and the trial." LaFave, Israel, and King, *Criminal Procedure* § 23.2 (3d ed. 2000).

b. "Death Qualified Juries"

In death penalty cases in which the jury decides both the question of guilt or innocence and the appropriate sentence, the prosecutor may excuse with a challenge for cause prospective jurors whose attitudes toward the death penalty would prevent them from imposing a death sentence. The rationale for this rule is that jurors who declare themselves unwilling to vote for a death penalty have in essence declared their refusal to follow instructions to consider a death sentence, and are therefore not impartial on the issue of sentence.

In *Witherspoon v. Illinois* (S.Ct.1968), the Court held that the trial court's application of a state jury selection statute that permitted the removal of jurors with "conscientious scruples" against the death penalty resulted in a violation of the defendant's right to an impartial jury on the issue of sentence. If, according to the Court, the prosecutor had excluded only those jurors who stated that they would not even consider returning a verdict of death, it could be argued that the resulting jury was simply neutral with respect to penalty. But the trial court permitted the prosecutor to go further than that, and to remove all those who "expressed conscientious or religious scruples against capital punishment" or who "opposed it in principle." Although the Court nowhere suggested that any of the individuals who served on the jury were biased, purging the panel of all those with "scruples" against capital punishment skewed the mix of views regarding the death penalty on the jury as a whole, and resulted in a jury slanted in favor of death.

The Court's opinion in *Witherspoon* seemed to suggest that due regard for the defendant's right to an impartial sentencing jury requires that prosecution challenges be limited to the removal of jurors who make it clear that they would refuse to vote for a death sentence under all circumstances. In the subsequent decision in *Wainwright v. Witt* (S.Ct. 1985), however, the Court approved a more generous standard for removal. The prosecution may, consistently with the defendant's constitutional rights, remove any juror whose views on the death penalty would "prevent or substantially impair the performance of his duties as a juror in accordance with his instructions and his oath."

In *Witherspoon* the Supreme Court reversed the defendant's death sentence, but allowed the guilty verdict to stand on the ground that the elimination of jurors with general objections to the death penalty did not impair the impartiality of the jury on the issue of guilt or innocence. Although the defendant had presented evidence that "death qualified" juries—juries from which persons opposed to the death penalty have been removed—are more conviction prone than non-death qualified juries, the Court considered this evidence "too tentative and fragmentary to establish that jurors not opposed to the death penalty tend to favor the prosecution in the determination of guilt."

The claim that death qualified juries are biased toward the prosecution in the determination of guilt reached the Supreme Court again nearly two decades after *Witherspoon* in *Lockhart v. McCree* (S.Ct. 1986). Although the social science evidence that death qualified juries are conviction prone presented in *McCree* was considerably stronger than what was before the Court in *Witherspoon*, the Court still found it wanting. Nevertheless, the Court proceeded to address the merits of the defendant's argument on the assumption that the empirical case had in fact been established. The Court held that even if death qualified juries are more prone to convict than other juries, the use of such juries does not violate the defendant's Sixth Amendment rights, since an impartial jury within the meaning of the Sixth Amendment consists of nothing more than *jurors* who will conscientiously apply the law and find the facts. The Court distinguished its cases holding that imbalanced *sentencing* juries fail to satisfy constitutional impartiality standards on the ground that requiring a mix of viewpoints is appropriate in the sentencing context where the range of jury discretion gives rise to greater concern over the possible effects of an "imbalanced" jury.

5.   PEREMPTORY CHALLENGES

All jurisdictions grant both the defense and prosecution the power to exclude a limited number of jurors—from as few as three to 20 or more—without having to provide any reason for the challenge. The procedure for exercising these "peremptory" challenges varies. In the most common jury selection method, twelve qualified jurors are seated in the jury box, at which point the prosecutor and defense counsel take turns exercising one challenge at a time. As each challenged juror is removed, another juror is randomly selected from the venire to keep the number of jurors under consideration at twelve. This procedure continues until both sides have either exhausted their reserve of peremptory challenges or approved the same group of twelve jurors. Under the so-called "struck system," a larger group of qualified jurors is assembled equal to the number of peremptory challenges available to both sides plus the number of jurors needed for the trial of the case. Thus, if each side is entitled to ten peremptory challenges, and the trial jury will consist of 12 jurors plus two alternates, the exercise of peremptory challenges begins with 34 jurors. The prosecutor and defense then alternate in their exercise of peremptory challenges until all the challenges have been used and the group is reduced to the size of the jury plus alternates.

The most widely accepted reason for granting peremptory challenges is that challenges for cause are not by themselves adequate to ensure an impartial jury. Because they need not be justified, peremptory challenges can be used to exclude jurors who are suspected of partiality, but who will not admit or do not recognize their bias. In *Holland v. Illinois* (S.Ct.1990), the Court endorsed the value of peremptory challenges as a mechanism for implementing the constitutional guarantee of an impartial jury, and rejected the claim that the Sixth Amendment limits the grounds on which peremptory challenges may be exercised. Another commonly stated justification for the peremptory challenge is that it enhances the legitimacy of the jury's verdict by giving the parties a voice in the composition of the jury. The primary criticisms of peremptory challenges are that the elimination of members of the venire through the use of peremptory challenges often has the effect of diminishing the representativeness of the jury, and that peremptories can be used to exclude jurors on illegitimate and invidious grounds.

In *Swain v. Alabama* (S.Ct.1965), the Court held that the equal protection guarantee applies to the prosecutor's use of peremptory challenges, and that purposeful discrimination in the exercise of peremptory challenges is a denial of equal protection. The Court also held, however, that the prosecutor's removal of Black jurors on the basis of the juror's race does not violate the constitution, provided the challenge is based on reasons related to the trial of the particular case. Thus, under *Swain*, a prosecutor could legitimately strike a Black juror if the prosecutor believed that a non-Black would be a better prosecution juror for the trial of that case. The Court further held, moreover, that there is a presumption that in any particular case the prosecutor is using the state's peremptory challenges to obtain a fair and impartial jury, and not in an invidiously discriminatory manner. In order to prove an equal protection violation, therefore, the defendant must show that the prosecutor used her peremptory challenges to exclude all Black potential jurors in all cases regardless of the circumstances. Only then, according to the Court, could it be inferred that the prosecutor's peremptory challenges were being used to deny Blacks an equal opportunity to serve on juries, rather than simply to obtain an impartial jury for the trial of the case at hand.

In *Batson v. Kentucky* (S.Ct.1986), the Court significantly tightened the equal protection restrictions on prosecutors' use of peremptory challenges, and lowered the burden of proof required for a defendant to prove an equal protection violation. The Court held that an equal protection violation occurs whenever the prosecutor's peremptory challenge is based on the juror's race. This is so even if the challenge is based on the prosecutor's belief that the juror, because of either the juror's race or what can be inferred about the juror because of her race, would be biased or otherwise inappropriate for the trial of the particular case. The fundamental difference in principle between *Swain* and *Batson* is that in *Swain* the Court found nothing constitutionally objectionable in a prosecutor challenging a Black juror if the prosecutor believed that a Black person could not fairly judge the issues in the case, whereas under *Batson* such a challenge is no longer permissible.

Under *Batson*, the defendant can prove a *prima facie* case of purposeful discrimination in the selection of the jury with evidence of the prosecutor's exercise of peremptory challenges at the defendant's trial. To prove a *prima facie* case the defendant must first show that the prosecutor has used peremptory challenges to remove from the venire potential jurors who belong to a cognizable racial group. In seeking to establish that such removal was based on the jurors' race, the defendant is entitled to rely on the fact that peremptory challenges constitute a jury selection practice that permits "those to discriminate who are of a mind to discriminate." The defendant must show that these facts, together with any other relevant circumstances, including the prosecutor's questions and comments during *voir dire* or a pattern of strikes against Black jurors, raise an inference that the prosecutor used peremptory challenges to exclude jurors on account of race.

Once the trial court rules that the defendant has made out a *prima facie* case of purposeful discrimination, the burden shifts to the prosecutor to come forward with a "race-neutral" explanation for the challenge. The Court stated that the prosecutor's assertion that she challenged the juror because she believed that persons of the juror's race could not judge the case impartially is not "race-neutral," since the core guarantee of the Equal Protection Clause would be meaningless if prosecutors were permitted to act on assumptions which arise solely from the juror's race. Nor may the prosecutor rebut the inference of purposeful discrimination merely by denying a discriminatory motive. To rebut the challenge the prosecutor's explanation for the challenge need not, however, rise to the level justifying a challenge for cause. Indeed, as the Court later held, the explanation need not even be "minimally persuasive," provided the offered explanation is the real reason for the challenge, and not a pretext for race. *Purkett v. Elem* (S.Ct.1995). Thus, a prosecutor's explanation that she challenged a juror because of the juror's long hair and beard satisfies the requirement that the explanation be race-neutral, even if the juror's hair length has no bearing on his fitness to try the case impartially.

In the third stage of the *Batson* inquiry, after the defendant has made out a prima facie case and the prosecutor has offered a race-neutral explanation, the trial judge must determine whether the defendant has established purposeful discrimination. This requires the trial court to make a factual determination of the prosecutor's intent in excluding the juror. In effect, the court must decide whether the prosecutor's explanation for the challenge is sincere or simply a pretext for race. In making this determination, the court may consider all relevant circumstances, including the plausibility of the explanation or the fact that the asserted grounds for removal will have the effect of eliminating jurors of a particular race. A justification which is implausible or fantastic is more likely to be found pretextual. The fact that the asserted grounds for removal will disproportionately impact jurors of a particular race does not by itself render the explanation improper, but the trial court may consider that fact as evidence that the prosecutor's stated reason is a pretext for racial discrimination.

In *Batson v. Kentucky* the Court stated that in order for a defendant to claim an equal protection violation in the use of peremptory challenges, the excluded juror and the defendant must both belong to the same cognizable racial group. This requirement was satisfied in the *Batson* case because both the defendant and the excluded jurors were Black. In *Powers v. Ohio* (S.Ct.1991), however, the Court held that a White defendant could claim an equal protection violation based on the prosecutor's purposeful discrimination against Black jurors. The rationale for this holding is that race-based peremptory challenges violate the equal protection rights of the excluded jurors, and that the defendant has standing to assert the constitutional rights of the jurors who will try her, regardless of the defendant's race.

The *Batson* decision applied solely to peremptory challenges exercised by prosecutors. In *Georgia v. McCollum* (S.Ct.1992) the Court extended the rule to apply to peremptories by defense attorneys. In reaching this result, the Court held that defense attorneys are state actors within the meaning of the Fourteenth Amendment, and that the interests underlying the *Batson* rule need not give way to the rights of the accused.

The *Batson* decision involved discrimination against jurors because of the jurors' race. In *J.E.B. v. Alabama ex rel. T.B.* (S.Ct.1994), the Court held that the Equal Protection Clause also prohibits peremptory challenges exercised on the basis of the jurors' gender. Lower courts have generally held the *Batson* rule applicable to challenges based on the juror's ethnicity, and have split on the question whether the rule applies to discrimination against jurors based on religion.

C. CHALLENGING THE JUDGE

The constitutional guarantee of due process includes the right to an impartial judge. The Supreme Court found this right to have been violated in a case in which the mayor who served as judge benefitted personally from the fees and costs imposed on the litigants. *Tumey v. Ohio* (S.Ct.1927). In a later case, the Court found a denial of the right to an unbiased judge even though the mayor-judge did not profit personally, but where the mayor exercised broad executive powers in the municipality, and a substantial portion of the municipal budget derived from fines the mayor levied as judge. *Ward v. Monroeville* (S.Ct.1972). The fact that defendants tried before the mayor's court were entitled to a trial *de novo* in another court with no presumption of correctness attaching to the first trial made no difference, since the defendant is entitled to a neutral detached judge in the first instance.

In a number of cases the Supreme Court has held that contempt citations imposed by judges against persons who appear before them are a denial of the defendant's right to an impartial judge, particularly when the contempt order is based on personal attacks on the judge. These cases have distinguished between contempt orders issued immediately and those made at the end of the trial. For reasons that have not been fully explained, the Court has approved contempt citations issued promptly after the offending behavior, but has held that due process requires that the contempt issue be decided by another judge when the trial court waits until the end of the trial.

The right to an impartial judge is not violated simply because the judge has participated in another aspect of the proceedings or acquired information relevant to the defendant's guilt that would be regarded as compromising the impartiality of a juror. Grounds for challenging a judge for cause are typically set forth in statute or court rule. Although these provisions may include specific grounds for disqualification, they also provide more generally for disqualification if the judge is biased.

In *Liteky v. U.S.* (S.Ct.1994), the Supreme Court rejected the contention that the federal judicial disqualification statute includes a strict "extra-judicial source" requirement. In reaching this conclusion the Court first acknowledged that the fact that the judge has acquired information relevant to the case from a source other than the courtroom proceedings is clearly relevant to whether the judge is biased. This is so because "bias" denotes a state of mind that is not only negative but also *wrongful* or *inappropriate*, and one circumstance that can render a judge's negative opinion of the accused or the issues inappropriate is that it is derived from an improper source.

The Court also held, however, that a demonstration of an extra judicial source is neither invariably required nor necessarily sufficient to establish judicial bias. In concluding that the defendants in the case before it had not proven bias requiring disqualification, the Court stated that the grounds put forth by the defendants—rulings and comments by the judge during a previous trial of some of the defendants—"[a]ll occurred in the course of judicial proceedings, and neither (1) relied upon knowledge acquired outside such proceedings nor (2) displayed deep-seated and unequivocal antagonism that would render fair judgment impossible."

Approximately one-third of the states grant the parties one opportunity to challenge the judge without having to demonstrate bias.

CHAPTER 13

THE TRIAL

A. PUBLIC TRIAL

1. THE SIXTH AMENDMENT RIGHT

The Sixth Amendment guarantees the accused the right to a "public trial." This right to keep the trial open to the public covers the entire trial, from jury selection to the return of the jury's verdict. It also applies to some pre-trial proceedings that resemble a trial, such as the preliminary hearing. The Supreme Court has held that the right to a public trial is among those Sixth Amendment protections that are binding on the states. *In re Oliver* (S.Ct. 1948).

The Sixth Amendment right to a public trial belongs to the defendant. The Sixth Amendment does not guarantee that the public, or the press on behalf of the public, have a right of access to criminal trials, though the Supreme Court has held that a right of public access is included in the First Amendment.

The defendant and the public in general benefit from keeping criminal trials open because openness helps ensure that the courts not be used as instruments of persecution. As the Supreme Court stated in *Oliver*, "[k]nowledge that every criminal trial is subject to contemporaneous review in the forum of public opinion is an effective restraint on possible abuse of judicial power." In addition to ensuring that judge and prosecutor act responsibly, preserving the openness of criminal trials also encourages witnesses to come forward and discourages perjury.

The right to a public trial is not absolute. The Supreme Court has stated that in order to close a hearing over the defendant's objection the party seeking closure must advance an overriding interest that is likely to be prejudiced by keeping the proceedings open. In addition, closure must be no broader than is necessary to protect that interest, the trial court must consider reasonable alternatives to closing the proceedings, and the court must make findings adequate to support the closure.

Applying this standard, the Court concluded in *Waller v. Georgia* (S.Ct.1984) that the threat to privacy interests of non-parties from playing intercepted telephone conversations did not justify closing the entirety of the suppression hearing when the playing of the tapes took up only two and one-half hours of the seven day hearing. Among the interests that have been recognized by lower courts as justifying a limited closure of the proceedings are protecting the privacy and safety of victims or witnesses, protecting the identity of undercover agents, and national security concerns.

2. FAIR TRIAL AND FREE PRESS

As a general rule, open trials benefit the defendant by protecting against the possibility of abuse of the judicial process that could occur if trials were conducted in secret. However, in a small proportion of cases that receive extensive media coverage and command wide public interest, publicity concerning the crime can pose a serious threat to the defendant's right to a fair trial.

Pretrial publicity may make it difficult or impossible to select an impartial jury, since information about the crime and the accused that is disseminated by the media may convince the community of the defendant's guilt even before the trial begins. When members of the public are then called for jury service, these prospective jurors may not be able to put aside their feelings or convictions and judge the defendant's guilt or innocence solely on the basis of the trial evidence. On the other hand, simply excluding during jury selection all jurors who have been exposed to publicity may undercut the representativeness of the jury, and may result in the elimination from the jury panel of precisely those public minded persons who are otherwise best qualified to serve.

3. RESTRICTING THE MEDIA

One possible method of protecting against the threat to the defendant's interest in a fair trial that is posed by pretrial publicity is to prohibit the media from publishing potentially prejudicial information. The Supreme Court has held, however, that prohibiting the media from reporting information that might prejudice the defendant's right to a fair trial will rarely, if ever, be permissible. In *Nebraska Press Association v. Stuart* (S.Ct.1976), the trial judge entered an order barring publication of 1) evidence presented at the defendant's preliminary hearing and 2) information derived from other sources that might implicate the defendant in the crime. Representatives of the press challenged the order as a violation of the First Amendment right to freedom of the press. In sustaining the challenge, the Supreme Court first flatly rejected the ban against publication of testimony from the preliminary hearing. The Court stated that "once a public hearing had been held, what transpired there could not be subject to prior restraint."

The Court also invalidated the ban on reporting information from sources other than the preliminary hearing. Although the Court did not declare a complete prohibition against prior restraints on publication of this type of information, its opinion made clear that the party seeking such a restraint bears a heavy burden to justify the action. After stressing that prior restraints on speech and publication represent the most serious and least tolerable infringement on First Amendment rights, the Court allowed the possibility that a publication ban might be ordered in a particular case based on consideration of 1) the nature and extent of pretrial news coverage, 2) the availability of other measures to mitigate its effects, and 3) the effectiveness of a restraining order in preventing the threatened danger. This possibility seems remote, however, in light of the strong disapproval of publication bans expressed in the concurring opinions in *Nebraska Press Association* and other First Amendment cases.

4. CLOSING THE COURTROOM

In *Nebraska Press Association*, the Supreme Court held that a ban against publication of testimony presented at the defendant's preliminary hearing is an impermissible method of protecting the defendant against the dissemination of potentially prejudicial information. Another possible technique for accomplishing the same objective is to deny the press access to the information by closing the proceedings, since the media cannot publish information which it does not possess. Closure of the trial or other proceedings—preliminary hearings, suppression hearings, jury selection proceedings—is also sometimes sought to accomplish objectives other than the protection of the interests of the defendant, such as protecting the privacy of jurors or crime victims.

The constitution nowhere expressly guarantees a right of access to criminal trials that would prevent closure of the courtroom. The Supreme Court has held, however, that a public right of access is embraced by the First Amendment, and that right is applicable to the states. *Richmond Newspapers v. Virginia* (S.Ct.1980). Although the Sixth Amendment grants the *defendant* the right to a "public trial," the Supreme Court has held that the Sixth Amendment does not create a right of access to the courtroom in either the public or the press, *Gannett Co. v. DePasquale* (S.Ct.1979).

In several cases the Court has held that the First Amendment right of access recognized in *Richmond Newspapers* applies to proceedings other than the trial itself, including the jury selection process, *Press-Enterprise Co. v. Superior Court* (S.Ct. 1984)(*Press-Enterprise I*), and the preliminary hearing, *Press-Enterprise Co. v. Superior Court* (S.Ct. 1986)(*Press-Enterprise II*). The Court's reasoning in these cases seems to guarantee a right of access to other proceedings as well, such as bail hearings and hearings on motions to suppress evidence. There is no public right of access to grand jury proceedings, which have traditionally been conducted in secret.

The First Amendment right of access to criminal trials and other proceedings is not absolute. The determination of whether a courtroom closure is permissible depends on a balancing of the First Amendment right of access against the right asserted in opposition to an open proceeding. The standard for deciding whether the courtroom must remain open when the interest that is asserted in favor of closure is the defendant's right to a fair trial was established in *Press-Enterprise II*.

That case involved a multiple murder prosecution that had received extensive press coverage. At the defendant's request, the trial court closed the preliminary hearing to protect the defendant from the risk that disclosure of inculpatory evidence from the preliminary hearing would prejudice potential jurors against him. On review of the closure order in the Supreme Court, the Court held that closure is permitted to protect the defendant's fair trial rights only if specific findings demonstrate: 1) there is a substantial probability that the defendant's right to a fair trial will be prejudiced by publicity that closure would prevent; and 2) reasonable alternatives to closure cannot adequately protect the defendant's fair trial rights.

Because the trial court had ordered closure on a lower standard of a "reasonable likelihood" of prejudice, and had not made specific findings that alternatives short of closure would protect the defendant against prejudice from pretrial publicity, such as voir dire of potential jurors, the closure of the preliminary hearing was improper. Although *Press-Enterprise II* involved the closure of a preliminary hearing, the standard stated there appears to be applicable to other proceedings as well.

When closure of criminal proceedings is sought on grounds other than the protection of the defendant's fair trial rights, the First Amendment right of access can be denied only if the closure is 1) necessitated by a compelling governmental interest; and 2) the denial of access is narrowly tailored to serve that interest. In *Globe Newspaper Co. v. Superior Court* (S.Ct.1982) the Court applied this standard to strike down a state statute that required exclusion of the press and the public from the courtroom during the testimony of minor victims of sex crimes. The Court held that the state had a compelling interest in protecting minors who testified in sex offense trials from trauma and embarrassment, and that this interest would justify closure on a case-by-case basis. The privacy rights of the victims did not, however, justify a blanket closure in all cases, as required by the statute.

In *Press-Enterprise I* the Court considered the claim that exclusion of the press from the courtroom during the voir dire questioning of prospective jurors was necessary to protect the jurors from public disclosure of embarrassing information. The Court held that the privacy interests of jurors could be a valid basis for closing the courtroom in some circumstances, but that closure could be ordered only upon a clear demonstration of necessity. Instead of closing the entire proceeding, as the trial court had done, the proper procedure is to advise potential jurors of their right to raise privacy concerns with the judge, and then order a limited closure only if an in camera interview with the juror reveals a valid basis for excluding the public.

5. RESTRICTING THE ATTORNEYS

Another possible technique for controlling pretrial publicity is to limit or prohibit extra-judicial statements by lawyers, parties, witnesses, or other participants in the criminal justice system. In *Sheppard v. Maxwell* (S.Ct.1966) a case in which the Court found that the defendant was denied a fair trial because of massive publicity, the Court stated that the trial judge should have made some effort to prevent the spread of prejudicial information. In particular, the Court wrote that "the trial court might well have proscribed extra-judicial statements by any lawyer, party, witness, or court official which divulged prejudicial matters." Despite the Court's seemingly definitive language, the permissibility of such a proscription under the First Amendment is far from certain.

In *Gentile v. State Bar of Nevada* (S.Ct.1991) the Court addressed the constitutionality of a state bar disciplinary rule that imposed restrictions on the extra-judicial statements of attorneys. Gentile, a lawyer, represented the owner of safe deposit box company who was charged with stealing drugs and money from one of the boxes. The stolen items had been stored in the box after police had seized them in an undercover police operation. The case received extensive media coverage because of reports circulating prior to the filing of charges which suggested that the drugs and money may have been stolen by a named police officer.

The day his client was indicted, Gentile held a press conference for the purpose of countering various statements emanating from the police and other sources, including reports that the two suspected police officers had submitted to lie detector tests, which they passed, but Gentile's client had refused to be tested. At the press conference Gentile stated, among other things, that his client was innocent, that the evidence pointed to a named police officer as the guilty party, and that claims by other box holders that they had also suffered thefts were not credible, since those persons were criminals who had accused Gentile's client in order to curry favor with the police.

Based on Gentile's statements in the press conference, the Nevada State Bar charged Gentile in a disciplinary proceeding with violating bar association rules regarding extra-judicial statements by lawyers regarding pending cases. The provision under which he was charged, which was virtually identical to the comparable provision in the ABA Model Rules of Professional Conduct, prohibits a lawyer from making "an extra-judicial statement that a reasonable person would expect to be disseminated by means of public communication," and which the lawyer should know "will have a substantial likelihood of materially prejudicing the trial." The rule specifies several types of statements that are deemed likely to materially prejudice the trial, including statements relating to the credibility of a likely witness.

In concluding that Gentile had violated the rule, the State Bar found that Gentile's statements related to the credibility of persons he expected to be called as witnesses—the police officer and the other box holders—and his purpose in calling the press conference was to influence public opinion by countering information offered by the prosecution and police. The Bar Association reprimanded Gentile. Gentile then challenged the Bar's action on the ground that it violated his First Amendment rights.

A five-to-four majority of the Supreme Court rejected Gentile's claim that the Nevada Bar Association rule was unconstitutional on its face. The Court was evenly divided on the question whether the Nevada rule was unconstitutional as applied.

In holding that the rule was not unconstitutional on its face, the Court rejected the argument that extra-judicial statements by lawyers should be governed by the same First Amendment standard that is applied to the press, stating that the speech of lawyers representing clients in pending cases may be subjected to greater restrictions than are permissible for the press. The reasons for permitting a more restrictive standard for lawyers, according to the Court, are that lawyers have access to more information through discovery and client communications than the press, and the statements of lawyers pose a special threat to the fairness of the proceedings, since their statements are likely to be received as especially authoritative.

The Court concluded that the "substantial likelihood of material prejudice" standard contained in the Nevada Bar rule strikes a constitutionally permissible balance between the First Amendment rights of attorneys in pending cases and the state's interest in fair trials. The Court identified two principal evils that the restriction on attorney speech is intended to combat: 1) comments that are likely to influence the outcome of the trial; and 2) comments that are likely to prejudice the pool of potential jurors, even if they do not prevent the selection of an impartial jury panel. The challenged rule, according to the Court, is narrowly tailored to achieve these objectives. The restriction is limited, covering only speech that is substantially likely to have a materially prejudicial effect; it does not favor any viewpoint, since it applies equally to all attorneys participating in the case; and it does not impose a permanent bar on any speech, but simply postpones the attorney's comments until after the trial.

Although a majority of the Court approved the constitutionality of the "substantial likelihood" standard, a different five-to-four majority concluded that the reprimand imposed on Gentile nonetheless violated his First Amendment rights because the rule's "safe harbor" provision was unconstitutionally vague. That provision, which was also adopted from the ABA Model Rules, states that, notwithstanding the general prohibition against extra-judicial comments, a lawyer "may state without elaboration ... the general nature of the claim or defense."

In holding this provision unconstitutionally vague, the Court stated that the right to explain the "general" nature of the defense without "elaboration" provides insufficient guidance because "general" and "elaboration" are both "classic terms of degree" that have "no settled usage or tradition of interpretation." In discussing the vagueness issue, the Court found it significant that Gentile had made an effort to conform his conduct to the requirements of the rule; he had researched the law relating to permissible extra-judicial comment before holding the press conference, and had told reporters during the press conference that he could not go into certain matters because of "ethics."

It is not clear from the *Gentile* decision what restrictions may be imposed on the speech of other participants in the criminal justice system, such as witnesses, parties, and other court personnel. On the one hand, the majority opinion's emphasis on the special powers and responsibilities of attorneys as the reason for a more restrictive standard suggests that the free speech rights of non-lawyer participants may be broader. At another point in the opinion, however, the majority spoke in terms of the speech rights of "those participating before the court," suggesting that the interests justifying restrictions on attorneys might be applicable to other participants as well.

B. DEFENDANT'S PRESENCE AT TRIAL

The Sixth Amendment guarantees the defendant the right "to be confronted with witnesses against him." The most fundamental component of this right of confrontation is the defendant's right to be physically present in the courtroom during the trial. A right of physical presence, grounded in due process, also extends to non-evidentiary trial proceedings which do not involve confrontation with adverse witnesses. The right to physical presence has been held to apply to jury selection, the giving of jury instructions, sentencing, and other proceedings that have a reasonably substantial relation to the defendant's opportunity to defend against the charge. The defendant has been held not to have a constitutional right to be present at some types of proceedings that relate solely to the resolution of questions of law, such as bench conferences and post trial motions for a new trial.

1. THE ABSENT DEFENDANT

The Supreme Court has long recognized that the defendant can make a knowing waiver of his right to be present during the trial. In *Taylor v. U.S.* (S.Ct.1973), the Court held that under some circumstances the trial can proceed in the defendant's absence even though the defendant has not entered an express waiver of her right to attend. Taylor, who was free on bail, had been present when the trial began, but then did not appear for the afternoon session after a lunch recess. The trial judge proceeded with the trial without the defendant, and the defendant appealed the resulting conviction on the ground that he had not knowingly waived his Sixth Amendment right to be present. The Supreme Court held that the defendant's voluntary absence after the trial had already begun constituted an effective waiver of his right to be present.

The Court based its holding in *Taylor* on its conclusion that a defendant who flees from the courtroom in the middle of the trial could reasonably be charged with knowledge that the trial would continue in her absence. Because the waiver theory adopted in *Taylor* is premised on the assumption that the defendant's initial appearance provides assurance that she knowingly relinquished her right to be present, it is unclear whether the constitution permits a defendant to be tried *in absentia* if she was not present when the trial began.

Under Rule 43 of the Federal Rules of Criminal Procedure the trial of an absent defendant is prohibited if the defendant was not present when the trial began. In *Crosby v. U.S.* (S.Ct.1993), the Court held that Rule 43 of the Federal Rules of Criminal Procedure prohibits the trial of a defendant who was not present at the beginning of the trial.

The principle established in *Taylor* is not applicable when the defendant's failure to appear is involuntary. A defendant who has been convicted following a trial from which she was involuntarily absent should be free to set aside the conviction on the grounds of violation of her right to attend.

2.   THE DISRUPTIVE DEFENDANT

The defendant's right to be physically present during the trial can be lost if the defendant's behavior in the courtroom makes it impossible to conduct an orderly judicial proceeding. In *Illinois v. Allen* (S.Ct.1970), the trial court excluded the defendant from the trial after repeated warnings from the trial judge that his disruptive and abusive behavior would lead to his removal. In upholding the trial court's action, the Supreme Court identified three constitutionally permissible methods of dealing with a disruptive defendant: 1) bind and gag the defendant in the courtroom; 2) cite the defendant for contempt; and 3) remove the defendant from the courtroom until she promises to conduct herself properly.

The Court's opinion in *Allen* suggests that in most situations the preferred method of dealing with a disruptive defendant will be removal. Binding and gagging the defendant in the presence of the jury prejudices the jury against her, prevents the defendant from communicating with her attorney, and is itself an affront to the dignity and decorum that should characterize judicial proceedings. Punishing the defendant with a contempt citation is unlikely to be effective against a defendant who is bent on disrupting the trial. In approving the trial court's action in removing Allen, the Supreme Court emphasized that the trial judge had repeatedly warned Allen that he would be removed if he persisted in his unruly behavior, and had also informed Allen he could return to the courtroom if he agreed to conduct himself in an orderly manner.

C. COMPETENCY TO STAND TRIAL

The Supreme Court has held that it is a denial of due process to try a person who is mentally incompetent at the time of the trial. (Note the distinction between the requirement of *competency to stand trial*, which focuses on the defendant's mental condition at the time of trial, and the *insanity defense*, which focuses on the defendant's mental state at the time of the commission of the crime.) The rationale for this rule is that the defendant's rights to be physically present at the trial and to confront her accusers are largely meaningless if the defendant lacks the mental capacity to understand the proceedings.

The test for competency to stand trial, first stated in *Dusky v. U.S.* (S.Ct.1960), requires only a minimal ability to understand and participate in the trial. As stated by the Court, the test asks whether the defendant has 1) "sufficient present ability to consult with his lawyer with a reasonable degree of rational understanding" and 2) "a rational as well as factual understanding of the proceedings." In *Godinez v. Moran* (S.Ct.1993), the Court held that the *Dusky* standard also governs the determination whether the defendant is competent to waive her right to counsel and enter a plea of guilty without the assistance of an attorney. The majority rejected the position taken by some lower courts that a higher standard of competency should be required for a valid waiver of constitutional rights, such as the right to counsel or to a trial, than is required for a defendant to proceed to trial with the assistance of an attorney.

The Supreme Court has held that the due process prohibition against trying an incompetent defendant imposes a constitutional obligation on the trial judge to inquire into the defendant's competency, without a request from the defendant, whenever "a sufficient doubt exists as to [the defendant's] present competence." *Pate v. Robinson* (S.Ct.1966). In

Robinson the Court held that the defendant's history of mental illness and erratic behavior, together with his assertion of an insanity defense, should have alerted the trial judge to the necessity for a hearing on the defendant's competency to stand trial, even though the defendant's behavior at trial did not suggest incompetency, and his attorney did not request an inquiry into competency.

Defendants who have been found incompetent to stand trial are typically hospitalized until such time as their mental condition improves to the point that they become competent. In *Jackson v. Indiana* (S.Ct.1972) the Court held that both the equal protection guarantee and the right to due process limit the state's power to confine persons who have been charged with a crime but never tried because of incompetency to stand trial. The defendant in the case was charged with minor theft crimes. Although the only legal basis for Jackson's confinement was to render him competent to stand trial, his confinement was effectively permanent, since there was little if any realistic possibility of his attaining competency.

The Court held that Jackson's confinement violated his right to equal protection because persons confined on the grounds of incompetency to stand trial were treated differently from persons subject to involuntary commitment under civil commitment statutes for the mentally ill. Persons confined on the grounds of incompetency to stand trial were subject to both a more lenient commitment standard and more stringent release criteria than those not charged with commission of a crime, who could be confined only under the state's civil commitment procedures. The Court also held that Jackson's due process rights were violated because the duration of Jackson's confinement, which was likely permanent, bore no rational relation to the purpose of his commitment. The Court concluded that a person who is committed solely on account of incompetency to stand trial cannot be held more than the reasonable time necessary to determine whether there is a substantial probability that she will attain competency in the foreseeable future. If it is determined that this is not the case, the state must either institute civil commitment proceedings or release the defendant.

D. BURDEN OF PROOF

It is a fundamental principle of American criminal law that conviction for a crime requires proof beyond a reasonable doubt. It was not until 1970, however, that this principle was held to be constitutionally mandated. In *In re Winship* (S.Ct.1970), the Court held that the Due Process Clause "protects the accused against conviction except upon proof beyond a reasonable doubt of every fact necessary to constitute the crime with which he is charged." The Court also held that the beyond a reasonable doubt standard is required in juvenile adjudications.

The constitutional requirement of proof beyond a reasonable doubt is given effect, first, by the requirement that the jury be instructed that it may convict only if it finds that the evidence establishes each of the elements of the offense beyond a reasonable doubt. Although the constitution does not require that any particular form of words be used in instructing the jury on the prosecution's burden of proving the defendant guilty beyond a reasonable doubt, jury instructions that fail adequately to convey the meaning of the reasonable doubt standard may violate the defendant's due process rights.

In one case, the Supreme Court held that a reasonable doubt instruction stating, among other things, that a reasonable doubt must be such a doubt as would give rise to a "grave uncertainty," is a "substantial doubt," and requires that jurors be persuaded to a "moral certainty," required a higher degree of doubt than is necessary for acquittal, and therefore authorized a guilty verdict on a lower standard of proof than the constitution demands. *Cage v. Louisiana* (S.Ct.1990).

In another case the Court held that an instruction which used the phrases "moral evidence" and "moral certainty" in defining reasonable doubt did not violate the defendant's Due Process rights, since the instruction as whole adequately conveyed to the jurors "the need to reach a subjective state of near certitude of the guilt of the accused." *Victor v. Nebraska* (S.Ct.1994) quoting *Jackson v. Virginia* (S.Ct.1979). Moreover, the Court has held that a constitutionally deficient reasonable doubt instruction cannot be harmless error and requires automatic reversal. *Sullivan v. Louisiana* (S.Ct.1993).

The reasonable doubt standard is also given effect through judicial review of the legal sufficiency of the evidence to support a conviction. This can occur both before the case is given to the jury, in response to a defense motion to direct a verdict of acquittal, or after the jury has found the defendant guilty, in response to a post-conviction motion or an appeal. The constitutional standard for the legal sufficiency of the evidence is "whether, after viewing the evidence in the light most favorable to the prosecution, *any* rational trier of fact could have found the essential elements of the crime beyond a reasonable doubt." *Jackson v. Virginia.*

1. DEFENSES

In *Mullaney v. Wilbur* (S.Ct.1975), the Court appeared to hold that the *Winship* requirement that the prosecution prove beyond a reasonable doubt every fact necessary to constitute the crime requires as well that the prosecution disprove beyond a reasonable doubt all defenses. In *Mullaney*, the Court held that a Maine statute that required the defendant to prove by a preponderance of evidence that she acted "in the heat of passion on sudden provocation" in order to reduce murder to manslaughter unconstitutionally shifted to the defense the burden of proving the "malice" element of homicide.

Two years after *Mullaney*, in *Patterson v. N.Y.* (S.Ct.1977), the Court repudiated a broad reading of *Mullaney*, and clearly held that the constitution permits imposing on the defendant the burden of proving at least some defenses. In *Patterson*, the Court rejected the defendant's Due Process challenge to a New York statute requiring that the defendant prove "extreme emotional disturbance" by a preponderance of the evidence in order to reduce an intentional killing from murder to manslaughter. The Court distinguished *Mullaney* on the ground that the statute involved in that case presumed a lack of provocation—which the Court regarded as equivalent to presuming the existence of malice—and therefore shifted to the defendant the burden of disproving an element of the crime. The extreme emotional disturbance statute at issue in *Patterson*, by contrast, was viewed by the Court as creating an affirmative defense that did not relieve the prosecution of the burden of proving any element of the crime.

Under *Patterson*, and the Court's subsequent decisions, the constitutionality of imposing on the defendant the burden of proving facts relevant to guilt or punishment is primarily a matter of legislative labeling. If the fact is labeled by the legislature as an element of the offense, the constitution requires that it be proven by the prosecution beyond a reasonable doubt. If the fact is defined as an affirmative defense, in most cases the fact need not be proven by the prosecution beyond a reasonable doubt, and the burden of proving the fact may be placed on the defendant. Thus, it is constitutionally permissible to impose on the defendant the burden of proving the defenses of insanity and self defense. *Martin v. Ohio* (S.Ct.1987).

The constitution presumably does not permit imposing on the defendant the burden of proving a "defense" which simply negatives a statutory element of the crime. The defense of alibi—the claim by the defendant that she did not commit the crime because she was elsewhere at the time of its commission—is an example of such a defense. The prosecution must *disprove* the defendant's claim of alibi, which is simply another way of saying that the prosecution must *prove* that the defendant committed the offense.

For a discussion of burden of proof requirements for facts identified as sentencing factors, see Ch. 15.

2. PRESUMPTIONS

The requirement that the prosecution bear the burden of proving the elements of the crime beyond a reasonable doubt also places limits on the use of presumptions in criminal cases. As the word is used in the law of evidence, a "presumption" is a rule of law prescribing that proof of one fact—called the "basic" or "foundational" fact—establishes or tends to establish the existence of another fact—called the "presumed" fact. Thus, if the law presumes that a gun found inside a car is possessed by any occupant of that car, proof that a gun was found inside the car (the basic fact) establishes that it was possessed by the occupant of the car (the presumed fact). As the illustration shows, a presumption enables a party to prove the existence of the presumed fact (possession of the gun) without having to introduce evidence of that fact.

The Supreme Court's cases dealing with the use of presumptions in criminal cases have distinguished four types of presumptions that differ in the type or strength of the relation between the basic fact and the presumed fact. The weakest type of presumption, which is not strictly speaking a presumption at all, is a permissive inference. A permissive inference exists if the fact finder (typically a juror) may, but need not necessarily, infer the existence of the presumed fact based on proof of the basic fact. Thus, referring to the basic fact as "A" and the presumed fact as "B," a permissive inference permits, but does not require, the juror to find the existence of B based on evidence of A alone (that is, without any evidence of B).

The second type of presumption, stronger than a mere permissive inference, is commonly referred to as a "bursting bubble" presumption. With a bursting bubble presumption, proof of A tends to establish B only until evidence is presented tending to show the non-existence of B. Once the presumption is rebutted through the introduction of evidence of the non-existence of B, the "bubble bursts" and the presumption disappears from the case. (Another way of saying this is that the presumption shifts the "burden of production" but does not shift the "burden of persuasion.") This second type of presumption is stronger than a permissive inference because, if the presumption is not rebutted, the presumption is conclusive and the jury is informed that it must accept the presumed fact as true.

A third type of presumption that is stronger still creates a bubble that does not burst with the introduction of contrary evidence. Even after the presumption is rebutted through the introduction of evidence tending to show that the presumed fact does not exist, the presumption retains some force as proof of the presumed fact, though it is not always clear how the artificial probative force created by the presumption is to be weighed with the evidence. This type of presumption is also known as a presumption that shifts the burden of persuasion.

Finally, a "conclusive" or "irrebuttable" presumption cannot be rebutted with evidence tending to show the non-existence of the presumed fact. In effect, a conclusive presumption simply substitutes proof of the basic fact for proof the presumed fact. Proof of the basic fact—a gun in the car—mandates a finding of the presumed fact—that the gun was possessed by the car's occupant. Such a conclusive presumption is really a substantive law rule and not a presumption at all.

The use of permissive inferences in criminal cases violates the Due Process Clause only if the suggested conclusion is not one that reason and common sense justify in light of the proven facts before the jury. In essence, a permissive inference is constitutionally unobjectionable provided the basic fact is logically relevant to the presumed fact. In order to be constitutional, it is also necessary that the jury instruction, by which the jury is informed of the permissive inference, explain the presumption with sufficient clarity to prevent the jury's interpreting the instruction as shifting the burden of proof to the defense.

The use of either mandatory presumptions or presumptions that shift the burden of persuasion (type 3 above) in criminal cases violates Due Process. The reason for this rule is that such presumptions relieve the prosecution of the burden of proving the necessary elements of crime beyond a reasonable doubt. The Supreme Court has not yet ruled on the constitutionality of a bursting bubble type presumption that shifts to the defense the burden of production but not the burden of persuasion.

E. PRESENTATION OF EVIDENCE

1. ORDER OF PROOF

After the jury is selected and sworn, the trial begins with opening statements by the attorneys for the parties. The basic purpose of opening statements is to outline the evidence that the parties intend to present to provide the jury with a framework for understanding the evidence.

Following opening statements, the prosecution presents its evidence in chief. This may consist of both testimonial evidence—the in-court testimony of witnesses—and real evidence—tangible objects and documentary evidence.

After the prosecution has rested, the defense routinely moves for a directed verdict of acquittal. The defendant is entitled to an acquittal if the prosecution's evidence in chief, even if believed, does not establish the defendant's guilt beyond a reasonable doubt. In some jurisdictions, the judge may either decide the motion immediately or delay decision until after the jury has returned a verdict. Postponing decision on the motion has the advantages of eliminating the need for a decision if the jury acquits, and preserving the prosecution's right to appeal a ruling in favor of the defense if the jury convicts.

Because the prosecution has the burden of proof on all of the essential elements of the crime, the defense is not required to present any evidence. The defense case, if there is one, may include the same types of testimonial and real evidence as presented by the prosecution. At the conclusion of the defense case, the prosecution has a right to respond to the defendant's proof with rebuttal evidence, and if the prosecution's rebuttal case raises new issues, the defense may be permitted to present rebuttal evidence as well.

Once the presentation of evidence is complete, the parties are given an opportunity to address the jury with closing arguments or summations. In many jurisdictions, the prosecution presents two closing arguments, one before and another one after the defense argument.

2. DEFENDANT'S RIGHT TO TESTIFY

The constitution nowhere expressly guarantees the accused's right to testify at her own trial. However, the Supreme Court has found such a right to be implicit in several constitutional provisions, including the Due Process Clause, which includes the right to be heard and give evidence, the Sixth Amendment Compulsory Process Clause, which logically includes the right to call oneself as a witness, and the Fifth Amendment guarantee against compulsory self-incrimination, which has as a necessary corollary the right to testify. *Rock v. Arkansas* (S.Ct.1987).

The accused's right to testify is not absolute, but may be limited to accommodate "legitimate interests in the criminal trial process." For instance, the state's interest in preventing the introduction of unreliable evidence justifies requiring the defendant to conform her testimony to the rules of evidence. Restrictions imposed on the defendant's right to testify may not, however, be either arbitrary or excessive in relation to the purposes they are designed to serve. Thus, in *Rock*, the case in which the Court first announced the right to testify, the Court held that a state statute imposing a *per se* ban on hypnotically enhanced testimony violated the defendant's constitutional right because it precluded all hypnotically refreshed testimony by the accused, without regard for the likelihood that the defendant's testimony in the particular case is unreliable.

3. DEFENDANT'S RIGHT NOT TO TESTIFY

The Fifth Amendment provides that no person "shall be compelled in any criminal case to be a witness against himself." The protections of the Fifth Amendment Self-incrimination Clause are applicable against the states through the Fourteenth Amendment. *Malloy v. Hogan* (S.Ct.1964).

The Fifth Amendment privilege against compelled self-incrimination entitles all witnesses, in both criminal and civil cases, to refuse to answer questions if the answers would either directly incriminate the witness or establish a link in a chain of evidence needed to prosecute the witness. For the accused in a criminal case, however, the protections of the Fifth Amendment are considerably broader. Unlike other witnesses, who have the privilege of refusing to answer, the Fifth Amendment protects the accused from being compelled to submit to questioning in the first instance. The defendant's Fifth Amendment privilege against compelled self-incrimination bars the prosecution from calling an accused as a witness in her own trial.

The Fifth Amendment privilege protects against *compelled* self-incrimination; it does not bar either the accused or an ordinary witness from waiving her rights and testifying voluntarily. The rules regarding waiver are different for the accused and all other witnesses. A witness who is not the accused in a criminal case will be deemed to have waived her Fifth Amendment privilege only if she gives incriminating testimony.

An accused who chooses to testify, however, thereby exposes herself to cross-examination under the rules governing cross-examination generally, and is deemed to have waived her privilege to refuse to answer any questions that are within the scope of permissible cross. In most jurisdictions the scope of cross-examination is determined by the witness's testimony on direct. This means that the accused who chooses to testify may be questioned on cross about any matters that are relevant to her testimony on direct. In some jurisdictions the scope of cross-examination is not limited to matters raised on direct, and the defendant's Fifth Amendment waiver is correspondingly broader. In these jurisdictions the testifying defendant waives her privilege with respect to any question that elicits facts relevant to the case. In all jurisdictions a defendant who testifies waives her privilege with respect to questions that are relevant for the purpose of impeaching the defendant's credibility as a witness.

In *Griffin v. California* (S.Ct.1965) the Court held that the Fifth Amendment privilege against compelled self-incrimination prohibits the prosecutor or the trial judge from commenting to the jury on the defendant's failure to testify. Prior to *Griffin*, some states had permitted the prosecutor to argue to the jury in closing argument that the defendant's silence at trial was an indication of her guilt. The reasoning behind such argument is that an innocent accused would not sit silent but would take the stand and proclaim her innocence. The *Griffin* decision held this practice penalizes the defendant's exercise of her Fifth Amendment privilege and is therefore unconstitutional.

The prohibition against commenting on the defendant's failure to testify prohibits comment that was either intended by the prosecutor or necessarily understood by the jury as a comment on the defendant's silence. Courts are frequently faced with deciding whether statements by the prosecutor which do not directly refer to the defendant's silence are nonetheless prohibited under *Griffin*. For instance, courts have given conflicting responses to the question whether a prosecutor's statement that the state's case was "unrefuted" or "uncontradicted" constitutes an impermissible comment on the defendant's failure to testify. A statement by the prosecutor that alludes to the defendant's silence is more likely to be found acceptable if it can be shown that the prosecutor was responding to arguments made by the defense. Even if a given comment is found to violate the *Griffin* rule, it may be, and often is, found to be harmless error on appeal.

In *Carter v. Kentucky* (S.Ct.1981), the Court held that the trial court, on request by the defendant, is constitutionally required to instruct the jury that it may not draw an adverse inference from the defendant's failure to testify. Defense counsel frequently refuse a so called "no inference" instruction on the belief that instructing the jury not to use the defendant's silence against her will do more harm than good by simply calling the jury's attention to the fact that the defendant did not testify.

In *Lakeside v. Oregon* (S.Ct.1978), however, the Court rejected the contention that the defendant is entitled to a reversal of his conviction when the trial court gives a no inference instruction over her objection. The Court refused to presume either 1) that the defendant's failure to testify might escape the jury's notice if no instruction were given or 2) that the jurors would disregard a no inference instruction and affirmatively give weight to what they had been told not to consider.

4. COMPULSORY PROCESS AND ACCESS TO EVIDENCE

The Sixth Amendment commands that the accused "shall have compulsory process for obtaining witnesses in his favor." In *Washington v. Texas* (S.Ct.1967), the Court held that this right to offer the testimony of witnesses and, if necessary, compel their attendance is a fundamental element of Due Process that is applicable to the states. In that case the Court held that a Texas statute that prohibited the defendant (but not the prosecution) from calling an alleged accomplice as a witness violated the defendant's right to compulsory process. If permitted to testify, the accomplice would have related that the defendant tried to prevent the homicide and fled before the accomplice fired the fatal shot. The Court held that the Texas statute arbitrarily denied the defendant the right to present relevant and material evidence, but cautioned that the Compulsory Process Clause does not guarantee defense access to evidence that is privileged or override other non-arbitrary limitations on the defendant's ability to present evidence.

The limited scope of the compulsory process guarantee and its relation to other constitutional doctrines relating to defense access to evidence is illustrated by the Supreme Court's decision in *Pennsylvania v. Ritchie* (S.Ct.1987). There the defendant sought to compel a state agency to turn over files relating to the case, which were privileged under a state statute. In rejecting the defendant's contention that the Compulsory Process Clause guaranteed him access to the files, the Court stated that it had never held that the Compulsory Process Clause guarantees a right to discover the *identity* of witnesses or to require the prosecution to produce exculpatory evidence. (A plurality of the Court also rejected the defendant's claim that denying him access to the files violated his Sixth Amendment confrontation rights because it interfered with his ability to cross-examine trial witnesses.)

The *Ritchie* Court went on to conclude that the defendant's entitlement to the information in the files should be evaluated under the Due Process standards for disclosure of exculpatory evidence. (See Chapter 5.) In another case, *U.S. v. Valenzuela–Bernal* (S.Ct.1982), the Court rejected the defendant's claim that his compulsory process rights were violated by the government's deportation of potential witnesses before the defendant had an opportunity to interview them. The Court emphasized that the government's practice of prompt deportation of illegal aliens is justified by its obligation to enforce the immigration laws, and stated that the government may be sanctioned for deporting witnesses "only if the criminal defendant makes a plausible showing that the testimony of the deported witnesses would have been material and favorable to his defense, in ways not merely cumulative to the testimony of available witnesses."

In addition to the constitutional compulsory process guarantee, all jurisdictions make the court's subpoena power available to the defendant by statute or court rule. Federal Rule of Criminal Procedure 17 provides that the court clerk shall "issue a subpoena, signed and sealed but otherwise in blank to a party requesting it, who shall fill in the blanks before serving it." The subpoena may be used either to compel the attendance of witnesses or to command the production of documents or tangible objects. Rule 17 also provides that the costs of subpoenaing and calling witnesses shall be paid by the government if the defendant demonstrates that she is indigent and that the presence of the witness is necessary.

5.   CONFRONTATION

The Sixth Amendment commands that "in all criminal prosecutions, the accused shall enjoy the right ... to be confronted with the witnesses against him." Read literally, this language would seem to require that all those who give evidence against the accused must testify in the physical presence of the defendant. In its application of the clause, however, the Supreme Court has focused on the *purpose* of the confrontation right, which the Court had identified, until its 2004 decision in *Crawford v. Washington* (S.Ct.2004), as ensuring the reliability of evidence presented against the accused, and has refused to interpret the clause as requiring direct face-to-face confrontation in all circumstances. In line with this focus on the purpose of the right, the Court has held that the Confrontation Clause also guarantees the defendant the right to cross-examine witnesses who appear in court and testify against her.

The confrontation right belongs to the defendant. The clause applies only to evidence presented *against* the accused; it does not apply to evidence presented *by* the defense. The Confrontation Clause is applicable in state prosecutions to the same extent as in federal court.

a.   Confrontation and "In Court" Testimony

In two cases the Supreme Court has addressed the constitutionality under the Confrontation Clause of courtroom procedures in which the witness testifies "in court" but not in face-to-face contact with the accused. Both cases arose out of child abuse prosecutions and involved procedures designed to protect child witnesses from the trauma of testifying in the presence of their abuser.

In *Coy v. Iowa* (S.Ct.1988), the child witnesses were separated from the accused by a screen that prevented the witness from seeing the defendant but allowed the defendant "dimly to perceive the witnesses." The state defended the practice as necessary to protect the two 13 year old sexual assault victims from trauma. Declaring that "[i]t is always more difficult to tell a lie about a person 'to his face' than 'behind his back,'" the Court held that the defendant's confrontation rights were violated because there had been "no individualized findings that these particular witnesses needed special protection."

Two years later in *Maryland v. Craig* (S.Ct.1990) the Court addressed the constitutionality of a procedure in which the witness testifies by way of one-way closed circuit television. Under the statute at issue in *Craig*, the procedure may be utilized only after the trial judge has made a determination that testimony by the child victim in the courtroom would result in the child suffering "serious emotional distress such that the child cannot reasonably communicate." Once that determination is made and the procedure is invoked, the witness, the prosecutor, and defense counsel withdraw to a separate room equipped with a television camera, and the judge, jury and defendant observe the witness's testimony on a video monitor in the courtroom. The defendant remains in electronic contact with defense counsel, and objections may be made and ruled on as if the witness were present in the courtroom. The witness, however, cannot see the accused.

In evaluating the constitutionality of this procedure, the Supreme Court relied on decisions addressing Confrontation Clause challenges to the admission of hearsay evidence under an exception to the hearsay rule. In those cases the Court identified the purpose of the Confrontation Clause as protecting the defendant against conviction by unreliable evidence. Confrontation guarantees the reliability of evidence in three ways: it ensures that the statements of witnesses will be made under oath; it forces the witness to submit to cross-examination; and it affords the jury the opportunity to observe the demeanor of the witness as an aid to evaluating the witness's credibility. Applying these principles to the case before it, the Court held that the Confrontation Clause does not prohibit the use of procedures that deprive the defendant of face-to-face confrontation if 1) the procedures are necessary to protect a child witness from trauma that would be caused by testifying in the physical presence of the defendant, at least where such trauma would impair the child's ability to communicate, and 2) the procedure used ensures the reliability of the evidence by subjecting it to rigorous adversarial testing.

Because the statute at issue in *Craig* required a judicial finding that testifying in the defendant's presence would cause the child witness emotional trauma such that she could not reasonably communicate, and because the closed circuit television procedure used in *Craig* incorporated all three of the safeguards of reliability associated with direct confrontation—oath, cross-examination, and demeanor—the Court held that it preserved the essence of effective confrontation and was constitutional.

b. Hearsay and Confrontation

All American jurisdictions have a hearsay rule that forbids the use of testimonial-type statements made out of court. But because all jurisdictions also recognize numerous exceptions to the hearsay ban, the admission of hearsay evidence at trial is a very common occurrence.

The introduction of hearsay evidence against the accused involves a potential violation of the Confrontation Clause, since the defendant is often deprived of the opportunity to confront the person who uttered the hearsay statement—the hearsay declarant. The admission of an out of court statement for a non-hearsay use does not raise issues under the Confrontation Clause.

In *Ohio v. Roberts* (S.Ct.1980) the Court established what it termed a "general framework" for evaluation of the constitutionality under the Confrontation Clause of the admission of hearsay evidence against the accused. In that case the defendant challenged as a violation of his confrontation rights the admission at trial of the preliminary hearing testimony of a witness who was no longer available at the time of trial. The evidence was admitted under a version of the former testimony exception to the hearsay rule.

The Court in *Roberts* established a two-part test for determining whether the admission of hearsay evidence violates the Confrontation Clause. The first prong of the test requires that the prosecution either produce the hearsay declarant at trial or demonstrate that the declarant is unavailable to testify. If the prosecution makes the declarant available for cross-examination by the defendant, the defendant's confrontation rights have been satisfied, and the inquiry need not proceed to step two. If, however, the prosecution demonstrates that the declarant is unavailable, the second part of the test requires that the hearsay evidence be shown to be *reliable*.

Reliability under the *Roberts* test can be demonstrated in two ways. First, hearsay that is admitted under a "firmly rooted" hearsay exception is presumed to be reliable, and no individualized demonstration of reliability is required. If the exception under which the evidence is admitted is not "firmly rooted," the prosecution must show from the facts of the case that the hearsay has "particularized guarantees of trustworthiness."

Although the Supreme Court professed continued adherence to the two part framework set forth in *Roberts*, subsequent decisions, even before *Crawford,* have considerably eroded the impact of the rule. In several cases culminating with *White v. Illinois* (S.Ct.1992) the Court appeared to eliminate a general requirement that the hearsay declarant be unavailable for hearsay evidence to be admissible. According to the Court in *White*, the Confrontation Clause requires a demonstration that the hearsay declarant is unavailable only when the out of court statements were made in the course of a prior judicial proceeding (as occurred in *Roberts*).

The Court had also signaled that most of the specific or class exceptions to the hearsay rule are "firmly rooted," and therefore evidence admitted under one of those exceptions is would be immune from challenge under the Confrontation Clause. The Court has held that the hearsay exceptions for co-conspirators statements, excited utterances, and statements for purposes of medical diagnoses are all firmly rooted.

Then, a plurality of the Court held that the exception for declarations against penal interest was not firmly rooted in *Lilly v. Virginia* (S.Ct. 1999). Furthermore, the Court also held that a state residual exception to the hearsay rule patterned after the residual exception contained in the Federal Rules of Evidence is not firmly rooted in *Idaho v. Wright* (S.Ct.1990). In order to introduce evidence under these exceptions, therefore, under the *Roberts* test of the Confrontation Clause, requires an individualized assessment of the reliability of the hearsay offered under the exception. This demonstration of reliability, according to the Court, must be based on the circumstances surrounding the making of the hearsay statement, rather than from other evidence in the case corroborating the truth of the hearsay.

Then came the Court's decision in *Crawford*, in which the Court adopted a Confrontation Clause test that treats "testimonial" statements under a standard different from the *Roberts* two-pronged test. Any evidence of an out-of-court statement found to be "testimonial" can only be admitted into evidence against a criminal accused, under *Crawford*, if the witness is shown to be unavailable *and* the accused had a prior opportunity to cross-examine that unavailable witness.

The *Crawford* Court did not fully define what constitutes "testimonial" evidence, nor did it eliminate the possibility of the *Roberts* rule applying to non-testimonial hearsay. The Court conceded that some categories of out-of-court statements are clearly testimonial, including: "Extrajudicial statements ... contained in formalized testimonial materials such as affidavits, depositions, prior testimony, or confessions" or "statements that were made under circumstances which would lead an objective witness reasonably to believe that the statement would be available for use at a later trial"

Moreover, the *Crawford* Court did not eliminate the possibility that the *Roberts* rule might survive as a measure of the validity of non-testimonial hearsay under the Confrontation Clause. The *Crawford* Court said it was not necessary to "definitively resolve whether [Roberts] survives our decision today" because the hearsay in *Crawford* would be inadmissible even if *Roberts* did not survive.

Confrontation Clause issues can also arise when two or more defendants are tried together and the prosecution introduces the out of court confession of one defendant that also implicates the co-defendant. Under the law of evidence, the out of court confession is admissible against the defendant who made the out of court statement, but not admissible against her co-defendants. Thus, if defendants A and B are tried together for a bank robbery, A's out of court confession that "B and I robbed the bank" is admissible against A but ordinarily not admissible against B. The standard solution to this problem of "limited admissibility" within the law of evidence is to instruct the jury that the out of court confession may be considered as evidence against the defendant who made the statement, but may not be considered as evidence against the defendant who did not.

In *Bruton v. U.S.* (S.Ct.1968), however, the Court held that such a "limiting instruction" is inadequate to protect the confrontation rights of the non-confessing defendant, since jurors cannot reasonably be expected to follow such an instruction and compartmentalize the evidence. In order to avoid a so-called "*Bruton* error," prosecutors must either conduct separate trials for the two defendants or redact the confession to eliminate all reference to the non-confessing co-defendant.

There are three situations in which the introduction of one defendant's confession does not violate the confrontation rights of co-defendants in the same trial. First, if the confessor defendant testifies and is subject to cross-examination, the confrontation rights of the co-defendants will have been satisfied. *Nelson v. O'Neil* (S.Ct.1971). Second, the admission of the out of court confession is not a violation of the Confrontation Clause if the confession is shown to be reliable under the Confrontation Clause standards for the admission of hearsay evidence. *Lee v. Illinois* (S.Ct.1986). Thus, if the confession qualifies for admission under a "firmly rooted" hearsay exception, its admission against nonconfessing defendants is not barred by the Confrontation Clause. Finally, the introduction of an out of court confession does not implicate the Confrontation Clause if the statement is admitted for some purpose other than to prove the truth of what is asserted in the statement. *Tennessee v. Street* (S.Ct. 1985).

c. Cross–Examination

The Supreme Court has long held that the Confrontation Clause protects the defendant's right to cross-examine witnesses and restricts the state's ability to impose limits on the nature and extent of cross-examination. The Court has been especially sensitive to restrictions on cross-examination that hamper the defendant's ability to demonstrate a prosecution witness's possible *bias*. In *Davis v. Alaska* (S.Ct.1974), for example, the Court held that the defendant's confrontation rights were violated when the trial judge prevented the defendant from cross-examining a key prosecution witness to show that the witness was on juvenile probation which could be revoked if the witness failed to assist the state. Although the Court acknowledged that the states have a legitimate interest in protecting the anonymity of juvenile offenders, the Court held that this interest was outweighed by the defendant's Sixth Amendment right to cross-examine the witness to expose a possible motivation to testify falsely. Similarly, in *Olden v. Kentucky* (S.Ct.1988) the Court held that the state's application of its rape shield statute to prevent the defendant from cross examining the alleged victim about her extra-marital relationship violated the defendant's confrontation rights where evidence of the relationship tended to establish a motive to falsify the rape charge.

The Confrontation Clause guarantees an opportunity for effective cross-examination. This does not, however, prevent courts from imposing reasonable limits on cross-examination based on concerns about witness harassment, prejudice, confusion of the issues, the witness's safety, or questioning that is repetitive or only marginally relevant.

In *Delaware v. Van Arsdall* (S.Ct.1986), the Court rejected the claim that a violation of the defendant's right to confront and cross-examine witnesses requires automatic reversal.

6. ATTORNEY ARGUMENT

Objections on the grounds of improper attorney argument during closing statement are common in criminal trials, and defendants frequently appeal their conviction on the ground that the prosecutor's argument deprived them of a fair trial. Because the Double Jeopardy Clause prevents the prosecution from appealing an acquittal, appellate review of defense arguments is rare.

The scope of permissible attorney argument is subject to the discretionary control of the trial judge, and the law governing what is proper and improper in closing argument cannot be stated with precision. A more or less standard categorization of types of prohibited argument is contained in the American Bar Association Standards for Criminal Justice. Although some commentators have argued that defense counsel should be and in fact are granted a broader leeway than prosecutors in arguing their case to the jury, the ABA standards for prosecutors and defense attorneys are the same, and courts generally purport to apply the same rules to both parties.

The ABA Standards identify four categories of prohibited argument. First, it is improper for attorneys to misstate the evidence or to make arguments that are not supported by evidence presented at the trial. In arguing their case to the jury, however, counsel may argue all reasonable inferences from the evidence, and may present arguments based on factual propositions that are matters of common knowledge. It is often difficult to distinguish arguments that are improper as not based on the record from arguments that are properly based on inferences drawn from the evidence.

Second, it is improper in closing argument to express a personal belief or opinion as to the truth or falsity of the evidence or the guilt or innocence of the accused. Counsel may, however, explain to the jury why it should accept or reject specific testimony, and urge the jury to draw certain conclusions from the evidence. Although attorneys should refrain from couching their arguments in the first person ("I believe, I think, or I know"), the line between proper argument and improper "vouching" is often unclear.

Third, attorneys are prohibited from making arguments that are "calculated to inflame the passions or prejudices of the jury." An example of an improper appeal to passion is the so-called "golden rule" argument, in which prosecutors invite the jurors to put themselves in the position of the victim of the crime. The prohibition against inciting the passions and prejudices of the jury does not prevent all appeals to emotion. For instance, it is generally not deemed improper to call the jury's attention to the seriousness of the crime and the harm suffered by the victim, even though such an argument injects an emotional element into the jury's consideration of the case.

Finally, the counsel should refrain from argument that would divert the jury from its duty to decide the case on the evidence, by injecting issues broader than the guilt or innocence of the accused, or by making predictions of the consequences of the jury's verdict. As with the prohibitions discussed above, the proscription against injecting extraneous considerations into the jury's decision does not produce a bright line rule. For instance, courts disagree on the propriety of a prosecutor arguing that a conviction of the defendant would deter others from committing crime.

In reviewing claims that prosecutors have crossed the line of appropriate argument, appellate courts frequently consider whether the prosecutor's arguments were responsive to arguments made by defense counsel. The Supreme Court discussed this "invited response" doctrine in *U.S. v. Young* (S.Ct. 1985). In that case the trial prosecutor had expressed his opinion that the defendant's actions constituted "fraud" after the defense counsel had stated in closing argument that even the prosecutor did not believe that the defendant had acted with a fraudulent intent. In responding to the defendant's claim that the prosecutor's actions entitled him to a reversal, the Court emphasized that the misconduct by defense counsel did not give the prosecutor a "license" to engage in similar misconduct, and that the proper response by the prosecutor to defense counsel's argument would have been an objection accompanied by a request for a warning to defense counsel against further misconduct and a curative instruction to the jury. The Court went on to state, however, that the fact that the prosecutor's argument was directly responsive to arguments by the defense was relevant to whether the prosecutor's statements unfairly prejudiced the defendant, and concluded on the facts before it that the harm from the prosecutor's remark was mitigated by the jury's understanding that the prosecutor was countering assertions by defense counsel.

The standards governing proper and improper attorney argument are primarily a matter of judicially fashioned local law. The Supreme Court has recognized, however, that misconduct by the prosecutor in arguing the case to the jury can result in a federal constitutional violation. The constitutional standard is violated if the prosecutor's argument "so infected the trial with unfairness as to make the resulting conviction a denial of Due Process." *Darden v. Wainwright* (S.Ct.1986). Because the Double Jeopardy Clause prevents the prosecution from appealing an acquittal, appellate review of defense arguments is rare.

7. JURY DELIBERATIONS AND VERDICT

a. Special Verdicts

In civil jury trials, it is relatively common to submit the case to the jury with a request for a "special verdict" in which the jury responds to a set of specific factual questions that are subsidiary to the ultimate issue in the case. In criminal cases, however, the use of special verdicts is disfavored, at least if the use of a special verdict is not requested or agreed to by the defendant.

General verdicts of either "guilty" or "not guilty" are preferred in criminal cases in order to protect the jury's nullification power. Jury nullification refers to the jury's power to return a verdict according to conscience and acquit an accused who is guilty under the law and the facts. As the United States First Circuit Court of Appeals explained in the leading case on the subject, "[t]here is no easier way to reach, and perhaps force, a verdict of guilty than to approach it step by step.... By a progression of questions each of which seems to require an answer unfavorable to the defendant, a reluctant juror may be led to vote for a conviction which, in the large, he would have resisted." *U.S. v. Spock* (1st Cir.1969). Where the questions included in a special verdict do not carry the risk of coercing a guilty verdict, the use of special verdicts is permissible.

Although the *Spock* decision suggested that the defendant's right to a general verdict may be grounded in the Due Process Clause, the Supreme Court has never held that there is a constitutional right to a general verdict in a criminal case. Because the prohibition against the use of special verdicts is rooted in the defendant's right to acquit against the law and the evidence, there should be no legal impediment to the use of a special verdict if agreed to by the defendant.

b.   Jury Deadlocks

It is not uncommon for juries to report to the judge in the course of their deliberations that they are unable to agree on a verdict. The trial judge is not required to dismiss the jury at the first indication of deadlock, but may order the jury to return to the juryroom and continue deliberations. The judge may not force a deadlocked jury to deliberate longer than is reasonable in light of the number and complexity of the charges they are considering. On the other hand, if the judge declares a mistrial and dismisses the jury without an adequate attempt to ensure that a verdict cannot be reached, re-trial may be barred by the Double Jeopardy Clause.

When faced with a jury that reports itself deadlocked, judges sometimes seek to encourage the jury to reach a verdict by giving a supplemental instruction. In the early case of *Allen v. U.S.* (S.Ct.1896), the Court approved the use of a charge which first advised the jurors that "the verdict must be the verdict of each individual juror, and not a mere acquiescence in the conclusion of his fellows," but then went on to charge that "if much the larger number [of jurors] were for conviction, a dissenting juror should consider whether his doubt was a reasonable one which made no impression upon the minds of so many men, equally honest, equally intelligent with himself." The charge also included language encouraging minority jurors favoring conviction to reconsider their position in light of the fact that a majority of the jury was in favor of acquittal.

In recent years some courts have concluded that use of this so-called "*Allen*" or "dynamite" charge carries too great a risk of coercing minority jurors to surrender their convictions, and have utilized charges that contain somewhat gentler encouragements to jurors to overcome their disagreements and reach a verdict. One alternative to the traditional *Allen* charge instructs jurors that they should not to hesitate to reexamine their views and change their opinions if convinced that they are erroneous, but, unlike the *Allen* charge, does not speak directly to minority jurors.

c.   Inconsistent Verdicts

In federal court and most states it is not necessary that the jury's verdicts on multiple counts or against multiple defendants be consistent with each other. This means that a defendant convicted by a jury on one count cannot attack that conviction on the ground that it is inconsistent with the jury's verdict of acquittal on another count or against another defendant in the same trial. (The collateral estoppel doctrine may compel a different result if separate juries return inconsistent verdicts in separate trials.) A jury's verdict is inconsistent if, for example, the jury convicts on a count requiring proof of "X" and "Y," but acquits on a count requiring proof of "X" only. A substantial minority of states hold that such an inconsistency is reversible error.

The rule tolerating inconsistent verdicts is justified as an adjunct to the jury's historic power to exercise leniency and acquit notwithstanding evidence of the defendant's guilt. Because the jury does not reveal the reasons for its decisions, however, the actual cause of the inconsistency in the jury's findings is never certain. It is possible that the inconsistent verdicts are the result of jury confusion rather than jury leniency.

In *U.S. v. Powell* (S.Ct.1984) the Court adhered to the position that a conviction on some counts cannot be attacked on the basis that it is inconsistent with an acquittal on other counts even if the circumstances do not support a conclusion that the jury was acting out of leniency in the acquittal. The defendant in *Powell* was convicted on a count charging use of the telephone to commit certain felonies (the "compound" offense), but acquitted on counts charging the commission of those underlying felonies (the "predicate" offense). The jury had been instructed that it must find the defendant guilty on the predicate offense in order to convict on the compound offense.

In rejecting the defendant's challenge to her conviction on the compound offense, the Court observed that any individualized assessment of the reasons for the jury's verdict in a particular case would be either speculative or violate long established practice against inquiry into the jury's deliberations. The Court also emphasized that the defendant is protected against jury irrationality or error by judicial review of the sufficiency of the evidence to support the conviction.

It is sometimes argued that a defendant should be permitted to attack a *judge's* verdict on grounds of inconsistency. The argument for applying different rules to verdicts by judges and juries is that judges do not possess the same power to speak the conscience of the community and acquit against the evidence as juries. In *Harris v. Rivera* (S.Ct.1981), however, the Court rejected the defendant's claim that he had a constitutional right to raise an inconsistency challenge to a judge's verdict, stating that "[t]he constitution does not prohibit state judges from being excessively lenient." The federal system and many states nevertheless apply different rules to judges and juries as a matter of non-constitutional local law.

d.   Impeaching Jury Verdicts

Attempts are sometimes made to invalidate or "impeach" the verdict of a jury on the ground that the jurors engaged in some form of misconduct during the trial or deliberations. However, a defendant's ability to upset her conviction because of juror misconduct is severely restricted by the evidentiary rule that prohibits most juror testimony regarding what occurred during deliberations if the testimony is offered for the purpose of invalidating the verdict.

Federal Rule of Evidence 606(b), which is similar to rules found in all jurisdictions, prohibits a juror from testifying to "any matter or statement occurring during the course of the jury's deliberations or the effect of anything upon that or any other juror's mind or emotions as influencing the juror to assent or dissent from the verdict ... or concerning the juror's mental processes in connection therewith."

This general prohibition against juror evidence is subject to two exceptions: a juror is not barred from testifying on the question 1) "whether extraneous prejudicial information was improperly brought to the jury's attention" or 2) "whether any outside influence was improperly brought to bear on any juror." The rule applies only to testimony or other evidence offered by jurors; there is no prohibition against the use of evidence from non-jurors to prove jury misconduct.

Because evidence of jury misconduct is rarely available from a source other than the jurors themselves, the effect of this evidence rule is virtually to prevent impeachment of jury verdicts on the grounds of juror misconduct unless the misconduct can be fit within one of the rule's exceptions. The courts have interpreted the first exception permitting testimony on "extraneous prejudicial information" to allow juror testimony that, for example, jurors read newspaper articles regarding the crime or made an unauthorized visit to the crime scene. Juror testimony that the jurors misunderstood or disregarded the trial judge's instructions on the law, or that they acted out of improper motives in convicting the defendant is not permitted. Courts have differed on whether juror testimony that the jurors conducted unauthorized experiments or tests with trial exhibits is admissible under this exception. Because the jury misconduct provable under this exception involves the jury's receipt of case specific information that must ordinarily be introduced in open court subject to adversarial testing, the courts have suggested that this exception may be constitutionally required, and that the jury's exposure to such information during deliberations may violate the defendant's Confrontation Clause rights.

The prime example of evidence admissible under the second exception for "outside influence" is juror testimony that jurors were bribed or threatened by non-jurors. Evidence that one of the jurors made threats against another juror during deliberations, by contrast, is generally not admissible as "outside influence."

In *Tanner v. U.S.* (S.Ct.1987), the Court construed the federal prohibition against juror testimony broadly to prohibit juror testimony that jurors consumed alcohol and illegal drugs during the trial and deliberations. The Court reasoned that juror intoxication was no more an *external* influence than physical or mental incompetence of jurors, which have been regarded as *internal* to the jury and not provable by the jurors. Although the evidence rule by its terms applies only to matters occurring during "deliberations," the Court in *Tanner* prohibited juror testimony that the jurors consumed drugs and alcohol during the trial as well.

After the defendant overcomes the initial hurdle and presents admissible evidence of juror misconduct, the defendant must still demonstrate that the alleged misconduct was prejudicial requiring an invalidation of the verdict. The prejudice inquiry focuses on the likelihood that the misconduct influenced the juror's evaluation of the case. For some types of serious misconduct, such as outside efforts to influence the jury or juror exposure to prejudicial information about the case, the courts adopt a presumption of prejudice that must be overcome by the prosecution in order for the verdict to stand. For less serious misconduct the defendant must prove prejudice. Because jurors are not permitted to testify to the effect of the misconduct on their decision making, the prejudice inquiry focuses on the likely impact of the misconduct on a reasonable juror.

CHAPTER 14

SENTENCING

The subject of sentencing—the decision about what consequences should be imposed for a violation of the criminal law—has been a matter of considerable debate in recent years, and both the law and public attitudes regarding sentencing have changed in important ways. There has occurred a general shift in emphasis away from rehabilitation as the purpose of criminal sanctions in favor of retribution or punishment. In addition, in many jurisdictions the law has been changed to make the sentencing decision less discretionary and more "structured," in that the decision is based on the application of legal rules to formal findings of fact. This shift toward more structured sentencing has raised new questions about the procedures to be followed in determining sentences.

A. THE GOALS OF SENTENCING

Decisions regarding what is the appropriate sentence for a person convicted of a crime depend to a great extent on the goal or goals that the criminal sentence is intended to achieve. One goal of sentencing is deterrence. The theory behind deterrent sentencing is that if the commission of a crime carries a threat of unpleasant consequences, the potential offender will refrain from committing crime in order to avoid those consequences.

There are two types of deterrence: specific deterrence and general deterrence. Specific deterrence is aimed at the individual who has already committed a crime, and is intended to deter that person from committing other crimes in the future. The aim is to punish the specific offender harshly enough so that the offender will not want to experience the discomfort of prosecution and punishment again, and will therefore not commit further crimes. General deterrence is designed to send a message to other potential offenders, so they will not commit crimes or the same type of crime. A single act of punishment can accomplish both specific and general deterrence, since it will serve both to deter the individual punished and send a message to others who might be inclined to become offenders.

Both types of deterrence rely on two assumptions. The first assumption is that before committing a crime, people weigh the consequences of their actions. The second assumption is that potential offenders believe that they will be caught and punished if they violate the law. Thus, if the criminal behavior involved is emotionally motivated and impulsive rather than calculated, there will be little likelihood that the individual will consider the threatened punishment as a deterrent. And even as to those crimes that are planned and calculated, deterrence will be effective only if the offender believes that detection of the crime and punishment are likely.

Another goal that sometimes underlies sentencing decisions is separation, also called incapacitation. The goal of separation or incapacitation is accomplished by segregating the offender from the rest of society, in a prison, or disabling the offender from committing further crimes, through such means as "chemical castration" or in some cases putting the person to death.

The efficacy of separation or incapacitation as a means of protecting society is beyond dispute. The recent popularity of "three strikes" sentencing laws and other sentencing schemes that increase the sentence for repeat offenders is probably explained in part by the aim of preventing persons perceived to pose a threat to society from committing additional crimes. Sentences designed to separate or incapacitate, such as three strikes sentences, are sometimes criticized as unjust if the sentence is deemed out of proportion to the offense. Imprisonment and the death penalty are also extremely costly to implement, both because of the cost of housing prisoners and because of lost productivity and other social costs from imprisoning large numbers of people.

A third goal of sentencing is rehabilitation. Rehabilitation refers to the effort to reform or transform the offender, or the offender's behavior, to enable the individual to become a productive member of society. This can take the form of education while in prison, job training, supervised release, drug or alcohol abuse treatment, counseling, or other efforts. Rehabilitation emerged as a principal goal of sentencing at the turn of the nineteenth century, and remained a dominant goal of sentencing through the 1970s. In recent decades, however, emphasis has shifted away from rehabilitation in favor of the fourth goal of sentencing, which is retribution.

Retribution, also referred to as punishment or vengeance, is rooted in the sense that those who violate social norms *deserve* to be punished. Although philosophers have had difficulty explaining why people who do bad things deserve to be punished or must "pay" for their crimes, the principle of retribution is deeply rooted in history, culture, and religion.

For those who believe in the principle of retribution or "just deserts," the punishment of an offender requires no justification beyond the fact of the commission of an offense. Because retribution is premised on the belief that the offender *deserves* to be punished, a retributive theory of punishment is strictly limited by the principle of proportionality. Retribution prohibits imposition of a punishment that is excessive in relation to the offense.

These four goals, or theories, of sentencing need not be mutually exclusive. That is, a legislature in enacting a sentencing law, or a judge in imposing a sentence, can be motivated by more than one goal or theory. For example, a sentence or a sentencing scheme may be intended to deter future crimes, but the severity of the sentence may be limited by the proportionality principle that is inherent in the idea of retribution.

Although the goals, or theories, of sentencing can, in some situations, work together, they are also sometimes incompatible. For instance, the goal of separation or incapacitation may, at least in some situations, be inconsistent with a goal of rehabilitating an offender. This is because a prison term may be an effective means of separation that will prevent the offender from victimizing others, but the prison experience may simply harden rather than rehabilitate the offender.

B. SENTENCING OPTIONS

The criminal justice system offers lawmakers and judges a number of sentencing options. The decision as to what sentence is appropriate for a particular offense and a particular offender will depend on the nature and seriousness of the crime and characteristics of the offender. In addition, the goals that the sentence is intended to accomplish are or should be an important factor in choosing among sentencing options.

In all American jurisdictions the law authorizes a sentence of incarceration for all felonies and most misdemeanors. While incarceration is authorized for almost all crimes, prison terms are not actually imposed as often as other types of sentences. The most frequently imposed sentence is probation. An offender who has been sentenced to probation is placed under the supervision of a probation officer and required to comply with specified conditions over some set time period. If the probationer adequately complies with the conditions through the entire probation term, the supervision is ended and the conditions lifted. Failure to abide by the probation conditions can result in an increase in the level of supervision, the addition of new conditions, or the revocation of probation, which usually means that the offender will be incarcerated.

The level of supervision probationers are subjected to varies considerably. For many probationers, the only supervision is a monthly meeting with the probation officer or a phone interview. In recent years some jurisdictions have experimented with a form of "intense supervision" which involves much more frequent meetings and even unannounced visits from the probation officer.

Judges generally enjoy broad discretion in determining the conditions of probation. In addition to such standard conditions as not committing crimes, it is common for judges to require of probationers such things as holding a job, supporting their family, or staying in school. In one California case a trial judge ordered, as a condition of probation, that the offender not play varsity or professional basketball during the probation period. On appeal, the court invalidated the condition on the ground that the basketball prohibition was more likely to impede, than to promote, rehabilitation. Such decisions are rare, however, since a judge's decision regarding the conditions of probation will generally be upheld unless the condition has no reasonable relation to the goals of the probation.

The Supreme Court has held that some constitutional rights apply differently to probationers than to other citizens. In *Griffin v. Wisconsin* (S.Ct.1987) the Court upheld a search of the probationer's home that was conducted without either a warrant or probable cause. The search was conducted by probation officers, but police were also present during the search. The search was carried out under authority of a state statute that required "reasonable grounds" to believe that contraband would be found in the place searched.

Because the decision to revoke probation involves a deprivation of liberty, the procedures used by the state in making the revocation decision must satisfy the demands of due process. However, the requirements of due process in the probation revocation setting are not as exacting as they are in the context of the trial. The Supreme Court has held that a probationer is entitled to a preliminary hearing to determine whether there is probable cause to believe a condition of probation has been violated, and a final hearing to make the ultimate decision whether to revoke probation. The final hearing is an adversarial proceeding in which the probationer is entitled to written notice of the claimed probation violation, disclosure of the evidence against him, an opportunity to be heard personally and to present evidence, the right to confront and cross-examine witnesses, a neutral and detached decision maker, and a written statement of the evidence relied on and the reasons for revoking probation. *Morrissey v. Brewer* (S.Ct.1972). There is no constitutional right to a speedy probation-revocation hearing, however. Because the decision to revoke probation is concerned with the success of defendant's rehabilitation, the added information about defendant's progress made available by delay may be advantageous to both the decisionmaker and the defendant. *Carchman v. Nash* (S.Ct.1985). Nonetheless, the rules of evidence do not apply during hearings to grant or revoke probation. Fed. R. Evid. § 1101(d)(3).

Whether an indigent probationer is entitled to appointed counsel at a revocation hearing is made on a case by case basis. To be entitled to counsel the probationer must establish the existence of a colorable claim either that no conditions of probation have been violated or that the violation was justified or mitigated by substantial reasons making revocation inappropriate, and those reasons are complex or difficult to present. *Gagnon v. Scarpelli* (S.Ct.1973).

Sentences of probation are often combined with other sanctions, including fines, restitution, or incarceration. Critics of sentencing practices in the United States have argued that the criminal justice system should make wider use of fines. There are clear advantages to imposing a monetary penalty on an offender rather than incarceration. While a fine exacts a penalty for the commission of the crime, and therefore serves the purposes of deterrence and punishment, fines do not carry the high social costs of incarceration. On the contrary, the fine can help offset the public expense of prosecution.

Those who urge wider use of fines in the U.S. often point to the countries of continental Europe as a model. One sentencing scheme used in Europe that some have suggested should be utilized in the U.S. is the system of day fines. Under a day fine system, the fine that is imposed for a particular offense is not a fixed dollar amount, but an amount calculated based on the seriousness of the offense and the offender's income. This approach avoids the problem of imposing fines that are too high, which the offender will not be able to pay, and also fines that are too low, which do not amount to a significant penalty for the offender.

The use of fines or other economic penalties can present constitutional problems if the offender's inability to pay the fine results in incarceration. In *Williams v. Illinois* (S.Ct.1970) an indigent defendant whose sentence included $505 in fines and court costs was required to spend 101 days in jail under a state statute that required unpaid fines to be "worked off" at a rate of $5 per day. The Court held that the incarceration of the defendant because of his indigence beyond the period that a nonindigent offender could be jailed for the same offense violated the defendant's right to equal protection of the law under the Fourteenth Amendment.

The subsequent case of *Bearden v. Georgia* (S.Ct. 1983) involved the revocation of the defendant's probation because of his failure to pay a fine. The Court avoided the equal protection issue, focusing instead on whether revocation of probation for failure to pay a fine violates the Due Process Clause. The Court held that an automatic revocation of probation for non-payment of a fine is fundamentally unfair, and therefore violates due process. However, if the defendant has the means to pay the fine and deliberately refuses, or fails to make a bona fide effort to acquire the necessary funds, revocation of probation for non-payment is permissible. If the defendant makes a bona fide effort to pay but is unable to do so, the court must determine whether there exist any adequate alternatives to incarceration before ordering the defendant's confinement. If there are no adequate alternatives, the court may order the defendant incarcerated because, according to the Court, "[a] defendant's poverty in no way immunizes him from punishment."

A fine is a monetary penalty that is paid to the government. In recent years there has been a growing interest in requiring convicted offenders to make restitution to the victim of the crime. In the federal system, for example, 18 U.S.C. § 3663 authorizes a court to order a defendant convicted of certain offenses to make restitution to the victim in the form of money, property or services. Monetary restitution can be ordered as compensation for lost or damaged property, payment of medical, funeral or other similar expenses, or payment for lost income.

C. STRUCTURING THE SENTENCING DECISION

In establishing a system for imposing sentences at least two issues must be resolved: who shall decide on the appropriate sentence, and what degree of discretion shall be entrusted to the sentencing authority. Sentencing schemes that give the sentencer discretion in deciding on the appropriate sentence raise an additional question regarding how the exercise of discretion shall be controlled.

The initial sentencing decision has generally been entrusted to the judge. The major exception to the general rule of judicial sentencing has been in capital cases, where juries are often called upon to decide whether to impose the death penalty. Although a judge typically decides on the sentence initially, the decision regarding the defendant's release from prison may be made by a parole board or other executive branch body.

1. INDETERMINATE SENTENCING

The sentencing system that involves the greatest degree of discretion is indeterminate sentencing. Under a system of indeterminate sentencing, the legislature authorizes broad ranges of prison terms for an offense or class of offenses. The top and bottom end of the range of permissible sentences increases with the seriousness of the crime.

The decision regarding the sentence to be imposed within the permissible range is made by the judge at the time of sentencing. In imposing sentence, the judge may be required to set only a minimum term, only a maximum term, or both a minimum term and a maximum term. The judge may also have the power to sentence the offender to a prison term and then suspend execution of the sentence, or defer sentencing and place the offender on probation. The actual term of incarceration beyond the minimum will be decided by the parole board, which has the power to order the offender's release based on a judgment about the offender's rehabilitation.

The system of indeterminate sentencing is designed to further the goal of rehabilitation. The broad discretion given the judge to fix the sentence reflects the view that the sentence should be based on an assessment of the rehabilitative needs of the individual offender. The indeterminate length of the sentence is designed to enable the parole board to monitor the progress of the offender with respect to rehabilitation, and to release the offender only when the rehabilitative process is complete.

The broad discretion in setting sentences that characterizes indeterminate sentencing schemes results in significant disparities in the sentences imposed on individual offenders. These disparities are tolerable or even desirable if they reflect the legitimate goals of the sentencing scheme, but they are clearly not tolerable if they are the result of such things as race or class. Dissatisfaction with disparity in sentencing, and a general shift in emphasis away from rehabilitation toward retribution as the primary goal of sentencing, has encouraged a trend to reduce the degree of discretion in determining sentences. Indeed, during "the 1970s each state followed an indeterminate sentencing scheme that offered the judge and the paroling authorities broad ranges within which to choose an appropriate sentence ... [d]uring the past thirty years that uniformity has disappeared." This occurred because of the lawmakers' "[c]oncerns about treating like cases alike, ensuring stiff penalties for certain crimes or criminals perceived to be particularly dangerous to society, and controlling corrections costs." WAYNE R. LAFAVE, JEROLD H. ISRAEL & NANCY J. KING, PRINCIPLES OF CRIMINAL PROCEDURE: POST-INVESTIGATION § 18.1(a) (2004).

2. DETERMINATE SENTENCING

Under a determinate sentencing scheme, the length of the sentence is definitively established by the judge at the time sentence is initially imposed, and there is no parole board or comparable authority with the discretionary power to determine the defendant's release date. Determinate sentencing systems also include mechanisms for limiting or eliminating the discretion of the judge in fixing the sentence.

One method of determinate sentencing that has been adopted in several states is known as presumptive sentencing. Under the presumptive sentencing system used in California, all felonies, except murder, are classified according to the seriousness of the crime. The law specifies three possible sentences for each class of felony: 1) a presumptive sentence, imposed in the absence of aggravating or mitigating circumstances; 2) a lower term that can be imposed if enumerated statutory mitigating circumstances are found to predominate; and, 3) a higher term that can be imposed if enumerated statutory aggravating factors predominate. The system of presumptive sentencing used in California does not include parole in the traditional sense, but the offender may qualify for release before the end of the term based on a record of good behavior in prison. In addition, all offenders are required to serve a three-year period of supervised release after leaving prison.

Another approach to determinate sentencing, that is now used in the federal system and some states, is a system of sentencing guidelines. The current federal sentencing system was adopted in 1984 with the Sentencing Reform Act. That Act abolished the federal parole commission and established a seven-member Sentencing Commission, which is charged with establishing guidelines to be used by judges in fixing sentences. The Sentencing Commission produced a sentencing manual of several hundred pages that guides the judge through a complicated process of fact finding and mathematical calculation that determines the sentence.

Under the federal sentencing guidelines an offender's sentence is based primarily on two factors—the "offense level," which is based on the characteristics of the offense, and the offender's "criminal history," which is based on the characteristics of the offender. A numerical score is calculated for both the offense level and the offender's criminal history based on the addition and subtraction of point values assigned to various factors under the guidelines. Once the judge has computed the offense level and the criminal history, the recommended sentence is determined by locating the sentence on a table, or grid, which assigns sentences for specific combinations of offense level and criminal history.

In calculating the offense level, the judge begins with the "base offense level" for the particular offense. The judge then adds or subtracts from this number based on "specific offense characteristics," such as the possession of a weapon in the commission of the offense, and "adjustments" for such factors as the defendant's role in the planning or commission of the crime and the defendant's acceptance of responsibility or cooperation with the prosecution. The number that represents the defendant's criminal history is computed by adding the score assigned in the guidelines for certain types of prior convictions.

In *Mistretta v. U.S.* (S.Ct.1989), the Court upheld the sentencing guidelines over challenges that they violated the doctrine of separation of powers, and that they involved an unconstitutional delegation of legislative power to the Sentencing Commission. The Supreme Court reviewed the constitutionality of the Federal Sentencing Guidelines in *U.S. v. Booker* (S.Ct.2005). The Booker Court was "deeply divided" and produced "two distinct majority opinions." One majority, led by Justice Stevens, held "the federal sentencing guidelines, when instructing judges to make factual findings to calculate increases in applicable sentencing ranges, transgressed the Sixth Amendment's jury trial right." Nonetheless, the remedy for this transgression, provided by the second majority, led by Justice Ginsburg, "was to declare the federal sentencing guidelines wholly advisory." Id. Therefore, "the guidelines are now an intricate set of suggestions for district judges: at sentencing, federal judges must continue to consult the guidelines, but no longer is a judge obliged to sentence within the ranges prescribed therein." *Id.* Nevertheless, "there are on-going debates within the U.S. Sentencing Commission and the U.S. Congress concerning whether an advisory guidelines system will facilitate and foster fair and effective federal sentencing."

D. PROCEDURAL ISSUES IN SENTENCING

In *Mempa v. Rhay* (S.Ct.1967) the Court held that the Sixth Amendment right to counsel applies to sentencing proceedings. Although the Court has not explicitly addressed the issue, the Court has also suggested that the right to counsel at sentencing includes the right to counsel that is effective.

Sentencing procedures must also comply with the requirements of the constitutional protection of due process. However, the courts have interpreted the demands of due process in the sentencing context differently from the trial context. The procedural safeguards required for sentencing are less stringent than those required for the trial. The courts also sometimes distinguish between capital sentencing and non-capital sentencing, demanding a higher level of protection for defendants who are sentenced to death.

1. FACTORS THAT MAY BE CONSIDERED IN SENTENCING

One important difference between the sentencing decision and the decision on guilt or innocence is that the judge in imposing sentence is permitted to consider a broad range of information that would not be admissible in evidence at the trial. While the character evidence rule generally prohibits introduction of evidence of the defendant's character at trial, information relating to the defendant's character is deemed highly pertinent to the judge's determination of sentence.

In *Williams v. N.Y.* (S.Ct.1949), for example, the Court condoned the sentencing court's consideration of prior burglaries for which the defendant had never been charged or convicted. The Court in *Williams* further stated that "the fullest information possible concerning the defendant's life and characteristics" is "highly relevant ... if not essential" to the selection of the appropriate sentence, and rejected the defendant's due process challenge to the state sentencing procedure which permitted the sentencer to consider information about the offender's "past life, health, habits, conduct, and mental and moral propensities."

U.S. v. Grayson (S.Ct.1978) addressed the defendant's due process challenge to the trial judge's imposition of a more severe sentence based on the judge's belief that the defendant had testified falsely at trial. The defendant argued that consideration of his allegedly perjurious testimony was improper for two reasons. First, the defendant argued that by increasing his sentence for testifying falsely the judge was in effect punishing him for a crime for which he had not been charged or convicted. The Court rejected this argument, stating that a defendant's willingness to testify falsely is probative of his attitude toward society and his prospects for rehabilitation, and therefore relevant to sentencing.

The defendant also argued that to permit the judge to use the defendant's suspected perjury as a factor in sentencing would have the effect of chilling the exercise of his right to testify on his own behalf. The Court rejected this argument as well, holding that the constitution guarantees only the right to testify *truthfully*, and that any chilling effect on the defendant's decision to testify falsely is entirely permissible.

In *Grayson* the Court premised its holding that there was no impermissible punishment for the exercise of a constitutional right on its conclusion that the constitution does not guarantee a right to testify falsely; the Court did not suggest that punishment for the exercise of a constitutional right, if demonstrated, is permissible.

In *N.C. v. Pearce* (S.Ct.1969) the Court held that the Due Process Clause does in fact prohibit punishing a defendant with a longer sentence for the exercise of his right to appeal his conviction. The defendant in that case obtained a reversal of his conviction for sexual assault on the ground that the trial judge erroneously admitted his confession at trial. Following a second trial and conviction for the same offense, the defendant was re-sentenced before the same judge, and received a harsher sentence than had been imposed after the first trial. The Court then held that the imposition of the longer sentence following the defendant's successful appeal violated his due process rights, stating that "vindictiveness against a defendant for having successfully attacked his first conviction must play no part in the sentence he receives after a new trial."

The *Pearce* rule does not require that the defendant offer proof of the actual subjective motivations of the judge in imposing the longer sentence in order to have the sentence set aside as a violation of due process. The Court established what amounts to a presumption that, in the circumstances presented in that case, the longer sentence was vindictive. To protect the accused from both retaliatory sentencing and the fear of retaliation, the Court in *Pearce* required that in order to impose a harsher sentence on re-sentencing the reasons for the harsher sentence must be on the record and must be based on facts occurring after the time of the original sentencing.

Since the decision in *Pearce*, the Court has narrowed the circumstances under which the presumption of vindictiveness applies. In *Chaffin v. Stynchcombe* (S.Ct.1973) the Court held that *Pearce* did not apply to jury sentencing. The potential for vindictive sentencing by a jury was "de minimus in a properly controlled retrial." Two factors were stressed. First, the jury sitting in the second trial would not know of the earlier sentence .. Second, "the second sentence is not meted out by the same judicial authority" that had its earlier proceeding reversed on appeal. The jury has no personal stake in the earlier proceeding, and it "is unlikely to be sensitive to the institutional interests that might occasion higher sentences by a judge desirous of discouraging what he regards as meritless appeals."

In *Texas v. McCullough* (S.Ct.1986) the defendant was initially sentenced by the jury rather than the judge. The trial judge granted the defendant's motion for a new trial, which resulted in the defendant's being tried a second time and re-convicted. After the second trial the defendant elected to be sentenced by the judge, who imposed a sentence more than twice as long as that originally imposed by the jury. The defendant then appealed claiming that the second longer sentence violated his due process right against vindictive sentencing.

The Court rejected the defendant's vindictive sentencing claim on three separate grounds. First, the Court held that the trial judge's action of granting the defendant's new trial motion demonstrated that the judge's sentence was not based on vindictive motives. The circumstances presented in *Pearce*, where the defendant obtains a reversal of the trial judge's ruling on appeal, gives rise to a presumption of vindictiveness because the trial judge who has been reversed may be motivated to engage in self-vindication. Where it is the trial judge herself who has granted the new trial, however, there is no realistic motive for vindictive sentencing, and the *Pearce* presumption does not apply.

The Court also held that the presumption of vindictiveness was inapplicable because the first sentence was imposed by the jury and the second was imposed by the judge. Where different sentencers have imposed the different sentences, the Court explained, it cannot be said that an "increase" in the sentence has occurred, but only that the judge and the jury assessed the relevant information differently.

Finally, the Court in *McCullough* held that even if the *Pearce* presumption of vindictiveness applied in that case, the presumption was rebutted by the trial judge's findings of her reasons for imposing the longer sentence. In imposing the longer sentence, the trial judge stated that she was relying on the testimony of two witnesses who testified at the second trial but not the first, and that she learned for the first time on the retrial that the defendant had been released from prison only four months before the crime was committed.

In *Alabama v. Smith* (S.Ct.1989) the Court held that no presumption of vindictiveness arises if the defendant receives a higher sentence following a vacated guilty plea and a subsequent conviction after trial. This is true even if both sentences were imposed by the same judge. The reason the presumption does not apply in this context is because the most likely explanation for the longer sentence is that the trial revealed new information not available at the time of sentencing following the guilty plea.

2.   NOTICE AND OPPORTUNITY TO BE HEARD

The previous section discussed potential limits on the range of information that may be considered by the judge in imposing a sentence. Another issue raised by the sentencing proceeding is whether the defendant has a right to notice and to be heard regarding the factors to be considered by the judge in deciding upon the sentence. The Supreme Court has held that, at least in capital cases, the defendant has a limited right to be informed of what is being used by the judge as the basis for the sentencing decision, and some opportunity to deny or explain that information.

The Supreme Court's leading recent decision on the right to notice and opportunity to be heard in sentencing is *Gardner v. Florida* (S.Ct.1977). In *Gardner* the defendant was sentenced to death based in part on confidential information contained in the pre-sentence report that was never disclosed to the defendant or his attorney. In response to the defendant's claim that this violated his right to due process of law, the state offered a number of justifications for its policy of non-disclosure.

The state first argued that without a guaranty of confidentiality, potential sources of information might be reluctant to disclose sensitive but relevant facts about the defendant's background and character. The Court found this argument unpersuasive, observing that consideration must be given to the quality as well as the quantity of information available to the sentencer, and that assurances of secrecy may be conducive to the transmission of information that is unreliable.

The state also argued that disclosure of sentencing information might unnecessarily delay the proceedings, and that some information contained in the pre-sentence report might disrupt the defendant's rehabilitation. The Court rejected both of these justifications for non-disclosure as well, noting that delays required to ascertain the truth of critical information are fully justified, and that concerns about possible adverse effects on the defendant's rehabilitation are not relevant when the defendant has been sentenced to death. The Court said that a defendant is denied due process of law when a death sentence is imposed on the basis of information that the defendant had no opportunity to deny or explain. Although this statement suggests that due process requires that the defendant be afforded both notice of the information to be used in sentencing and some opportunity to contest its reliability, the Court has not specified what procedures are necessary to satisfy the defendant's right to be heard.

The Court in *Gardner* distinguished its earlier decision in *Williams* from the facts of *Gardner*. In *Williams*, like *Gardner*, the sentencing judge had relied on information contained in the pre-sentence report, and the report had not been made available to the defendant. But unlike *Gardner*, in *Williams* the facts concerning the defendant's background that were contained in the pre-sentence report were described in detail by the trial judge in open court. In holding that Williams' right to notice and opportunity to be heard was not violated, the Court relied on the fact that neither Williams nor his counsel had challenged the accuracy of the information described by the judge, and the judge had not been asked to disregard the information or asked to afford the defendant an opportunity to explain or refute the judge's statement of the facts. Twenty years after *Gardner*, in *Gray v. Netherland* (S.Ct. 1996), the Court clarified that the scope of the notice guaranteed by Gardner in capital cases does not include discovery of that information in advance of sentencing.

Both *Gardner* and *Williams* involved the imposition of a death sentence. The Court has not clarified the scope of the constitutional right to notice and opportunity to be heard in non-capital cases. It is settled, however, that the defendant has no right to cross-examine adverse witnesses. This is true for both capital and non-capital sentencing proceedings.

3.　FACTFINDING AT SENTENCING

Another due process issue relates to sentencing procedures that concern the allocation of who has the burden of proving the existence of aggravating or mitigating factors, and the standard by which sentencing factors must be proven. In *Walton v. Arizona* (S.Ct.1990) the Court held that the Due Process Clause does not prohibit imposing on the defendant the burden of proving mitigating factors in a death penalty sentencing proceeding. The Court had answered some of the questions concerning the prosecution's burden of proving aggravating factors in *McMillan v. Pennsylvania* (S.Ct.1986).

McMillan involved a challenge to a Pennsylvania sentencing statute requiring the sentencing judge to impose a mandatory minimum sentence of five years in prison on defendants convicted of certain specified crimes, if the judge found by a preponderance of the evidence that the defendant "visibly possessed a firearm" during the commission of the crime. The defendants claimed that this statute violated both the due process requirement that every element of the crime be proven beyond a reasonable doubt, and the Sixth Amendment right to have the question of guilt or innocence decided by a jury. The Supreme Court rejected both arguments. The Court held that the prosecution was not required to prove possession of a firearm beyond a reasonable doubt, and the defendant was not entitled to have that question decided by a jury, because under the Pennsylvania statute, the defendant's possession of a firearm was a "sentencing factor" rather than an element of the offense.

In concluding that the Pennsylvania statute made possession of a weapon a sentencing factor rather than an element of the crime, the Court emphasized that the Pennsylvania legislature had expressly designated visible possession of a firearm as a sentencing factor that comes into play only after the defendant has been found guilty beyond a reasonable doubt of one of the applicable crimes. The Court acknowledged that the constitution imposes limits on a legislature's power to avoid due process and Sixth Amendment requirements through simple legislative labeling. The Court declined, however, to define those limits with precision.

In concluding that the Pennsylvania legislature had not exceeded its power in *McMillan*, the Court found it significant that the statute at issue did not increase the maximum penalty for the crime of conviction, nor did it create a separate offense with a separate penalty. Instead, according to the Court, the statute "operates solely to limit the sentencing court's discretion in selecting a penalty within the range already available to it without the special finding of visible possession of a firearm."

In *Apprendi v. N.J.* (S.Ct.2000) the Court clarified the constitutional limits on the legislature's power to characterize factual determinations as sentencing factors for the judge rather than elements of the offense for the jury. The defendant in *Apprendi* was convicted of possession of a weapon for an unlawful purpose. That crime was classified as a second-degree offense, which under New Jersey law was punishable by imprisonment for a term of between five and ten years. Because it had evidence that the incident that was the basis for the charge was racially motivated, the state sought an enhancement of the defendant's sentence under a separate statute described as a "hate crime" law.

This statute authorized the judge to impose an "extended term" of imprisonment if the judge determines, by a preponderance of the evidence, that the defendant, in committing the crime, acted with a purpose to intimidate an individual or group of individuals because of, among other things, race or color. The extended term authorized by the hate crime statute for a second degree offense was imprisonment between ten and 20 years. When it applies, this extended term is added to the sentence for the underlying offense.

In response to the prosecutor's motion, the trial judge held an evidentiary hearing on the issue of the defendant's purpose in firing the gun. Upon finding that the evidence showed by a preponderance that the defendant's actions were motivated by racial bias, the court determined that the hate crime enhancement applied. As a result of this finding, the judge was required to impose a sentence of between ten and 20 years in prison, twice the sentence authorized for the commission of the crime without the enhancement. The judge then sentenced the defendant to 12 years in prison.

On appeal the Supreme Court held that enhancement of the defendant's sentence based on the trial judge's finding of racial motivation by a preponderance of the evidence violated the defendant's rights under the Sixth Amendment jury trial guarantee and the Fourteenth Amendment Due Process Clause.

The Court distinguished *McMillan* on the ground that the sentencing statute at issue in that case simply limited the judge's discretion in deciding on the sentence within the range of authorized penalties established for the crime for which the defendant had been convicted. The hate crime statute in *Apprendi*, by contrast, increased the penalty for the crime beyond the prescribed statutory maximum. The underlying weapons offense carried a maximum prison term of ten years; the maximum increased to 20 years upon a finding by the judge at sentencing that the defendant acted with a racial motive. The Court held that, with one exception, discussed below, "it is unconstitutional for a legislature to remove from the jury the assessment of facts that increase the prescribed range of penalties to which a criminal defendant is exposed," and "that such facts must be established beyond a reasonable doubt.''

The rule established in *Apprendi* is subject to one important exception. In *Almendarez–Torres v. U.S.* (S.Ct.1998), a case decided before *Apprendi*, the Court held that the prohibition against increasing the penalty beyond the statutory maximum based on facts not found beyond a reasonable doubt by the jury, does not apply when the enhancement is based on the defendant's having been previously convicted of a crime. Thus, it is permissible for the legislature to increase the prescribed sentence beyond the maximum for the crime of conviction based upon a finding by the judge that the defendant has previously been convicted of a crime. In *Blakely v. Washington* (S.Ct.2004), the Court held ''the statutory maximum for *Apprendi* purposes is the maximum sentence a judge may impose solely on the basis of the facts reflected in the jury verdict or admitted by the defendant. In other words, the relevant statutory maximum is not the maximum sentence a judge may impose after finding additional facts, but the maximum he may impose without any additional findings.'' *Id.*

CHAPTER 15

APPEAL AND COLLATERAL ATTACK

Direct appeal and collateral attack are alternative procedures for challenging the correctness of rulings made in the processing of a criminal case. Historically, the distinction between appeal and collateral attack was based on the fact that an appeal was a continuation of the original criminal proceeding, whereas a collateral attack was a separate civil action attacking the result in the criminal case.

Although that conceptual distinction has been eliminated for federal habeas corpus actions, which are now regarded as part of the original federal criminal case, two important practical implications of the original distinction remain. First, collateral attack is not subject to the same strict time limitations of direct appeal. Second, while appeals courts are bound by the factual record developed by the trial court, courts considering collateral attacks may undertake independent fact finding and expand the record beyond what was generated in the trial court.

A. THE RIGHT TO A DEFENSE APPEAL

There is no federal constitutional right to appeal a criminal conviction. All jurisdictions, however, guarantee a convicted defendant at least one appeal. The federal system and most states now have two tiers of appeals courts. Typically, the defendant is granted an "appeal as of right" to the first level appellate court. Review by the highest court in the jurisdiction is for most types of cases discretionary with the court. A defendant convicted in state court can seek review in the United States Supreme Court only of questions of federal law.

Although the constitution does not include a right to an appeal, the Supreme Court has held that the constitution does guarantee the defendant certain protections once a right to an appeal is granted. In *Griffin v. Illinois* (S.Ct.1956) the Court held that the Equal Protection Clause of the Fourteenth Amendment was violated by a state rule that required the defendant to supply a transcript of the trial record in order to obtain appellate review, but which did not provide for a free transcript for defendants who could not afford to pay for one.

In *Douglas v. California* (S.Ct.1963) the Court relied on the Equal Protection and Due Process Clauses to hold that an indigent defendant must be provided with an attorney when the state guarantees the defendant the right to an appeal. The Sixth Amendment right to counsel, which applies to "criminal prosecutions," does not encompass the right to an attorney on appeal. The Court has also held that the Due Process Clause includes the same protection against ineffective assistance of counsel on the defendant's first appeal as of right that is guaranteed at trial by the Sixth Amendment.

In *Ross v. Moffitt* (S.Ct.1974), however, the Court held that the constitution does not guarantee indigents the right to the assistance of an attorney in seeking discretionary review in the state supreme court or the Supreme Court of the United States. In reaching this result the Court noted that the defendant in the case had received the assistance of an attorney in presenting his appeal to the intermediate appellate court, and that he was in possession of the trial transcript and the legal brief submitted to the intermediate court that could be used in pursuing further review of the case in the state supreme court.

Two other constitutional doctrines relevant to the appellate process are discussed elsewhere in this Nutshell. In a line of cases beginning with *Anders v. California* the Supreme Court has addressed the obligations of appointed appellate counsel when counsel concludes that the trial record contains no meritorious appellate issues. Those cases are discussed in Chapter 11 on assistance of counsel.

Another important constitutional doctrine relevant to the appellate process is the set of due process rules prohibiting vindictive sentencing. These rules are discussed in Chapter 14 on sentencing.

B. THE FINAL JUDGMENT RULE

In the course of a criminal prosecution the trial judge may make many legal rulings that are potentially appealable. Under what is known as the final judgment rule, the defendant is generally not permitted to delay or suspend the processing of the case in the trial court by taking an immediate or "interlocutory" appeal of those rulings. Instead, the defendant is required to postpone her appeal until after the case has been terminated in the trial court with a conviction, and must consolidate all of her appellate claims in a single appeal.

The Supreme Court has identified three general interests supporting the federal version of the final judgment rule: 1) preserving the respect due to trial judges by preventing appellate interference with ongoing prosecutions; 2) expediting the prompt resolution of criminal cases by prohibiting time consuming appeals; and 3) promoting judicial efficiency by preventing unnecessary appeals and combining all claims in a single appeal.

All jurisdictions recognize exceptions to the final judgment rule and permit interlocutory appeals under some circumstances. The federal rule, which is also followed by many state courts, permits interlocutory appeals only for a small category of cases falling within the "collateral order" exception to the final judgment rule. To come within this exception, the trial court order must meet three conditions. The order must: 1) conclusively determine the disputed question; 2) resolve an important issue completely separate from the merits of the action; and 3) be effectively unreviewable on appeal from the final judgment.

The Supreme Court has interpreted the exception to the final judgment rule strictly, and recognized only a small number of types of orders that meet the three part test. The Court has held that a pretrial order denying a defense motion to reduce bail may be appealed immediately because: 1) the issue of whether bail is unconstitutionally excessive is finally resolved by the trial court order; 2) the question of the amount of bail is independent of the issues to be tried; and 3) the question whether bail has been set too high becomes moot if review is postponed until after trial.

The Court has also authorized interlocutory appeals from orders denying motions to dismiss charges on double jeopardy grounds. The Court has emphasized that double jeopardy is not simply the right not to be convicted a second time; it is the right not to be *tried* for the crime. If the defendant's appeal of her double jeopardy claim is delayed until after trial and conviction, the conviction can be vacated if the appeal is successful, but the right against being subjected to a second trial will have been irretrievably lost. For similar reasons the Court has upheld interlocutory appeals of claims asserting immunity from prosecution, since the underlying right protects against being tried, rather than simply convicted. The Court has also allowed an interlocutory appeal from an order requiring a defendant to be medicated during trial. If allowed to go unchallenged, the defendant would be forced to take medication during trial, the very action she seeks to avoid. *Sell v. U.S.* (S.Ct. 2003).

The requirements for recognizing an exception to the final judgment rule are clarified by an examination of the kinds of cases that have been held not to qualify for interlocutory appeal. For instance, the Supreme Court rejected interlocutory review of pre-trial orders denying speedy trial claims on the ground that a motion to dismiss on speedy trial grounds is not separable from the issues at trial, since the degree to which the defense has been impaired by delay of the trial is an important factor in judging whether the right to a speedy trial has been violated.

For similar reasons the Court has disallowed interlocutory appeals of pre-trial orders denying Fourth Amendment motions to suppress evidence. Because the evidence that is the subject of search and seizure motions is often critical trial evidence, the issues raised in suppression motions are not independent of the merits of the case.

The Court has also held that the right against vindictive prosecution is fully protected by post-conviction review because, according to the majority, the vindictiveness claim is a right whose remedy requires dismissal of the charges, rather than a right not to be tried. Finally, the Court has rejected interlocutory appeal of a pre-trial order disqualifying defense counsel from joint representation in a multiple defendant trial, reasoning that the right to joint representation is merely a right not to be convicted in certain circumstances, and therefore is not lost irretrievably if the defendant is tried in violation of that right.

C. PROSECUTION APPEALS

The scope of prosecution appeals is considerably narrower than is available to the defense. The primary reason for the broader appealability of defense claims is the Double Jeopardy Clause, which prohibits the prosecution from appealing any prior rulings whenever the case ends in an acquittal. Independent of the constitutional double jeopardy doctrine, however, the scope of prosecution appeals is limited by the common law doctrine requiring express statutory authorization for prosecution appeals. Almost all jurisdictions authorize prosecution appeals in at least some circumstances.

Prosecution appeals are subject to the final judgment rule, but the rule is applied less strictly to the prosecution than to the defense. The reason the prosecution is allowed to appeal non-final orders that would not be appealable by the defense is because the Double Jeopardy Clause, which bars any prosecution appeal from a final judgment of acquittal, may prevent the prosecution from obtaining any appellate review of the issue if it is required to await a final judgment.

One type of interlocutory order that is routinely appealable by the prosecution is a pre-trial order granting a defense motion to suppress evidence. A prosecution appeal of a suppression order does not abridge the defendant's double jeopardy rights because jeopardy has not yet "attached" at the time the suppression order is entered. In addition, there are strong policy justifications for permitting an appeal. Frequently, granting the defendant's suppression motion will effectively terminate the prosecution. This is because the unavailability of the suppressed evidence often renders the prosecution evidence legally insufficient, and compels the prosecutor to move for dismissal of the charges. If the prosecution is not permitted to take an interlocutory appeal of the suppression order, some defendants who ought to be convicted will be set free. On the other hand, not permitting prosecution appeals of suppression orders might also disadvantage the defendant. Some judges might deny the defendant's suppression motion in order to force the defendant to appeal the suppression order after she has been convicted as the only means of obtaining appellate review of the issue.

The prosecution is also typically permitted to appeal trial court orders entered after jeopardy has attached that dismiss the charge on some ground other than a finding that the evidence is insufficient to convict. In addition, the prosecution can generally appeal dismissal orders which are based on the sufficiency of the evidence, but only if the dismissal occurs *after* the defendant has been convicted. These limitations are based on the double jeopardy doctrine, which is discussed in Chapter 9.

D. THE SCOPE OF APPELLATE REVIEW

One important limitation on the scope of appellate review is the "raise or waive" doctrine, which requires that most claims must have been raised in the trial court before they will be considered by the appeals court. If a claim has not been "preserved" for appellate review in the trial court, the appeals court may deny the appeal without reaching the merits of the claim.

The basic rationale for the raise or waive doctrine is judicial economy. The theory behind the rule is that costly appeals and second trials can be avoided if claims of error are raised at a time when they can still be corrected.

The timing and manner of preserving a claim for appellate review depend on the type of claim, and may not be precisely specified. In general, preservation of appellate issues in the trial court requires that the issue be presented to the trial judge in such a way as to permit the trial court to correct it. That means, first, that the issue must be raised in a timely fashion, so that any corrective action ordered by the trial judge will be effective in remedying the error. In addition to being timely, the objection made in the trial court must make clear the nature of the claim so that the trial judge will have a sufficient understanding of the allegation of error to rule on its merits.

All jurisdictions recognize exceptions to the raise or waive doctrine that authorize appeals courts to consider some types of claims that have not been preserved at trial. Rule 52 of the Federal Rules of Criminal Procedure, for example, authorizes appeals courts to consider "plain errors or defects affecting substantial rights" even though the errors "were not brought to the attention of the [trial] court." The Supreme Court has interpreted the concept of "plain error" under Rule 52 as including three issues. *U.S. v. Olano* (S.Ct.1993).

The first requirement for a finding of plain error is that there must be an "error" in the sense of a "deviation from a legal rule" that has not been waived. In explaining this point, the Court distinguished between a waiver, which is an intentional relinquishment of a known right, and a forfeiture, which is a failure to make a timely assertion of a right. A right that has been forfeit can nevertheless be considered on appeal if the other requirements for plain error have been satisfied, but a right that has been waived cannot. Thus, a defendant who pleads guilty cannot claim on appeal that she was denied the right to a trial, because the right was waived at the time the guilty plea was entered.

The second requirement for plain error is that the error be plain, which the Court defined as meaning "clear" or "obvious." The appeals court cannot consider an appellate claim unless the mistake was obvious under existing law.

The third and most difficult requirement is that the error "affect[ed] substantial rights" of the defendant. The Court explained that this requirement means that the defendant must ordinarily show that the error was prejudicial in the sense that it must have affected the outcome of the district court proceedings. In other words, the defendant must normally, though not necessarily always, demonstrate that the error was not harmless under the standard for harmless error.

If the requirements for plain error are satisfied, the appeals court has the authority to correct the error, but is not required to do so. Rule 52 states that plain errors that affect substantial rights "may" be noticed by the appeals court, not "must" be noticed. In explaining the circumstances under which a court should exercise its discretion to correct unpreserved errors, the Supreme Court has stated (in *Olano*) "the Court of Appeals should correct a plain forfeited error affecting substantial rights if the error 'seriously affect[s] the fairness, integrity or public reputation of judicial proceedings.' "

E. HARMLESS ERROR

Because of the complexity of the rules governing American judicial trials, error free trials are rare or non-existent. In order to avoid endless reversals and re-trials, all jurisdictions have "harmless error" rules that enable appeals courts to avoid reversals for most kinds of trial error. Thus, in order to win a reversal on appeal, a defendant must show both the existence of an error or errors in the proceedings and also that the error was harmful under the standards for harmless error.

Harmless error doctrine distinguishes between errors that have their source in constitutional rights and errors that do not. In general, constitutional errors are thought to be more serious and more readily require reversal, though this is not necessarily the case.

1.   NON-CONSTITUTIONAL ERRORS

The standard for non-constitutional harmless error in the federal system is contained in Federal Rule of Criminal Procedure 52, which states that "[a]ny error, defect, irregularity or variance which does not affect substantial rights shall be disregarded." In applying this rule a distinction is often made between errors that involve violations of rights that bear on the "structure of the proceedings" and errors that involve violations of rights that relate to the "presentation of the case." An example of an error that involves structural rights is an error in the application of the venue rules. When one of this category of rights is violated, the error is deemed harmful and reversal is required if 1) the right that was violated is a right that is deemed "substantial," and 2) the violation deprived the defendant of the basic benefit of that right.

The second category of non-constitutional errors—errors in the presentation of the case to the factfinder—include such things as errors in the admission or exclusion of evidence, improper argument by counsel, and errors in the instructions to the jury on the law. The harmless error test used for this kind of error evaluates whether the error was harmful by looking at the impact of the error on the outcome of the case. The courts disagree, however, over how this test is to be applied. One approach seeks to evaluate the impact of the error by evaluating whether the jury reached the correct result regardless of the error or its effect upon the judgment. Under this approach, an error will be deemed harmless even if the error might have influenced the jury's decision, so long as it appears that the jury reached the correct result in light of the evidence that was properly admitted. The Supreme Court has rejected this so-called "correct result" approach for the federal courts in favor of an approach that seeks to evaluate the probable effect of the error on the actual decision. This approach requires an evaluation of the entire record to determine whether the error likely influenced the jury in its decision to convict.

Although most courts now follow the approach that looks to the effect of the error on the judgment, courts disagree over the degree of impact or risk of impact that must be found before an error will be deemed harmful and a reversal of the conviction ordered. Some courts require a finding of a "high probability" that the error did not contribute to the verdict for an error to be considered harmless, while other courts require a showing that the error more probably than not did not affect the decision. There are other formulations of the standard as well. Regardless of how the test is stated, any inquiry into the probable effect of error in the proceedings on the jury's decision is inherently speculative and uncertain, since rules regarding the secrecy of jury deliberations prevent the reviewing court from determining whether the error in fact played any role in the jury's decision making.

2.   CONSTITUTIONAL VIOLATIONS

A different set of harmless error rules applies to errors that involve violations of constitutional rights. Some constitutional errors require automatic reversal without regard for the impact of the error on the outcome of the case, while other constitutional errors are subject to harmless error analysis.

The Supreme Court first held that a constitutional violation can be found harmless in *Chapman v. California* (S.Ct.1967). The defendants in that case appealed their murder convictions on the ground that the prosecutor in closing argument commented on their failure to testify in violation of their Fifth Amendment right against compulsory self-incrimination. The Court held that while some constitutional violations require automatic reversal, there are other constitutional errors which in the setting of a particular case are so unimportant that they can be deemed harmless. The Court in *Chapman* treated the Fifth Amendment violation involved in that case as an error that might in an appropriate case be found harmless, but did not explain except by illustration how the two categories of constitutional errors are to be distinguished.

In *Arizona v. Fulminante* (S.Ct.1991) the Court attempted to clarify the line between those constitutional errors which require automatic reversal and those that do not. The Court distinguished between "structural defects in the constitution of the trial mechanism," which require automatic reversal, and "trial errors," which are subject to harmless error analysis. The Court cited as examples of structural defects a total deprivation of the right to trial counsel, trial before a biased judge, denial of the right to self-representation, denial of public trial, and exclusion of members of the defendant's race from the grand jury. These errors require automatic reversal because of the difficulty of evaluating the impact of the error on the outcome of the case.

In addition, automatic reversal is required when the remedy for the constitutional violation is a bar on re-prosecution, such as a denial of the right to speedy trial or violation of the double jeopardy protection. A third category of constitutional errors not subject to harmless error analysis is violations of constitutional standards which themselves require a showing of prejudice to the defendant, such as the right to effective assistance of counsel and the right to disclosure of exculpatory evidence.

In contrast to structural defects that defy harmless error analysis, the effect of trial error in the presentation of the case to the jury can, according the Court in *Fulminante*, be "quantitatively assessed in the context of other evidence" to determine whether it was harmless. Examples of trial error subject to harmless error analysis include

various types of errors in jury instructions, erroneous admission or exclusion of evidence, admission of
evidence obtained in violation of the Sixth Amendment right to counsel or the Fourth Amendment
right against unreasonable search and seizure, improper comment on the defendant's failure to testify, restriction on the defendant's right to cross-
examination in violation of the Sixth Amendment
Confrontation Clause, and, as a divided Court held
in *Fulminante*, admission of a coerced confession.

Once it is determined that the error is of the type
that is subject to harmless error analysis, there
remains the question of how the test for harmless
constitutional error is to be applied. In defining the
test for harmless constitutional error the *Chapman*
Court stated that the burden of establishing that a
constitutional error was harmless must be borne by
the beneficiary of the error, the prosecution. The
Court also held that in order to carry its burden the
prosecution must prove beyond a reasonable doubt
that the error did not contribute to the verdict.

The Court in *Chapman* made clear that in evaluating whether a constitutional error is harmless the
question is not simply whether the fact finder
reached the correct result based on the evidence
that was properly admitted. Rather, the court must
assess the likely impact of the error on the jury's
decision. To find the error harmless the appellate
court must find beyond a reasonable doubt that the
error did not contribute to the verdict. Although the
presence of overwhelming evidence of guilt is not
determinative, the strength of the evidence is clear-

ly a relevant factor in the reviewing court's analysis, since the stronger the evidence of guilt the lower the risk that the error influenced the jury's decision.

F. FEDERAL HABEAS CORPUS

The English common law writ of habeas corpus (which means, "have the body") provided a procedure by which a person could challenge the legality of incarceration. When the U.S. constitution was written, the writ was recognized in Article I, which prohibits suspension of habeas corpus except in specified circumstances. Congress included procedures governing habeas corpus in the Judiciary Act of 1789, but at the same time made clear that under the Act the writ was available only to prisoners being held by the federal government; it did not apply to state prisoners. In an early decision construing this statute, the Supreme Court held that the limitation to federal prisoners was consistent with the right to habeas corpus recognized in the constitution.

In 1867 Congress passed the Habeas Corpus Act, which made the writ of habeas corpus available to state prisoners as well. While extending the procedure to state prisoners, the 1867 Act also limited federal habeas corpus to claims that the person was being held in violation of federal law; claims of violations of state law are not cognizable. Congress amended the Act most recently in 1996 as part of the Anti-terrorism and Effective Death Penalty Act.

The current version of the federal Habeas Corpus Act is contained in 28 U.S.C. §§ 2241–2266. The statute provides for essentially similar remedies for state and federal prisoners, but under different labels. Title 28, § 2254 authorizes federal courts to grant a writ of habeas corpus for a state prisoner, while 28 U.S.C. § 2255 authorizes a motion to vacate, set aside, or correct a sentence.

1. CUSTODY

The writ of habeas corpus was historically used as a means of challenging in court the legality of detention by the Crown of persons who had not been convicted of a crime. Although the writ later became available to challenge the validity of a conviction as well, the requirement that the applicant be in custody in order to qualify for the remedy was retained. The current explanation for the custody requirement is that the extraordinary remedy of habeas corpus, which can involve intervention by a federal court in a state conviction that has long since become final, should not be available except for severe restraints on individual liberty.

To be considered "in custody" for purposes of seeking a writ of habeas corpus, the petitioner need not be actually incarcerated. A person who has been convicted of a crime is deemed to be in custody if the person is free on probation or parole, or has been released on recognizance while awaiting execution of sentence. However, a person who has served out any sentence and been unconditionally released is not in custody simply by virtue of potential collateral consequences of the conviction, such as enhancement of the sentence for some future crime.

The determination whether the petitioner is in custody is made at the time the petition for habeas corpus is filed. Therefore, a person who is released from custody while the petition is pending is still entitled to pursue the claim.

2.   EXHAUSTION OF STATE REMEDIES

The statute that governs habeas corpus petitions by state prisoners, 28 U.S.C. § 2254, requires that an application for a writ of habeas corpus by a person in state custody "shall not be granted unless it appears that the applicant has exhausted the remedies available in the courts of the State, or that there is either an absence of available State corrective process or the existence of circumstances rendering such process ineffective to protect the rights of the prisoner." This "exhaustion" requirement bars federal habeas relief if, at the time of the federal petition, there exist state procedures in which the federal claim could be presented.

The exhaustion requirement does not bar federal habeas corpus if the state procedure is no longer available at the time of the federal petition, even if the defendant failed to pursue the state remedy when it was still an option. (*But see O'Sullivan v. Boerckel* (S.Ct.1999) describing the defendant's failure to seek discretionary state supreme court review of federal claim as failure to exhaust state remedies, even though state supreme court review was no longer available at the time of the habeas petition.)

The amendments to the habeas corpus statute contained in the 1996 Anti–Terrorism and Effective Death Penalty Act contained two revisions of the exhaustion requirement. First, the Act authorizes the federal courts to deny a habeas application on the merits, notwithstanding the applicant's failure to exhaust state procedures. This provision enables a federal judge to prevent an applicant from presenting a non-exhausted claim to the federal courts for a second time after returning to the state courts to comply with the exhaustion requirement. Second, the Act provides that the state shall not be deemed to have waived the exhaustion requirement, or be estopped from asserting the requirement, unless the state has made an express waiver, and that waiver was made by counsel. The effect of this provision is to strengthen the exhaustion requirement by preventing the defendant from relying on a claim of implied waiver based on the state's failure to raise the exhaustion issue as a bar to the habeas petition. In 1996, § 2254 was amended to clarify the meaning of exhaustion of remedies: "An applicant shall not be deemed to have exhausted the remedies available in the courts of the State, within the meaning of this section, if he has the right under the law of the State to raise, by any available procedure, the question presented."

3. COGNIZABLE CLAIMS

a. Federal Question

Since its creation in the 18th century, federal habeas corpus has required a showing that the defendant is being detained "in violation of the Constitution or laws or treaties of the United States." Thus, a state prisoner is not entitled to habeas corpus on the ground that the trial court misapplied state law, such as a misapplication of the rules of evidence. Because state criminal trials rarely involve application of non-constitutional federal law, the vast majority of habeas corpus petitions by state prisoners allege a violation of the constitution. While a federal prisoner can seek to attack her sentence for both constitutional and non-constitutional errors, to be entitled to relief based on a violation of non-constitutional federal law the petitioner must show that the error constituted a fundamental defect which inherently results in a complete miscarriage of justice, a difficult standard to meet. As a result, most federal habeas corpus petitions, by either state or federal prisoners, are based on a claim that the defendant is being detained in violation of the U.S. constitution.

The requirement that the petition be based on a violation of federal law is illustrated by the case of *Herrera v. Collins* (S.Ct.1993). The issue in *Herrera* was whether a prisoner claiming actual innocence based on newly discovered evidence was entitled to have his claim heard in a federal habeas corpus action. The petitioner in the case, who had been sentenced to death for the murder of a police officer, offered evidence that had been discovered years after the trial that purported to demonstrate that the murder for which he had been convicted was committed by his brother.

The Supreme Court denied Herrera's petition, and held that a claim of innocence based on newly discovered evidence will seldom, if ever, be considered in a federal habeas corpus action. In the first part of its opinion, the majority strongly suggested that a claim of actual innocence does not raise a constitutional issue cognizable in a habeas corpus action. The Court rejected the view that the State of Texas's 30 day time limit for new trial motions based on newly discovered evidence, which prevented Herrera from raising his claim in state court, was fundamentally unfair in violation of due process. The Court also distinguished Herrera's claim from a claim that the evidence presented at trial was legally insufficient, which does raise a constitutional due process issue cognizable in a federal habeas corpus action. Finally, the Court drew a distinction between claiming innocence as the basis for habeas relief, which the Court said had never been recognized, and the rule that a showing of actual innocence may enable a defendant to obtain a hearing on a habeas petition that would otherwise be procedurally barred.

The main thrust of the Court's opinion was directed toward showing that claims of actual innocence based on newly discovered evidence do not state a ground for federal habeas relief in the absence of an independent constitutional violation occurring in the state criminal proceeding. But then at the end of its opinion, the Court left open the possibility that "in a capital case a truly persuasive demonstration of 'actual innocence' made after trial would render the execution of a defendant unconstitutional, and warrant federal habeas relief if there were no state avenue open to process such a claim." The Court stressed that the threshold showing of innocence for such a claim would be "extraordinarily high." The reason the Court gave for refusing to permit the use of federal habeas corpus to raise innocence claims based on newly discovered evidence except in extraordinary circumstances is that allowing such claims would disrupt the need for finality in capital cases, and retrials of such claims would impose enormous burdens on the states.

b. Fourth Amendment Claims

In *Stone v. Powell* (S.Ct.1976) the Court created an exception to the general rule that constitutional errors occurring during the processing of a criminal case can be raised in federal habeas corpus proceedings. The defendant in *Stone* sought habeas corpus relief on the ground that evidence that had been seized in violation of his Fourth Amendment right against unreasonable search and seizure had been introduced at his trial. The Court held that a defendant who has been afforded the opportunity for a "full and fair litigation" of a Fourth Amendment claim by the state courts is not entitled to raise that claim in a federal habeas corpus proceeding. This rule applies even if the state courts erroneously allowed the admission at trial of evidence obtained in violation of the Fourth Amendment. The reason for the "full and fair litigation exception" relates to the policy underlying the exclusionary rule, which is to deter the police from violating the Fourth Amendment. The Court reasoned that the incremental benefit in terms of additional deterrence of applying the exclusionary rule in collateral proceedings does not justify the cost.

The Court's opinion in *Stone v. Powell* suggested that the exception to the federal courts' authority created in that case might extend to other types of constitutional claims as well. But subsequent cases have rejected all attempts to expand the "full and fair litigation" exception beyond Fourth Amendment claims. In *Rose v. Mitchell* (S.Ct.1979) the Court held that the petitioner's claim that the grand jury that indicted him was selected in violation of the Equal Protection Clause was cognizable in a federal habeas corpus proceeding, even though the defendant had an opportunity to litigate the claim in state court. In *Kimmelman v. Morrison* (S.Ct.1986), the Court held that a claim that the defendant was denied effective assistance of counsel as guaranteed by the Sixth Amendment was cognizable in a habeas corpus proceeding, even though the ineffective assistance claim was based on counsel's failure to object to the admission of evidence seized in violation of the Fourth Amendment. Most recently, in *Withrow v. Williams* (S.Ct.1993) the Court refused to extend the *Stone v. Powell* rule to habeas petitions claiming improper admission of a confession taken in violation of the defendant's rights under *Miranda v. Arizona* (S.Ct.1966).

The amendments to the habeas corpus statute passed in 1996 do not expressly recognize the exception to the courts' authority for Fourth Amendment claims. Nevertheless, the courts have continued to recognize the exception on the ground that elimination of the exception would have been inconsistent with the general purpose of the amendments, which was to restrict rather than expand habeas corpus jurisdiction.

c.   Novel Constitutional Doctrines

The Supreme Court created an additional limitation on the federal courts' habeas jurisdiction in *Teague v. Lane* (S.Ct.1989). In *Teague* the Court held that in deciding whether a habeas petitioner is being detained in violation of the constitution, the conviction should be reviewed based on the law as it existed at the time the conviction became final. This means, first, that a defendant challenging her conviction in a habeas corpus action is not entitled to relief based on a retroactive application of a new constitutional rule that was established *after* the petitioner's conviction became final. In addition, the *Teague* rule also prohibits the federal courts from declaring new rules of constitutional law in cases being heard on habeas corpus review.

Both of the limitations announced in *Teague* are illustrated by the facts of that case. The petitioner in *Teague* claimed that the prosecutor's use of peremptory challenges to exclude African American jurors during jury selection violated his rights under the U.S. constitution. Prior to the time Teague filed his petition, but after his conviction had become final, the Supreme Court had decided *Batson v. Kentucky*, which held that a prosecutor's use of peremptory challenges to exclude African American jurors because of the juror's race violated the Equal Protection Clause. As one line of attack, Teague challenged his conviction based on an argument that the *Batson* rule should be given retroactive application to his case. In addition to his equal protection argument, however, Teague also requested the habeas court to hold that racially discriminatory use of peremptory challenges violates the Sixth Amendment guarantee of trial by an impartial jury. At the time of Teague's petition, the Supreme Court had not yet ruled on the applicability of the Sixth Amendment to the use of peremptory challenges. The Supreme Court rejected both of Teague's arguments, because neither of his challenges would have been available under the law as it existed at the time his conviction became final.

There are two narrow exceptions to the rule of *Teague*. First, a habeas petitioner may claim the benefit of a new constitutional rule if the rule is one that places the conduct that is the basis for the conviction beyond the power of the state to criminalize. An example of such a rule is the decision in *Robinson v. California* (S.Ct.1962), in which the Supreme Court held that the constitutional prohibition against cruel and unusual punishment prohib-

its a state from punishing a person for being addict-
ed to narcotics because it amounts to punishing a
person for the status of being an addict.

The second exception to the prohibition against
applying new rules of constitutional law in habeas
corpus proceedings is for new rules that constitute
"bedrock procedural element[s]" that "implicate
the fundamental fairness of the trial" and "without
which the likelihood of an accurate conviction is
seriously diminished." An example of a rule that
implicates fundamental fairness and is central to an
accurate determination of innocence or guilt is the
decision in *Gideon v. Wainwright* (S.Ct.1963) establishing the right of indigent defendants to appointed
counsel. As the Court stated in *Teague*, most of the
watershed principles of constitutional criminal procedure have already been identified, and it is unlikely that many such components of basic due
process have yet to emerge. Thus, the circumstances under which this exception will apply can be
expected to be very rare.

Congress appears to have codified and perhaps
extended the rule (but not the exceptions) of *Teague*
in the amendments to the habeas corpus statute
contained in the Anti-terrorism and Effective Death
Penalty Act. Subsection (d) of 28 U.S.C. § 2254 now
provides that writs of habeas corpus "shall not be
granted with respect to any claim that was adjudicated on the merits in State court proceedings unless the adjudication of the claim ... resulted in a
decision that was contrary to ... clearly established

Federal law as determined by the Supreme Court of the United States."

In a recent decision construing this language, the Supreme Court stated that this phrase "refers to the holdings, as opposed to the dicta, of this Court's decisions as of the time of the relevant state court decision." *Williams v. Taylor* (S.Ct.2000). The Court further stated that, with one caveat, "whatever would qualify as an old rule under our *Teague* jurisprudence will constitute 'clearly established Federal law as determined by the Supreme Court' " under the statute. The one difference between *Teague* and the statute is that the statute restricts the source of clearly established federal law to the Supreme Court's jurisprudence, as opposed to decisions by other courts.

4.   PROCEDURAL FORECLOSURE

a.   Procedural Default

In most situations a defendant will not be permitted to raise a federal constitutional claim in a habeas corpus action if, because of the defendant's "procedural default," the constitutional claim was not properly raised in the state courts. "Procedural default" refers to the defendant's failure to comply with procedural requirements for raising or preserving a legal claim. Thus, for example, a defendant may be barred from presenting a constitutional claim in a habeas corpus petition if the defendant failed to appeal the claim within the time limit specified under state law. Although the discussion here assumes an attack on a state conviction, a comparable limitation applies to federal prisoners who seek to vacate their sentence under 28 U.S.C. § 2255.

The reason for the rule denying habeas review of defaulted claims is that the defendant's failure properly to raise the constitutional claim in the state court has the effect of depriving the state courts of the opportunity to rule on the claim in the first instance. There is, however, a certain irony and inequity in the rule which, as Justice Black explained in 1953, grants a second review to defendants who have already received consideration of their claim in the state courts, but denies any review at all to defendants whose claims have not been considered by the state courts because of the defendant's procedural default.

Because the purpose of the procedural default rule is to protect the state courts' opportunity to rule on constitutional claims, the rule operates as a bar to federal habeas review only if the state court judgment rests on grounds that are both "adequate" and "independent" of the federal constitutional claim. The independence requirement means that the state court judgment must be actually based on the defendant's procedural default, rather than on the merits of the claim. Thus, if the state court refers to the defendant's procedural default, but then proceeds to address and reject the constitutional claim on the merits, the state courts have not relied on the default as an independent basis for the judgment. The purpose of the adequacy require-

ment is to assure that the state procedural rules are
not applied in a capricious or discriminatory fashion. A state procedural rule is not adequate if it is
not applied consistently and regularly.

The procedural default rule is subject to two
exceptions—the "cause and prejudice" exception,
and the "actual innocence" exception. Both exceptions are difficult to satisfy and rarely successful.

b. Exception to Procedural Default—Cause and Prejudice

At one time a defendant's procedural default
would not bar habeas review of the defaulted claim
unless the defendant "deliberately bypassed" state
procedures in order to present the claim to the
federal court. The Supreme Court has now replaced
the deliberate bypass rule with the much stricter
cause and prejudice standard. In order to obtain a
hearing on a defaulted claim, the defendant must
show both "cause" for the default and "prejudice"
as a result of the alleged violation of federal law.

In order to establish cause for not presenting the
constitutional claim to the state courts, the defendant must show that some objective factor, external
to the defense, prevented presentation of the claim.
The Supreme Court has identified three circumstances that qualify as cause excusing default of
federal claims. First, a defendant can establish
cause by showing that either the legal or factual
basis for the claim was not reasonably apparent at
the time it should have been presented to the state
courts. The first aspect of this rule—which excuses

non-presentation of claims that are based on novel *legal* principles—has been significantly undermined by later decisions by the Court that have held that federal courts may neither declare nor apply new rules of constitutional law in federal habeas corpus proceedings. As discussed above, under the rule of *Teague*, a federal habeas corpus court may not base its decision on a new constitutional rule unless the rule is one that either deprives the trial court of the power to hear the case or is necessary for an accurate determination of guilt or innocence. Thus, the same showing that is necessary to excuse the defendant's procedural default has the effect of denying the defendant a hearing in federal court. Although the *Teague* principle does not impugn the rule permitting presentation of claims based on new *facts*, the Court will likely require a strong showing that the facts could not have been discovered prior to trial.

A second type of cause recognized by the Court occurs when interference by the state prevents the defendant from presenting the claim to the state courts. Suppression by state officials of information necessary to present the claim is an example of the kind of state interference that would excuse the defendant's failure to present the claim in the state courts.

Finally, the Court has recognized that cause excusing procedural default exists if the assistance of counsel in the state courts was constitutionally ineffective under the standards established in *Strickland v. Washington*. To prove cause on this ground, the defendant must demonstrate that counsel's performance in failing properly to present the constitutional claim in the state courts was constitutionally deficient, and that the defendant was prejudiced by counsel's error, in that there is a reasonable probability that presentation of the claim would have changed the outcome.

The second prong of the cause and prejudice exception to the procedural default rule requires that the defendant demonstrate that she was prejudiced by the procedural default. The Supreme Court has not yet specified what degree of prejudice must be shown. It seems likely, however, that the Court will require the same showing of prejudice that is required for a violation of the Sixth Amendment right to effective assistance of counsel, which means that the defendant must demonstrate a reasonable probability that the error affected the outcome of the proceeding.

c. Exceptions to Procedural Default—Actual Innocence

The second exception to the general ban on habeas review of defaulted claims applies when it is shown that the constitutional violation resulted in the conviction of a defendant who is probably innocent. The Supreme Court's discussion of this exception suggests that to qualify for the exception the defendant must demonstrate "factual innocence," such as the conviction of the wrong person, rather than "legal innocence," such as a conviction based on erroneous jury instructions. When the defendant is claiming that the violation resulted in a wrongful *conviction*, the defendant must show that it is *more likely than not* that no reasonable juror would have convicted. The Court has applied this same preponderance of the evidence standard to collateral attacks on convictions that are based on the defendant's plea of guilty. When the defendant is attacking a *death sentence*, however, the defendant must meet the higher clear and convincing standard. This means that the defendant must show by *clear and convincing evidence* that no reasonable juror would have imposed a sentence of death had it not been for the constitutional violation.

The assertion of innocence as an exception to the ban on habeas review of defaulted claims must be distinguished from the assertion of innocence as a substantive ground for habeas relief. Under the exception to the procedural default rule, a showing of probable innocence gains the defendant a hearing on a separate constitutional claim, whereas in *Herrera* discussed above, the alleged conviction of an innocent person was asserted as the constitutional violation urged in support of the issuance of a writ of habeas corpus.

d. Successive Petitions

Because a habeas corpus petition was historically conceived as a separate civil suit, a defendant was not barred from filing multiple petitions attacking the same conviction. A second or subsequent petition could raise either the same claim that was raised in the earlier petition or raise a different claim.

Although multiple habeas petitions from the same prisoner were not absolutely barred, the courts have developed rules designed to limit the filing of repeat petitions. The "successive petition doctrine" generally prohibits a second or subsequent petition that raises a claim that had already been adjudicated in a prior petition. The "abuse of writ doctrine" bars an attempt by the defendant to raise in a second or subsequent petition a claim that was not presented in the earlier petition.

The 1996 amendments to the habeas corpus statute clarified and strengthened both of the doctrines relating to second or subsequent petitions. With respect to second or subsequent petitions by state prisoners that raise the same claim raised in an earlier petition, the new rules appear to bar all successive petitions, without exception. The Act states flatly that "[a] claim presented in a second or successive habeas corpus application under section 2254 that was presented in a prior application shall be dismissed." Notwithstanding this language, there remains some room for a defendant to argue that a second petition raising the same claim may be heard because the second claim is not "successive" within the meaning of the Act. This argument may succeed when the first petition was denied based on technical or procedural grounds, such as a failure to exhaust state remedies.

The 1996 Act expressly authorizes a second petition raising a different claim, but only in narrowly defined circumstances. The Act provides that second petitions raising claims not presented in the prior petition shall be dismissed unless one of two conditions is met: First, a claim can be heard if it relies on a new rule of constitutional law that the Supreme Court has made retroactive to cases on collateral review. Second, a claim can be heard if the factual predicate for the claim could not have been discovered previously through the exercise of due diligence, and the facts underlying the claim establish by clear and convincing evidence that no reasonable factfinder could have found the defendant guilty but for the constitutional error.

In addition to limiting the circumstances under which second or subsequent claims may be presented, the 1996 Act imposes new procedural requirements for the presentation of second or successive petitions. The Act states that prisoners seeking to file a second petition must move in the appropriate court of appeals for an order authorizing the district court to consider the petition. The court of appeals is to issue the order only if the applicant makes a prima facie showing that the requirements for a successive petition described above have been satisfied.

5. THE STATUS OF STATE FACT FINDING

Unlike an appeals court, which must confine its review to the factual record developed in the trial court, a habeas court has the authority to hold an evidentiary hearing in which the parties present evidence bearing on the claimed constitutional violation. This authority to receive evidence raises two questions. First, under what circumstances should a federal habeas court order an evidentiary hearing, and second, if the state courts have already received evidence related to the federal claim, what degree of deference should the habeas court accord to the factual findings of the state court.

In *Townsend v. Sain* (S.Ct.1963) the Court originally defined the circumstances under which a habeas court is required to convene an evidentiary hearing. The Court held that the habeas court *must* hold an evidentiary hearing if the defendant did not receive a full and fair hearing in the state court. More specifically, a hearing is required if: 1) the merits of the factual dispute were not resolved in the state court; 2) the state's factual determination is not fairly supported by the record; 3) the state fact finding process was not adequate to afford a full and fair hearing; 4) there is a substantial allegation of newly discovered evidence; 5) the material facts were not adequately developed at the state court hearing; or 6) for any reason it appears that the state trier of fact did not afford the habeas applicant a full and fair hearing. In the absence of circumstances mandating an evidentiary hearing, the decision whether to hold a hearing is discretionary with the federal court considering the habeas application.

As a part of the 1996 amendments to the federal habeas corpus statute, Congress narrowed the circumstances under which a hearing will be held based on the ground that the material facts were not adequately developed in the state court, per *Townsend*. The statute now provides that if the applicant has failed to develop the factual basis for a claim in state court proceedings, the federal court shall not hold an evidentiary hearing unless the claim is based on either 1) a new rule of constitutional law that the Supreme Court has made retroactive to cases on collateral review; or 2) a factual predicate that could not have been previously discovered through due diligence, and the facts underlying the claim would establish by clear and convincing evidence that no reasonable factfinder could have found the defendant guilty but for the constitutional violation. 28 U.S.C. § 2254(e)(2). In a recent case construing this provision, the Supreme Court rejected the view that an applicant has "failed to develop the factual basis" for the claim within the meaning of this provision whenever the defendant's habeas claim was not the subject of a state evidentiary hearing. The Court held that "a failure to develop the factual basis of a claim is not established unless there is a lack of diligence, or some greater fault, attributable to the prisoner or the prisoner's counsel." *Williams v. Taylor* (S.Ct. 2000).

Congress first addressed the question what degree of deference federal habeas courts must give state court determinations of factual issues in 1966.

An addition to the habeas corpus statute enacted at that time provided that a state court determination of a factual issue that is based on a hearing on the merits and set forth in writing shall be presumed to be correct. 28 U.S.C. § 2254(d). The statute also included a list of eight circumstances in which the presumption of correctness does not apply. The presumption did not apply when, for example, the merits of the factual dispute were not resolved in the state court, or an indigent applicant was denied appointed counsel in violation of the constitution. Congress amended this part of the statute again in 1996. The statute now states simply that "a determination of a factual issue made by a State court shall be presumed to be correct. The applicant shall have the burden of rebutting the presumption of correctness by clear and convincing evidence." 28 U.S.C. § 2254(e)(1). The new statute does not contain a list of situations in which the presumption of correctness does not apply. Although the significance of this change is not entirely clear, the purpose of the revision appears to be to increase the degree of deference accorded state court factual determinations in federal habeas corpus proceedings.

Prior to the passage of the 1996 amendments to the habeas corpus statute, habeas courts treated purely factual questions differently from "mixed questions of law and fact." Although the distinction is not always clear, in general a mixed question of law and fact involves the application of a legal standard to historical facts. Under pre–1996 rules, the presumption of correctness that is due state court factual determinations did not apply to state court determinations of mixed questions.

As part of the 1996 amendments, Congress added new language to the habeas corpus statute which requires federal court deference to state court determinations of mixed questions. Sub-section (d) of 28 U.S.C. § 2254 now states that writs of habeas corpus "shall not be granted with respect to any claim that was adjudicated on the merits in State court proceedings unless the adjudication of the claim . . . involved an unreasonable application of clearly established Federal law as determined by the Supreme Court of the United States." In *Williams* (S.Ct.2000) the Court construed this language to require federal habeas courts to defer to state court applications of federal law provided the application of the law by the state court was "objectively reasonable." The Court emphasized, moreover, that an application of the law can be reasonable and therefore entitled to respect even if it is "incorrect." The effect of this decision is to extend the requirement of federal court deference to state court determinations of mixed questions of law and fact, though the degree of deference required for such determinations is not specified.

†